当代国际商务文化阅读丛书
Readings for Modern International Business Culture

华尔街梦魇
——『商界风云』篇

Nightmare on Wall Street
The Business Circle

【英汉对照】

吴斐　编著

武汉大学出版社

图书在版编目(CIP)数据

华尔街梦魇:"商界风云"篇:英汉对照/吴斐编著. —武汉:武汉大学出版社,2016.5
 当代国际商务文化阅读丛书
 书名原文:Nightmare on Wall Street:The Business Circles
 ISBN 978-7-307-13998-5

Ⅰ.华… Ⅱ.吴… Ⅲ.金融市场—研究—美国—英、汉 Ⅳ.F837.125

中国版本图书馆 CIP 数据核字(2014)第 181969 号

责任编辑:郭园园 金 军 责任校对:鄢春梅 版式设计:韩闻锦

出版发行:**武汉大学出版社** (430072 武昌 珞珈山)
（电子邮件:cbs22@whu.edu.cn 网址:www.wdp.com.cn）
印刷:武汉中远印务有限公司
开本:880×1230 1/32 印张:10.125 字数:223 千字
版次:2016 年 5 月第 1 版 2016 年 5 月第 1 次印刷
ISBN 978-7-307-13998-5 定价:28.00 元

版权所有,不得翻印;凡购买我社的图书,如有缺页、倒页、脱页等质量问题,请与当地图书销售部门联系调换。

前　言

　　人类社会进入21世纪后，国家间的商务往来更加频繁，商务交际手段随着互联网的诞生和电子信息的进步日新月异，国际化企业的文化和理念千差万别，商务话题的表达和沟通能力无疑是人们所遇到的最大障碍。　在我们熟知的生活英语、学术英语之外，商务英语不仅是我国目前从事或即将从事涉外商务人员英语实际应用能力不可多得的辅助工具，更是商务工作人员在这个国际化的高科技时代商务竞争能力、外贸业务素质和英语水平的重要体现。《当代国际商务文化阅读》(英汉对照)丛书以从事国际商务活动所必需的语言技能为经,以各种商务活动的具体情景作纬，将商务精神和商务元素巧妙融合，展示时尚而又经典的商务文化世界流行风，为广大读者提供一套语言规范、内容新颖、涉及面广、趣味性强、具有实用价值、富于时代精神的读物，既注意解决人们在国际商务环境中遇到不熟悉的专业词汇而无法与外国合作者就工作问题交流沟通的难题，又着力解决人们学外语单纯地学语言而缺乏商务专业知识的弊端。

　　《当代国际商务文化阅读》(英汉对照)丛书由10个单行本组成:《拥抱新欢亚马逊（Embracing Amazon Service）——电子商务篇(E-Commerce)》、《华尔街梦魇（Nightmare on Wall Street）——商

前言

界风云篇（The Business Circles）》、《路易斯·波森的朋克摇滚（The Punk Rock of Louis Posen）——商界精英篇（Business Elites）》、《希波克拉底誓言（Hippocratic Oath）——商务交际篇（Business Communication）》、《强烈的第一印象（A Powerful First Impression）——商务礼仪篇（Business Etiquette）》、《企业帝国继承权之争（Corporate Empires' Grappling with Succession）——商务文化篇（Business Culture）》、《紫色血液（The Purple Blood）——商务心理篇（Business Psychology）》、《多米诺骨牌效应（The Domino Effects）——商务知识篇（Business Knowledge）》、《公开的赌注（Public Stakes）——商务演讲篇（Business Speeches）》、《伊斯特林悖论（The Easterlin Paradox）——感悟财富篇（Comprehension of Wealth）》。这套丛书的编写旨在帮助读者在国际商务环境下，能够读懂英文的商务信息和商务新闻，并能对某一商务话题的知识有全面透彻的了解，领悟当代时尚商务文化成长的环境和思维方式，提高在全球化高科技时代的商务竞争能力、外贸业务素质和英语交际水平。丛书中的阅读材料力求做到题材广泛，内容精辟，语言规范，遵循趣味性、知识性和时效性原则，培养读者在商务环境下的英语竞争能力和综合应用能力。丛书融时代性与经典性为一体，内容经得起时间考验，文字经得起反复咀嚼，保证其可读性。读者在阅读过程中接收大量的语言输入，为合理组织和娴熟运用英语语言表达自己的思想打下牢固的基础。丛书的单行本包括以一个主题为中心的 30 篇文章，每篇文章包括题记、英语原文、汉语译文、生词脚注和知识链接。"题记"用丰富生动的语言点评文章的精髓，对文章的内容起到提炼和画龙点睛的作用。"英语原文"主要摘自当代国际主流报纸杂志，具有语

前言

言规范、内容新颖、涉及面广、趣味性和时代感等特点。"汉语译文"力求准确流畅,既关注译文的文化语境及其内涵,也重视译文的外延和现当代标志性语言符号。"生词脚注"的难度把握在大学英语六级和研究生英语词汇程度,以帮助读者即时扫清阅读障碍。"知识链接"根据文章内容,或精解一个专业术语,或阐释一种新的商务理念,或介绍叱咤商界的企业或公司,以帮助读者培养游弋商海、运筹帷幄的能力,具备洞悉中西文化的国际视野。

《华尔街梦魇(Nightmare on Wall Street)——"商界风云"篇(The Business Circles)》为读者揭示了公司的成功案例和失败案例、卓越企业建设、公司历史、金融风暴、次贷危机、金融秩序与金融发展、商场博弈、成功秘诀、社会信用、道德风险等跌宕起伏的金融生态,他们或险象环生,或春风得意;或瘫痪崩溃,或傲视群雄。 不同的人对商界风云有不同的解读。 金融学家眼中的商界风云可能是资金链的延伸或断裂,一如沃尔特·迪士尼一手创办的迪士尼主题公园,它不仅改变了迪士尼公司的财富,还复苏了惨淡经营的美国娱乐公园行业;或一夜之间陷入全面崩溃境地的两家房贷抵押机构房地美和房利美,因次贷危机造成的信贷紧缩引发了持续的市场恐慌,资不抵债,濒临破产。 经济学家眼中的商界风云可能是信息技术带动的品牌创新或冒险,一如苹果运用全新的经营模式为美国企业树立的黄金标准:创建品牌,树立形象,在乱象重生的时代获得再生;或如与美国固特异和日本普利司通的激烈竞争中的米其林,叱咤风云,纵横驰骋,以绝对的实力在中国轮胎领域独占鳌头,"滚动"出一条经营奇迹。 心理学家眼中的商界风云可能是人类历史上的大众心理博弈,一如广告行业的最大玩家们强烈反

对全球最大搜索引擎谷歌与全球第一家提供互联网导航服务网站的雅虎签署的非排他性搜索广告合作协议；或如苹果坚决抵制美国音乐出版商协会等提出的提高数字音乐下载版税分成的要求。社会学家眼中的商界风云可能是企业结构的变化和发展，一如星巴克书写的一段美妙而浪漫的文化传奇，让人们循着绿色美人鱼的标志性微笑步入咖啡馆，在沁人心脾的咖啡香味和舒适优雅的环境中放松下来，轻松地享受一段美好的时光；或如成功汽车生产商的典范丰田公司，开发出适应知识经济时代工业生产的全新管理模式，将生产手段变为"深度智慧"，发掘每位员工、经销商、业务合作伙伴头脑中的知识和经验。哲学家眼中的商界风云可能是企业的文化内涵和资本精神，一如高盛集团创造出的一种与人的本能和恐惧相反的文化，有效地整合并利用强大的专业队伍、强烈的责任心、伙伴关系制度以及商业理念等四种管理模式；或如苹果的灵魂人物史蒂夫·乔布斯以其卓越远见和领导能力创造的苹果激情，为工程师们提供克服设计和工程障碍的动力，使他们满腔热情、奋不顾身地参与改变世界数码工业的革命。

今天，商界的每一个细节都扮演着一个部分，每个部分都不可或缺；每次失败都孕育着成功，每次成功又开始了新的前行。让我们跟随时代潮流，在华尔街惊世梦魇的每一个清晨迎接东方升起的太阳，享受世界流行文化创造的快乐、荣誉、价值和成就感！

作　者

2016 年 1 月

目 录

Nightmare on Wall Street	/2
华尔街梦魇	/3
Reverse Engineering Google's Innovation Machine	/12
会思考的搜索引擎：GOOGLE	/13
Apple's High-wire Act	/22
苹果的冒险行为	/23
Business Risk as Culture for Goldman Sachs	/32
高盛的商业风险文化	/33
Opening new worlds: The Disability Boom	/42
"残疾人之家"开辟新商机	/43
Changing the Rules of the Game	/52
改写游戏规则	/53
A Bridge between Companies and Cultures	/60
企业和文化之间的桥梁	/61
The Seamless Handover	/70
权力移交天衣无缝	/71
The Rise and Fall of Enron	/80
安然公司的浮沉	/81

目 录

Unravel Lehman Structure	/92
剥离雷曼架构	/93
The Banks that Robbed the World	/102
掠夺世界的银行	/103
The Global Concerted Action	/112
全球协同行动	/113
Retrying the Andersen Case	/122
安达信案件重审	/123
The Last Days of Bear Stearns	/132
贝尔斯登最后的日子	/133
Key Facts on Fannie Mae and Freddie Mac	/144
房利美和房地美的关键事实	/145
Panic in the Financial City of London	/154
伦敦金融城陷入恐慌	/155
Walt Disney's "Theme Park" Development	/164
迪士尼"主题公园"的发展	/165
Apple Defeats Music Rate Hike	/174
苹果拒绝音乐版税涨价	/175
Google Dealing with Yahoo Draws Opposition	/184
谷歌雅虎交易遭到反对	/185
Wells Bids for Wachovia	/196
富国银行竞购美联银行	/197
DHL Holds Hands with UPS	/206
敦豪快递携手联合包裹服务公司	/207

目 录

Merrill Is Sold	/216
出售美林	/217
Fighting for Survival-Reorganizing AIG	/228
奋力求生：重组美国国际集团	/229
Toyota—The Open Secret of Success	/238
丰田公司成功的秘诀	/239
Amazon into Apparels	/248
亚马逊进军服装业	/249
Michelin Green Wheels in China	/260
米其林绿色轮胎在中国	/261
The Lesson from Barings' Straits	/272
巴林银行陷入困境的教训	/273
Money Markets—Blocked Pipes	/284
货币市场：封闭的管道	/285
The BCG Global Approach	/294
波士顿咨询公司全球业务巡礼	/295
Starbucks Voyage of Success	/304
星巴克成功之旅	/305

题 记

  令人神往的华尔街在2008年经历了一场风声鹤唳的惊世梦魇：两房的次贷风波，雷曼兄弟破产，美林证券出售，股民信心波动，股价油价下跌……然而噩梦并没有就此止步，仍在华尔街的翻云覆雨间持续加剧：金融秩序与金融发展、金融创新失衡，金融监管缺位，社会信用恶化，道德风险蔓延……金融危机不可遏止地迅即蔓延到整个世界。当多米诺骨牌逐个倒下时，其他敏感的金融巨们头争先恐后地自我救赎或者筹集足够的资本以避免类似的命运。相对安全的美国长期国库券收益大幅贬值，雷曼的终结凸显了行业的无能，节俭出名的华盛顿互惠银行正在新老板的带领下为生存而战，美国最大的保险公司美国国际集团由于对关联抵押债务债券义务的信用违约掉期的轻率行动，陷入更为焦虑的状态。美联储救助贝尔斯登和财政部接管两房贷款抵押公司房利美与房地美的措施根本无法缓解人们内心的恐惧，他们眼睁睁地看着雷曼兄弟步履蹒跚地离开"世界金融第一街"……

Nightmare on Wall Street

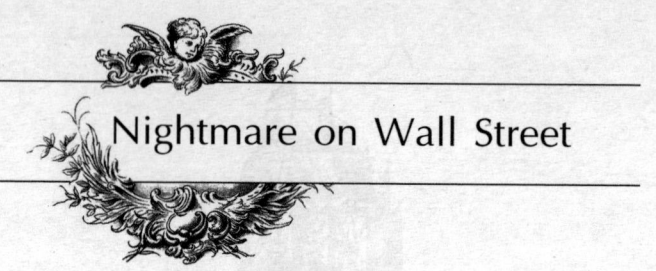

A weekend of high drama reshapes American finance.

Even by the standards of the worst financial crisis for at least a generation, the vents of Sunday and the day before were extraordinary. The weekend began with hopes that a deal could be struck, with or without government backing, to save Lehman Brothers, America's fourth-largest investment bank. Early Monday morning Lehman filed for bankruptcy protection. It has more than $613 billion of debt.

Other vulnerable financial giants scrambled to sell themselves or raise enough capital to stave off a similar fate. Merrill Lynch, the third-biggest investment bank, sold itself to Bank of America (BofA), an erstwhile① Lehman suitor, in a $50 billion all-stock deal. American International Group (AIG) brought forward a potentially life-saving overhaul and went cap-in-hand to the Federal Reserve. But its shares also slumped on Monday.

The situation remains fluid, and investors stampeded② towards the relative safety of American Treasury bonds. Stock markets tumbled around the world though some Asian bourses were closed, and the oil price plummeted to well under $100 a barrel. The dollar fell sharply, and the

---

① erstwhile [ˈəːstwail] adj. 从前的
② stampede [stæmˈpiːd] n. 惊跑

华尔街梦魇

一个极富戏剧性的周末重塑了美国的金融体系。

即使参考近30年来最严重的金融危机标准,周日及头天的突发事件仍然非同寻常。 人们本来对这个周末充满希望,期盼政府出台关于是否出面拯救美国第四大投资银行雷曼兄弟的协议。 周一早间,雷曼兄弟提请破产保护。 它的负债已超过6 130亿美元。

其他敏感的金融巨头们争先恐后地自我救赎或者筹集足够的资本以避免类似的命运。 第三大投资银行美林证券将全部股份以500亿美元出售给曾经起诉过雷曼兄弟的美国银行(BofA)。 美国国际集团(AIG)提出了潜在的救生改革方案,并将结果毕恭毕敬地向美联储做了汇报。 但其股价周一仍然大幅下跌。

金融局势风云变幻,投资者们惊慌失措地转向相对安全的美国长期国库券。 尽管部分亚洲交易所已经关闭,全球证券市场仍然风声鹤唳,石油价格暴跌至每桶100美元以下。 对美联储周二例会宣布降息的期望使美元大幅贬值,两年期国库券的收益不足2%。 美国股票的未来同样深陷负债之门。 而已经抬高的风险信贷规模还在不断扩大。

形势的变化促使金融危机进入一轮全新并极其危险的阶段。 一旦雷曼资产在清算中被倾销,其他公司账簿上的类似资产将不得不

Nightmare on Wall Street

yield on two-year Treasury notes fell below 2% on hopes the Federal Reserve would cut interest rates at a scheduled meeting on Tuesday. American stock futures were deep in the red too. Spreads on risky credit, already elevated, widened further.

With these developments the crisis is entering a new and extremely dangerous phase. If Lehman's assets are dumped in a liquidation, prices of like assets on other firms' books will also have to be marked down, eroding their capital bases. The government's refusal to help with a bail-out of Lehman will strip many firms of the benefit of being thought too big to fail, raising their borrowing costs. Lehman's demise highlights the industry's inability, or unwillingness, to rescue the sick, even when the consequences of inaction are potentially dire.

The biggest worry is the effect on derivatives markets, particularly the giant one for credit-default swaps. Lehman is a top-ten counterparty in CDSs, holding contracts with a notional value of almost $ 800 billion. On Sunday, banks called in their derivatives traders to assess their exposures to Lehman and work on mitigating risks. The Securities and Exchange Commission, Lehman's main regulator, said it is working with the bank to protect clients and trading partners and to "maintain orderly markets".

Government officials believed they had persuaded a consortium of Wall Street firms to back a new vehicle that would take $ 40 billion-70 billion of dodgy assets off Lehman's books, thereby facilitating a takeover of the remainder. But the deal died when the main suitors, BofA and Barclays, a British bank, walked away on Sunday afternoon. Both were unwilling to buy the firm, even shorn of the worst bits, without some sort of government backstop.

But Hank Paulson, the treasury secretary, decided to draw a line and refuse such help. After the Fed had bailed out Bear Stearns in March and the

华尔街梦魇

被减值,资产基数也相应缩水。 如果政府拒绝帮助雷曼摆脱困境,就将夺走很多公司的利益,提高他们的借款成本,他们原本认为公司规模很大,不致倒闭。 雷曼的终结凸显了行业的无能,或不愿拯救危机,即使这些无作为存在隐性的恐怖后果。

最大的焦虑来自衍生市场的影响,尤其是信贷违约互换的大型公司。 雷曼位列信贷互惠前十,持有名义价值约为800亿美元的合同。 周日,各家银行纷纷通知自己的衍生产品经销商,评估对雷曼的敞口,尝试减轻风险。 雷曼的主要监管者美国证券交易委员会声称,它将与该银行并肩作战,保护客户和贸易伙伴,"维护有序市场"。

政府官员相信他们已经成功说服由华尔街公司的财团支持一项新举措,剥离雷曼账户上的400~700亿美元的资产,推动对剩余资产的接管。 但是,当美国银行和英国巴克利银行等主要起诉人在周日下午脱身而退之时,这项交易烟消云散。 即使去除损失最严重的部分,没有政府的某种援助,两家银行并不愿收购雷曼。

但美国财长汉克·鲍尔森却决定与其划清界限并拒绝此类帮助。 美联储三月救助贝尔斯登和上周末财政部接管两房贷款抵押公司房利美与房地美之后,民众对其继续帮助雷曼公司有着很高的期望。 而这恰恰是问题所在:它证实了联邦政府站在金融体系全方位的风险承担之后,既制造了需要数年才能解除的道德危机,又几乎无限地扩大了纳税人的债务。 美国国会有可能已经令人信服地否决了鲍尔森先生所需要的这笔资金,纵然他一直倾向于帮助雷曼兄弟渡过难关。

这使得雷曼兄弟除了做好破产的准备之外别无他选。 尽管这家

Nightmare on Wall Street

Treasury had taken over Fannie Mae and Freddie Mac last weekend, expectations were high that they would do the same for Lehman. And that was precisely the problem: it would have confirmed that the federal government stood behind all risk-taking in the financial system, creating moral hazard that would take years to undo and expanding taxpayers' liability almost without limit. Conceivably, Congress could have denied Mr. Paulson the money he needed even if he had been inclined to bail Lehman out.

This left Lehman with no option but to prepare for bankruptcy. Though the bank has access to a Fed lending facility, introduced after Bear's takeover by JP Morgan Chase, the collapse of its share price left it unable to raise new equity and facing crippling downgrades from rating agencies. Moreover, rival firms that had continued to trade with it in recent weeks—at the urging of regulators—had begun to pull away in the past few days. The inability to find a buyer is a huge blow to Lehman's 25,000 employees, who own a third of the company's now-worthless stock; in such a difficult environment, most will struggle to find work at other financial firms. It also makes for an ignominious① end to the career of Dick Fuld, Lehman's boss since 1994, who until last year was viewed as one of Wall Street's smartest managers.

Merrill's rush to sell itself was motivated by fear that it might be next to be caught in the stampede. Despite selling a big dollop of its most rotten assets recently, the market continued to question its viability. Its shares fell by 36% last week, and hedge funds had started to move their business elsewhere. Its boss, John Thain, concluded that it needed to strike a deal before markets reopened. It approached several firms, including BofA and Morgan Stanley, but only BofA felt able to conduct the necessary due

---

① ignominious [ˌɪgnəˈmɪniəs] *adj.* 耻辱的

华尔街梦魇

银行在摩根大通公司收购贝尔斯登之后,有权使用美联储贷款,但其股价的瓦解使它无法筹集新股,只能面对评级机构的临界下调趋势。 此外,在管理者的极力主张下,近几周继续与其进行交易的竞争企业已在过去几天中开始脱身。 无力找到购买者对雷曼的25 000名雇员无疑是一个巨大的打击,他们拥有公司当前一文不值的股份的三分之一。 在如此艰难的环境中,大部分人都将奋力去其他金融公司寻找工作。 同时,这也给迪克·富德职业生涯的终结蒙上了耻辱——自1994年担任雷曼老总以来,至上年为止,他一直被视为华尔街最明智的管理者之一。

美林急于将自身出售是唯恐成为这场风波的下一个受牵连者。尽管近期已经售出最大的一块不良资产,市场对其生存能力仍持怀疑。 它的股价上周下降了36%,对冲基金已经开始向其他行业转移。 美林老总约翰·塞恩推断,在市场重启之前,它需要大赚一笔。 该公司与多家企业进行了交涉,包括美国银行和摩根大通,但只有美国银行认为,必要时可及时谨慎处理。

华尔街拥有众多正在痛苦中挣扎的公司。 节俭出名的华盛顿互惠银行正在新老板的带领下为生存而战。 美国最大的保险公司美国国际集团由于对关联抵押债务债券义务的信用违约掉期的轻率行动,陷入更为焦虑的状态。 投资人纷纷逃离,担心公司在目前筹资200亿美元的基础上还需注入更多的新资金。 美国国际集团受周末翻云覆雨的刺激,周一提出重组方案。 预计该计划包括飞机租赁和其他业务。 另据报道,美国国际集团正在争取从美联储获得400亿的过渡性融资,一旦销售完成便可偿还,希望这将吸引可能来自私营资产公司的新资金。

Nightmare on Wall Street

diligence in time.

Wall Street has company in its misery. Washington Mutual, a big thrift, is fighting for survival under a new boss. Even more worryingly, so is AIG, America's largest insurer, thanks to a reckless foray into CDSs of mortgage-linked collateralized-debt obligations. Investors have fled, fearing the firm will need a lot more new capital than the $20 billion raised so far. Prompted by the weekend bloodletting, AIG brought forward to Monday a restructuring. This was expected to include the sale of its aircraft-leasing arm and other businesses. It is also reported to be seeking a $40 billion in bridge loan from the Fed, to be repaid once the sales go through, in the hope that this will attract new capital, possibly from private-equity firms.

With Lehman left dangling, official attention is now turning to putting more safeguards in place to soften the coming shock to markets and the economy. The first step has been to encourage Lehman's counterparties to get together and try to net out as many contracts as possible. On Sunday the Fed also expanded the list of collateral it will accept for loans at its discount window, to include even equities; and dealersmay lend any investment-grade security, not just triple-A rated, to the Fed in exchange for Treasury bonds. As spectacular as this weekend was, more drama is on the way.

(1,043 words)

华尔街梦魇

随着雷曼兄弟步履蹒跚地离开,政府注意力现在已转移到别处,以在适当的地方设置更多的安全措施,缓和即将袭击证券市场和经济的震动。第一步是鼓励雷曼兄弟的交易对手加强团结,签出尽可能多的合同。周日,美联储也扩大了附属担保品清单,将在贴现窗口接受借款,甚至包括普通股。经销商可以向美联储提供任何安全级别的投资来兑换国债,而不仅仅是三A评级。如同本周末的惊世壮举,更多戏剧化的情节将会接踵而至。

知识链接

美林证券 美林(Merrill Lynch)曾是世界最著名的证券零售商和投资银行之一,总部位于美国纽约,在曼哈顿四号世界金融中心大厦占据了整个34层楼,拥有17 000名财务顾问。2008年金融危机之际,受次贷危机拖累,美林证券蒙受了超过500亿美元的损失以及资产减计。2009年1月,美国银行完成其对美林证券330亿美元的收购,给美林证券长达95年的独立公司经营道路画上了一个句号。

题 记

在众多的网络公司名流当中，谷歌的文化独树一帜。谷歌拥有自身所处的生态系统，也是这个系统的营运者，它可以控制系统的演变过程，并且很有效率地取得系统创造的大部分价值。谷歌利用自身的生态系统完成IT和业务构建、实验、即兴创作、分析决策制定、参与产品发展，以及其他相关非同常规的创新。谷歌把创新排入员工的工作时间表，员工按照公司规定的创新时间分配制度工作，人人把创新当成分内的事。因此谷歌不仅吸引大量的高素质员工，也创造了大量的新构想和新产品。图片管理工具 Picasa、在线视频 Youtube；在线广告 DoubleClick、卫星图片 Keyhole（现已成为谷歌地球）、网页分析 Urchin（现已成为谷歌分析）等信息管理工具现已成为谷歌麾下的子公司。组织全世界的信息并使之能被广泛地获取和使用是谷歌的任务，虽然看起来是如此宽泛，以至于像是一个帝国的目标，但谷歌确实是在认真地执行这个任务。

Reverse Engineering Google's Innovation Machine

Every piece of the business plays a part, every part is indispensable, every failure breeds success, and every success demands improvement.

In the pantheon of internet-based companies, Google stands out as both particularly successful and particularly innovative. Not since Microsoft has a company had so much success so quickly. Google excels at IT and business architecture, experimentation, improvisation①, analytical decision making, participative product development, and other relatively unusual forms of innovation. It balances an admittedly chaotic ideation process with a set of rigorous, data-driven methods for evaluating ideas. The company culture attracts the brightest technical talent, and despite its rapid employee growth, Google still gets 100 applicants for every open position. It has developed or acquired a wide variety of new offerings to augment the core search product. Its growth, profitability, and shareholder equity are at unparalleled levels. This highly desirable situation may not last forever, but Google has clearly done something right.

Indeed, Google has been the creator or a leading exponent② of new

---

① improvisation [ˌimprəvaiˈzeiʃən] n. 即兴创作
② exponent [ikˈspəunənt] n. 典型

会思考的搜索引擎:GOOGLE

商业的每一个细节都扮演着一个部分,每个部分都不可或缺,每次失败孕育着成功,每次成功都需要改进。

在网络公司的众多名流中,谷歌表现得既特别成功又极富创新力。微软之后就没有其他任何一家公司成长得如此之快。谷歌擅长IT和业务构建、实验、即兴创作、分析决策制定、参与产品发展,以及其他相关非同常规的创新机制。不可否认,谷歌运用一系列严谨、数据驱动的方法评估思想,平衡无序的构思过程。尽管谷歌的员工人数激增,但公司的文化依旧吸引着才华横溢的顶尖技术天才,每一次公开招聘依旧会有数百个求职者。谷歌广泛开发或收购一系列新产品,扩大核心搜索产品。公司的增长、利润率以及股东权益均处于史无前例的水平。尽管这种高度赏心悦目的状况不可能一直持续下去,但谷歌显然取得了一定的成就。

事实上,谷歌已经成为商业和经营改革新方法的创始人或主要代表者。虽然谷歌所做的很多工作植根于它传奇般的IT基础设施,但公司的技术和战略密不可分并相互渗透,很难说技术是否战略的核心或者其他的相关方法。不管是哪种说法,谷歌在过去的数

Reverse Engineering Google's Innovation Machine

approaches to business and management innovation. Much of what the company does is rooted in its legendary IT infrastructure, but technology and strategy at Google are inseparable and mutually permeable①—making it hard to say whether technology is the DNA of its strategy or the other way around. Whichever it is, Google seems to embody② the decades-old, rarely fulfilled vision of IT pundits that technology should do more than just support the business; it should engender strategic opportunity and be architected with that purpose in mind. As such, Google may well be the internet-era heir to such companies as General Electric and IBM as an exemplar of management practice.

We haven't spent a lot of time in the Googleplex, and between us we've consumed only one of the company's tasty and free cafeteria meals. One of us impulsively tried to question Sergey Brin in the Googleplex courtyard, but he beat a hasty retreat and came close to calling security. Fortunately, however, the company is quite open, there are scores of official and unofficial blogs accessible through the company's website, for example, and non-insiders can find countless clues as to how the company approaches innovation. Many of those clues we unearthed, appropriately enough, through Google searches. Based on our years of observing how Google does what it does so well, we have identified a number of key innovation practices that others can profitably adopt. To be sure, some of Google's attributes—two are its category-killing search engine and a massive, scalable IT infrastructure—would be very hard and very costly to

---

① permeable [ˈpɜːmiəbl] adj. 能渗透的
② embody [imˈbɒdi] vi. 体现

十年中极少迎合 IT 专家们的想象力，即技术不仅要支撑企业，更应该创造战略机遇，按照大脑的意图构建技术。 同样，谷歌有充分的理由像通用电气和国际商用机器公司等管理工作的典范一样，成为互联网时代的继承者。

  我们没有在谷歌总部消耗大量的时间，在合作期间，我们只享受了一次公司的美味自助餐。 我们中有个人很冲动，曾试图在谷歌总部大院对谢尔盖·布林提问，但他还是放弃了这种草率的想法，以确保稳妥。 幸运的是，公司很开放，例如，公司的网页上有几十个相互链接的官方或非官方博客，外部人员能找到无数个公司如何改革的通道。 我们运用谷歌搜索发掘了很多链接，足以满足工作的需要。 根据多年对谷歌良性运行的观察，我们认定了一批核心创新方法，供其他公司采用并获利。 确切地讲，谷歌具有的某些特性——分类捕获搜索引擎和大规模、可升级的 IT 基础设施，这两点不仅很难仿效，即使仿效成本也很高。 但其他方面——明确的技术创新机制加上深思熟虑的组织和文化战略——都可以坚持在很多行业的公司成功运用。

  谷歌"组织世界的信息、让全人类获取和使用信息"的任务是如此宽泛、甚至崇高，但谷歌显然在认真贯彻此方针。 在核心搜索和广告业务之外，公司已经着手投资在线生产、博客、电台、电视广告、在线支付、社交网络和手机操作系统，以及更多的信息领域。

  谷歌已经获得了尚未开发的信息管理工具：图片管理工具

emulate①. But others—technology explicitly architected for innovation coupled with a well-considered organizational and cultural strategy—can be applied diligently and successfully by businesses across many industries.

Google's mission " to organize the world's information and make it universally accessible and useful" is so broad as to be imperial, yet Google clearly takes it seriously. Beyond its core search and advertising capabilities, the company has embarked on ventures involving online productivity, blogging, radio and television advertising, online payments, social networks, mobile phone operating systems, and many more information domains.

What information management tools the company hasn't developed it has acquired: Picasa for photo management; YouTube for online videos; DoubleClick for web ads; Keyhole for satellite photos (now Google Earth); Urchin for web analytics (now Google Analytics). Google seeks to master not only bits but also electrons: It recently announced an ambitious project to generate low-cost green electricity. While few of these ventures make money today, they are all bricks in the wall of its ambitious strategy, and few doubt Google's resolve or its ability to make progress toward the ultimate goal. Almost every day the company announces a new product or feature that chips away at information disorganization.

With such a farsighted mission, the short-term profitability of a new offering doesn't seem to matter as much to Google as it might to other businesses. The company's managers are strategically patient. CEO Eric Schmidt has estimated that it will take 300 years to achieve the mission of organizing the world's information. His 1,200-quarter forecast might invite smirking; still, it illustrates Google's long-term approach to building value

---

① emulate [ˈemjuleit] n. 仿效

Picasa；在线视频Youtube；在线广告DoubleClick；卫星图片Keyhole（现已成为谷歌地球）；网页分析Urchin（现已成为谷歌分析）。谷歌不仅寻求掌握储存能量，还有电子：它近期雄心勃勃地宣布了一项发展低耗绿色电能的计划。尽管谷歌的这些冒险现在很少能够赚钱，但它们都是其雄心勃勃的战略基础，极少有人怀疑谷歌向它最终目标进发的决心或能力。它几乎每天都在宣布新产品或新特点，剔除信息混乱。

可能对其他公司相当重要的新的交易方式的短期盈利能力，对谷歌来说似乎无关紧要，就因为它拥有一个如此有远见的目标。公司的管理者在战略上非常耐心。首席执行官埃里克·施密特估计，谷歌将用300年的时间完成组织世界信息的任务。他的这个"1 200季度"的预言也许会招来嗤笑，但它说明了谷歌建立价值体系和能力的长期途径。谷歌与其他公司不一样，其基于搜索的广告是一项利润丰厚的业务，能够为其他非盈利业务提供支持，所以能承担广泛的任务和大量的创新。公司当然也关心积累客户，但它的执行官们认为，随着时间的流逝，商业模式和货币均会自行运转。施密特在贝尔斯登的一次会议上这样说："先推广，再赚钱……如果你能够建立一个足以吸引眼球的企业，你总能找到赚钱的好方法。"

换句话说，并不是每件事都要花上300年。如果谷歌表达的任务是组织世界信息，它还有一个不那么高尚、但同等重要的商业目标没有明说：通过消费者的搜索和其他在线行为赚钱。基于搜索的广告是这种任务最成功的例子。公司目标清晰，关注细节，从而使

and capability. Google, unlike many companies, can afford its broad mission and collection of innovations simply because its search-based advertising is a fantastically profitable product that provides cover for many unprofitable ones. The company certainly cares about accumulating customers, but its executives believe that over time the business model and the money will take care of themselves. At a Bear Stearns conference, Schmidt put it this way: "Ubiquity① first, revenues later…If you can build a sustainable eyeball business, you can always find clever ways to monetize them."

In other words, not everything will take 300 years. If Google's expressed mission is to organize the world's information, it has a somewhat less exalted but equally important unexpressed commercial mission: to monetize consumers' intentions as revealed by their searches and other online behavior. Search-based advertising is the first highly successful instantiation of this mission. What makes strategic patience work for Google are the company's clarity of purpose and attention to detail. Everything Google does extends its reach. It is informational kudzu, always putting down new roots based on the thoroughly internalized principle that information shall be organized by analyzing users' intentions. Companies aiming to learn from Google must first understand that clear, simple directives underlie the vast infrastructure and ostensible chaos.

(906 words)

---

① ubiquity [juːˈbikwəti] *n.* 普遍存在(性)

谷歌的战略耐心成功运转。谷歌所做的每件事都在扩展其范围。它是信息的葛藤，总是将新的根扎在彻底内在化的准则之上，即依靠分析用户的意图组织信息。打算向谷歌学习的公司首先必须理解：明确而简单的方针位于大量的基础架构和表面的混乱之下。

知识链接

Googleplex Googleplex 是 Google 公司总部的名字，位于美国加州圣克拉拉县的山景城。"Googleplex"来源于英文单词"googolplex"（古戈尔普勒克斯），而"Google"转变于单词"googol"（古戈尔）。Googleplex 也是道格拉斯·亚当斯(Douglas Adams)所著的《银河系漫游指南》一书中的"超级电脑"的缩写名。

题 记

　　谁会想到像苹果这样一个品牌能够唤醒如此大的市场？iPod数码音乐播放器把听音乐的体验做到了极致，iTunes音乐商店最大化地捕捉用户需求和市场状态，iPhone将软件、硬件、内容整合在一个干净漂亮的系统中，牢牢巩固了苹果行业霸主的地位，iPad简易的操控和便携式的独特操作体验，让所有人为之热血澎湃。苏格拉底把曾经高山仰止、高高在上的哲学变成与人休戚相关的学科；苹果开发的一系列产品，开创了PC时代，重新定义了移动互联网，改写了动漫、音乐、出版、线下零售，把电脑和电子产品不断变得简约化、平民化，让曾经是昂贵稀罕之物变为现代人生活的一部分。创新改变世界。苹果的冒险行为和游戏规则，是科学与艺术的完美结合。苹果的哲学就是将所有的资源投入极少数的产品，并把它们做到极致。苹果还在继续冒险，它的iCloud、iTV、iCar、iHouse、iTown、iEarth仍在前行……

Apple's High-wire Act

The creator of the iPod and iPhone sets a dazzling new standard for innovation and mass appeal, driven by an obsessive CEO who wants his products to be practically perfect in every way.

The mass market is supposed to be dead, but you would never know it from Apple. The iTunes Store became the second-largest music retailer in the U.S., right behind Wal-Mart. The iPod is to music players what Kleenex is to tissue or Xerox is to copiers. Almost everything Apple makes transcends gender, geography, age, and race. An Apple Store is a demographic melting pot, with computer games for kids and a Genius Bar for their parents and so much cool stuff to touch that it's a magnet for teens and twenty somethings.

Apple scoffs① at the notion of a target market. It doesn't even conduct focus groups. "You can't ask people what they want if it's around the next corner," says Steve Jobs, Apple's then CEO and cofounder. At Apple, new-product development starts in the gut and gets hatched in rolling conversations that go something like this: What do we hate? (Our cellphones.) What do we have the technology to make? (A cellphone with a Mac inside.) What would we like to own? (You guessed it, an iPhone.)

---

① scoff [skɔf] *vi.* 嘲笑

苹果的冒险行为

iPod 和 iPhone 的创建者为产品创新和吸引大众的注意力制定了一套令人眼花缭乱的新标准,并由一名首席执行官强制推行,该首席执行官必须从全方位将产品打造得完美无缺。

大众市场通常被认为是死路一条,但苹果从不这么想。iTunes 商店成为紧排在沃尔玛之后的美国第二大音乐零售商。iPod 与音乐播放器的关系就像舒洁与手纸或者施乐与打印机的关系一样。苹果制造的所有产品几乎都超越性别、地域、年龄和种族。一家苹果商店就是一个汇聚各种人群的熔炉:儿童电脑游戏,父母的天才吧,以及吸引十几、二十岁的年轻人的超酷的玩意儿。

苹果看不起那种只盯住目标市场的理念。它甚至没有确定的目标群体。苹果曾经的首席执行官、也是创始人之一的史蒂夫·乔布斯认为,"你不能去问别人,他们在下一阶段需要什么"。在苹果公司,新产品的发展始于勇气,并在反反复复的讨论中孵化出来,过程往往如此:你讨厌什么?(我们的手机)我们拥有的技术可以制造什么?(内置 Mac 的手机)我们想拥有什么?(你猜,一部 iPhone)乔布斯说:"对苹果来说,关键之一就是我们生产的产品要根据我们

Apple's High-wire Act

"One of the keys to Apple is that we build products that really turn us on," says Jobs.

With that simple formula, Apple not only has upstaged the likes of Microsoft but has set the gold standard for corporate America with an entirely new business model: creating a brand, morphing it, and reincarnating① it to thrive in a disruptive age. Now, just several years after it unveiled the first iPod, fully half of Apple's revenues come from music and iPods. Interest in the iPod and iPhone has rubbed off on the Mac, whose sales growth outpaces the industry's. Apple has demonstrated how to create real, breathtaking growth by dreaming up products so new and ingenious that they have upended one industry after another: consumer electronics, the record industry, the movie industry, video and music production.

In the process the company that ranks as the new No. 1 among America's Most Admired Companies has become a roaring financial success. In the five years, sales tripled to $24 billion and profits surged to $3.5 billion, up from $42 million. While Apple's stock is slumping along with the market, tumbling 40% sometimes on worries about less-than-stratospheric sales growth, it doesn't usually stay down for long. Apple ranks No. 1 among Fortune 500 companies for total return to shareholders over both the past five years (94%) and the past ten (51%).

The era coincides exactly with the return of Jobs as Apple's maestro, leaving behind his particular mix of genius and obsession, as well as a tendency to play by his own rules. His utter dedication to discovery and excellence has created a culture that has made Apple a symbol of

---

① reincarnate [riːˈinkɑːneit] vt. 使化身

苹果的冒险行为

自身的条件而定。"

利用这个简单的公式,苹果不仅超越了同行微软,而且还以全新的经营模式为美国企业树立了黄金标准:创建品牌,树立形象,在乱象重生的时代获得再生。 现在,尽管距离它发布第一款 iPod 仅仅几年的时间,但苹果至少有一半的收入来自音乐和 iPod。 iPod 和 iPhone 的利润已经超过 Mac,尽管 Mac 销量的增长速度超过其他行业。 苹果已经证明如何创造真正的、令人惊叹的增长,即创造全新的、设计精巧的产品,颠覆一个又一个的行业:消费电子、唱片业、电影业、影像和音乐产品。

在此期间,苹果位列美国新晋的最受欢迎的公司首位,在赢利方面取得了巨大成功。 5 年间销售额增长了 3 倍,达到 240 亿美元,利润从 4 200 万美元飙升至 35 亿美元。 尽管苹果的股票有时随市场一起暴跌,降幅达 40%,引起低于超常水平的销售增长焦虑,但不会长期处于低位。 无论在过去的 5 年中,还是在过去的 10 年中,苹果的总体资本回报率都居财富 500 强公司的第一位,分别是 94%和 51%。

这个时代仍然与乔布斯这位苹果的艺术大师的回归完全吻合,他留下了天赋与痴迷的特殊混合体以及自己的游戏规则。 他绝对献身于对发现和卓越的追求,使苹果成为创新的标志。 在位于加州库比提诺无限循环大道上的苹果总部,在任何一张公告或宣传页上都找不到创新这个单词。 创新在这儿是一种生活方式,并不像佳洁士牙膏那样变化多端。 在苹果,每次努力都是一缕月光。 公司时有

Apple's High-wire Act

innovation. You won't find that word on a placard or a piece of propaganda at One Infinite Loop, Apple's headquarters in Cupertino, Calif. There innovation is a way of life. But it isn't like creating new variations on Crest toothpaste. At Apple, every endeavor is a moon shot. Sometimes the company misses, but the successes are huge. Apple's goal for iPhone sales at present is rapid growth.

Apple requires a special kind of workforce. The place is divided by product but also by function along what COO Tim Cook calls "very faint lines." Collaboration is key. So is a degree of perfectionism. Apple hires people who are never satisfied. A designer has to be a borderline fanatic to care about the curve of a screw on the underside of a MacBook Air or the apparent weightlessness of the tiny door that hides its connectors. You don't get a foot in the door here unless your eyes light up when you talk about your Mac. Head designer Jonathan Ive referred to a new MacBook Air as "this guy" as he pointed out features in a recent interview. The place is loaded with engineers, but it's not just the skills that are important, it's the ability to emote. The passion is what provides the push to overcome design and engineering obstacles, to bring projects in on time—and a peer pressure so great it sometimes causes a team to eject① a weak link or revolt against an underperforming boss. "Apple," says Cook, "is not for the faint of heart."

Here there is no such thing as hedging your bets. "One traditional management philosophy that's taught in many business schools is diversification. Well, that's not us," says Cook. "We are the anti-business school." Apple's philosophy goes like this: Too many companies spread

---

① eject [iˈdʒekt] *vt.* 驱逐

苹果的冒险行为

失败,但仍然成效卓著。 苹果目前的目标是iPhone的销售量迅猛增长。

　　苹果需要特殊类别的人力资源。 这块领地的划分不仅取决于产品,而且需要责任感,但营运总监蒂姆·库克认为"界限非常模糊"。 合作才是关键。 还要有点完美主义。 苹果喜欢雇佣永不满足的雇员。 设计师毫无疑问是爱质疑的狂热分子,关注苹果笔记本风扇下面螺钉的曲线,或隐藏连接器小门外观的厚薄。 除非一谈到苹果你就两眼放光,否则根本不可能在此立足。 首席设计师乔纳森·埃维在近期的一次访谈中,指着一个新苹果笔记本风扇称呼"这个家伙"。 这儿的工程师人满为患,但重要的不是技术,而是焕发激情的能力。 激情提供了克服设计和工程障碍的动力,使项目按期完成。 而同事之间的压力是如此之大,有时它会使一个团队抛弃弱者,或者厌恶不称职的老板。 库克认为,"苹果不适合心脏脆弱的人"。

　　这儿完全没有双面赌注。 库克认为,"许多商学院教授的一种传统管理哲学是多样化。 然而,它并不适合我们。 我们是反商学院"。 苹果的哲学是这样的:太多的企业试图同时干太多的工作,制造形形色色的产品降低风险,所以在平庸中陷入困境。 苹果的做法是将所有的资源投入极少数的产品,并把它们做到极致。 苹果残酷地淘汰劣质、过时的产品:在引进更好的纳米产品、获得更高的边际收益之时,公司抛弃了最受欢迎的迷你型iPod。 为什么要稀释你的资源呢?

Apple's High-wire Act

themselves thin, making a profusion of products to defuse risk, so they get mired in the mediocre①. Apple's approach is to put every resource it has behind just a few products and make them exceedingly well. Apple is brutal about culling past hits: The company dropped its most popular iPod, the Mini, on the day it introduced the Nano, a better product, higher margins, why dilute your resources?

Apple might look like a high-wire act. But while success is never guaranteed, it's not random either. Ownership of its operating system gives Apple an unusual degree of control over its ability to design, change, and adapt. That allows Apple to follow the product—with no preconceptions about where it will end up. The iPod has evolved from a device the size of a deck of cards to a Nano to a Shuffle and now to a Touch. The Touch, says Cook, "has another roadmap in front of it" if it becomes, as he predicts, the first mainstream Wi-Fi mobile device.

"Apple's DNA has always been to try to democratize technology," once said Jobs, in the belief that if you make something "really great, then everybody will want to use it." Who would have thought that a cult brand like Apple would be resuscitating a mass market? Jobs and his true believers have proved that if you're bold enough to build it, they will come!

(1,022 words)

---

① mediocre [ˌmiːdiˈəukə] *adj.* 平庸的

苹果的冒险行为

苹果公司可能看起来是在冒险，但是成功既无保障，也不可能随机。经营体系的所有权在产品设计、改变和调整方面赋予苹果超乎寻常的控制力。这使苹果可以跟随产品的潮流，无法预测它的尽头。iPod 的体积经历了从卡片大小、纳米技术、随机播放、再到现在的可触式一系列变化。库克说，可触式成型"之前有另一张路线图"，如他所预测的，即第一部主流 Wi-Fi 移动装置。

乔布斯曾说，"苹果的基因使它经常试图使科技民主化"。他深信，如果你做的东西"真的非常伟大，那么每个人都想使用它"。谁会想到苹果这样一个风靡一时的品牌唤醒了大众市场呢？乔布斯和他的忠实追随者们已经证明：尽可能大胆地去做，你终将获得回报！

知识链接

Kleenex 舒洁是美国金佰利公司旗下的一款产品，也是全球最知名的面巾纸品牌，代表着最佳品质、柔软舒适的感觉和如家的温馨，多次被美国《商业周刊》评为全世界 100 个最有价值的品牌之一。

Xerox 美国施乐公司是全球最大数字与信息技术产品生产商，是一家全球 500 强企业。施乐公司是复印技术的发明公司，具有悠久的历史，目前在复印机市场占有率，特别是彩色机器的市场占有率，据全球第一的位置，其彩色的技术方面是全球领袖企业。

题 记

　　自霍夫斯泰德提出民族文化维度以来，文化对企业经营活动的影响日益引起人们的关注。当各种文化系统在企业经营活动中相遇时，这种文化差异便潜在地构成了无法避免的文化风险。高盛集团之所以能成为全球领先的投资银行、证券及投资管理公司，与其将企业的经营风险纳入战略和组织、从而形成一种独特的企业风险文化密切相关。强大的专业队伍为高盛复杂的贸易和衍生交易提供了必需的量化和理性的精确数据支撑；强烈的责任心能够确保某些风险回报标准能够始终如一地贯彻到全公司；伙伴关系制度使合伙人十分谨慎地管理公司的资金，照料自己的财产；坚持商业原则使员工根据风险、灵活性、法律和其他强大的控制职能自己做出判断，保持独立的观点和维护公司的声誉。商业风险文化培植了高盛集团丰富的地区市场知识和国际运作能力，帮助客户无论在世界何地都能敏锐地发现和抓住投资的机会，独树一帜。

Business Risk as Culture for Goldman Sachs

As the markets for risk have evolved, it has become clear that a company's success is closely linked to the role risk plays in its culture. In the financial sector there is no better model than Goldman Sachs, arguably the world's leading investment banking, securities, and investment management firm. Today Goldman is essentially in the business of managing risk: Trading and principal investments account for 68% of its net revenues, whereas only 17% come from the traditional investment-banking and advisory business for which it was once best known.

Yet despite its reliance on highly volatile① trading revenues (and the company's trading revenues are more volatile than any of its peers'), Goldman has so far avoided the large losses that have afflicted its leading competitors. In the publics' view, this is because the firm's culture embraces rather than avoids risk the antithesis of the typical corporate approach. Goldman makes money by being willing to risk losing it. When

---

① volatile [ˈvɔlətail] *adj.* 不稳定的

高盛的商业风险文化

随着市场风险的演变，人们已经清楚地意识到，企业的成功和风险与企业文化发挥的作用密切相关。在金融行业，没有一个公司的管理模式能够比得上高盛——它称得上是世界领先的投资银行、证券及投资管理公司。如今，高盛主要从事管理风险业务：贸易和主要的投资占公司净收入的68%，仅有17%的收入来自传统的投资银行业务和咨询业务，这些业务曾经是高盛的招牌业务。

尽管高盛依赖于高风险贸易收入（高盛的贸易收入与其他同类公司相比稳定性更差），但到目前为止，高盛避免了大量的损失，而这些损失令其主要竞争对手苦不堪言。公众认为，这是因为公司的企业文化与常规的公司治理方法相背，强调容纳风险而不是规避风险。高盛在赚钱的同时就已准备承担损失的风险。证券市场动荡沉浮之际，价值的买卖选择权上升，经验丰富的风险管理自然也随之升值。高盛确保公司的管理者熟悉并适应风险，鼓励毫无顾忌的自由辩论，敢于在必要时迅速做出决策。高盛在2007年次级抵押贷款市场中采取的积极有效的防护措施就是这种企业文化的典范。高盛拥有灵活和幸运两种特质。它的灵活显示在它能够感知危机的

securities markets become more volatile, options rise in value; naturally, the value of experienced risk management rises also. Goldman ensures that its managers are familiar and comfortable with risk, can debate it freely without fear of sanctions, and are willing to make decisions quickly when necessary. The company's aggressive hedging in 2007 in markets related to subprime mortgages was a striking example of this. Goldman was both skillful and lucky. It was skillful in sensing that trouble was brewing① and deciding to move quickly to reposition itself. It was lucky in getting both the decision and the timing correct.

Creating a culture so contrary to people's instincts and fears isn't easy.Goldman's success stems from four factors. None is unique to the company, but Goldman very effectively employs all four.

Quantitative professionals. Beginning in the early 1980s, Goldman recruited experts in mathematical modeling, who came to be called quants. Perhaps the most notable hire was Fischer Black, brought over from MIT by Robert Rubin, who was then a general partner. Black led the firm's Quantitative Strategies group, working on, among other things, modern portfolio management and modeling interest-rate movements in order to value fixed-income options. Goldman also hired Emanuel Derman, a PhD in theoretical physics and one of Black's successors as head of Quantitative Strategies; and Bob Litterman, a PhD in economics and a co-developer of the Black-Litterman global asset allocation model. People like these

---

① brew [bru:] *vi.* (不愉快的事)即将降临

高盛的商业风险文化

来临,并迅速采取措施应对危机;它的幸运在于在正确的时间做出了正确的决策。

创造一种与人的本能和恐惧相反的文化并不容易。高盛的成功来源于四个因素。尽管任一因素对公司并非独特,但高盛却有效地整合利用了所有这四种因素。

强大的专业队伍。20世纪80年代早期,高盛开始聘请数学建模方面的专家,他们被称为数量化投资。由当时的一位高层合伙人罗伯特·鲁宾引荐、来自麻省理工的费舍尔·布莱克也许是最著名的受雇专家。除其他的工作之外,布莱克领导公司的定量化战略决策团队,研究现代证券管理,建立利率变动模型评估固定收益选择的价值。高盛还雇佣了理论物理学博士伊曼纽尔·德曼,作为布莱克定量化战略领导接班人之一。而经济学博士雷德曼,则是布莱克·雷德曼全球资产分析模型的开发者之一。这些人提供了必需的量化和理性的精确数据,以支持高盛复杂的贸易和衍生交易。

强烈的责任心。1994年,一场意外的全球利率增长使很多证券公司损失惨重,高盛当时的大型特许地位导致其利润大幅度下滑,并产生了道德危机。针对这一情况,刚担任公司高层领导的乔恩·科赞重组了高盛的风险控制系统,并成立了企业全面风险委员会,监督市场和全球信贷风险。该委员会每周举行例会,目的是确保某些风险回报标准能够始终如一地贯彻到全公司。每日风险报告详细地描述了公司暴露出的问题,例如,观察记录表显示各种宏观风险因素的变化对公司产生的潜在影响;压力测试显示各种情况造成的

provided the quantitative and intellectual rigor needed to support Goldman's complex trading and derivatives businesses.

Strong oversight. In 1994, when an unexpected rise in global interest rates caused severe losses on many bond-trading desks, Goldman's large proprietary positions led to a substantial decline in profitability and a crisis in morale. In response, Jon Corzine, who had just assumed leadership of the company, restructured Goldman's risk-control systems, establishing the Firm-wide Risk Committee to oversee market and credit risk worldwide. The committee, which meets weekly, aims to ensure that certain risk-return standards are applied consistently across the firm. Daily risk reports detail the firm's exposure with, for example, summary sheets showing the potential impact of changes in various macro risk factors and stress tests showing potential losses under a variety of scenarios, such as a widening of credit spreads, as happened in the autumn of 1998. Some Goldman executives claim they can fairly accurately estimate the firm's daily P&L just by looking at the risk reports and knowing the market's movements that day. Other forms of risk are taken equally seriously: Operational and reputational risks are addressed by the Business Practices Committee, loan and underwriting① risks are addressed by the Capital and Commitments committees, and liquidity risk is managed by the Finance Committee.

Partnership heritage.From its earliest days in 1869 to its IPO in 1999, Goldman was funded largely by its own partners. But while Lazard Frères

---

① underwrite [ˌʌndəˈraɪt] vt. 承保

高盛的商业风险文化

潜在损失,如1998年秋发生的信贷扩大利差。 高盛的有些高管声称,他们只需查看风险报告和了解当天的市场动向,就可以相当准确地估计公司的每日盈亏。 其他形式的风险同样被认真监管:商业实践委员会管理运营和声誉风险;资本和担保委员会管理贷款和承保风险;财务部门管理流动性风险。

伙伴关系制度。 从1869年成立伊始到1999年上市,高盛的资金主要由自己的合作伙伴提供。 当拉扎德兄弟公司和其他私人公司每年将超过80%的收入分配给股东时,高盛的合伙人却把税后利润的80%留在公司,退休时才大量回撤资金。 合伙人十分谨慎地管理公司的资金,因为这些都是他们自己的财产。 高盛的大多数高层主管秉承了这一传统,同时,员工也拥有相当一部分股份,这有助于增强这种伙伴关系文化。

坚持商业原则。 最后,高盛的价值观强调许多风险管理理念。绝大多数人受益于公司的信誉。 新雇员被告知,公司的成功尽管不是个人的努力,但任何人都可能玷污公司的声誉。 当潜在的分歧出现时,公司鼓励员工根据风险、灵活性、法律和其他强大的控制职能做出判断,保持独立的观点。 被高盛解雇的最快方式不是赔钱,而是单方面做出危害公司声誉的决定。

知识链接

Goldman Sachs 高盛集团成立于1869年,总部设在纽约,并在东京、伦敦和香港设有分部,在23个国家拥有41个办事处,是全球历史最悠久、规模

and other private firms distributed more than 80% of their earnings each year, Goldman's partners usually left as much as 80% of their after-tax earnings in the firm, withdrawing substantial amounts of capital only at retirement. The partners were careful stewards① of the firm's capital because it was their own. Goldman's most senior executives continue this heritage, and the fact that employees still own a significant portion of equity helps reinforce the partnership culture.

Business principles. Finally, Goldman's values reinforce many of these risk-management lessons. The company's reputation is prized most of all. New hires are taught that although no single individual can make the firm successful, anyone can harm its reputation. They are encouraged to solicit② independent views from risk, compliance, legal, and other powerful control functions when potentially controversial choices arise. The fastest way to get fired at Goldman is not to lose money but to make a unilateral decision that endangers the reputation of the firm.

(792 words)

---

① steward [ˈstjuːəd] n. 管理员
② solicit [səˈlisit] vt. 征求

高盛的商业风险文化

最大的投资银行之一。高盛集团的所有运作都建立在紧密一体的全球基础上,由优秀的专家为客户提供服务,向全球提供广泛的投资、咨询和金融服务,拥有大量的多行业客户,包括私营公司、金融企业、政府机构以及个人。

题 记

在平常人的眼中，残疾人是上天的弃儿，是社会的弱者，是正常人呵护的对象。然而，"残疾人之家"(Disaboom)却讲述了一个截然不同的故事。"残疾人之家"的创办人之一格伦·豪斯自己也是一名四肢瘫痪达20多年的残疾人，他以自己的亲身经历向世界宣告："残疾并不是世界末日，而是一个新的起点。"美国统计局的数据显示，自"残疾人之家"网站(Disaboom.com)建立以来，残疾人的自我雇佣率从12%上升到15%，而其他健康人的自我雇佣率却依然停留在8%。事实证明了残疾人在伟大的科技新领域畅通无阻。如果与正常人有什么区别的话，那就是他们自身拥有的决心提供了一种明显的商业优势。"残疾人之家"还在努力建造其他的社会网络，它不仅为残疾人、他们的家人、朋友、亲戚和看护提供了帮助，也为社会各阶层的人士了解他们的工作、生活和需求打开了一扇窗。

Opening new worlds: The Disability Boom

Led by a hot social network, disabled entrepreneurs are doing well by selling products that help the handicapped—and the rest of us.

Despite his wheelchair, and often because of it, Dr. Glen House has always enjoyed doing what he isn't supposed to. Take the time he persuaded his neighbor in Colorado Springs, J.W. Roth, to join him on vacation in the ice fields of Taku, Alaska. The trip entailed flying to a remote lodge in a tiny ski plane that was ill-equipped for disabled passengers: Boarding was via a rope ladder. "They said no wheelchairs," Roth recalls. "So we signed up."

That 2006 trip was a turning point for House and Roth. The boarding process was dicey: Roth gave House a fireman's lift up the plane's ladder, which dangled over the ice. "If I go down, you're going with me," House snarled on the way up. But later the pair sat in the Taku lodge, wondering how they might bring such exhilarating① experiences to other disabled people. "They're sick of doctors," House told Roth. "They want to know how to live forward with their conditions."

---

① exhilarating [igˈziləreitiŋ] *adj.* 令人喜欢的

"残疾人之家"开辟新商机

残疾人企业家在热门社会网络的引导之下,热火朝天地销售着他们的产品,在帮助了残疾伙伴的同时,也给我们提供了便利。

格伦·豪斯博士坐在轮椅上——就因为经常如此,才能始终愉快地做着自己始料不及的事情。他曾花了很多时间劝说科罗拉多州溪流地区的邻居 J. W 罗斯和他一起去阿拉斯加塔酷的滑雪场度假。去那儿必须乘坐小型滑雪机到一个遥远的山林小屋,而滑雪机的残疾人装备不足:只能通过绳梯登机。罗斯回忆说:"他们说没有轮椅,我们只好就此签约。"

2006 年的旅行对豪斯和罗斯来说都是一个转折点。登机过程险象环生:罗斯将消防队员爬飞机用的梯子递给豪斯,梯子在冰雪中不停地摇摆。豪斯边往上爬边咆哮:"我要是掉下去了,你也别想活命。"但后来两人还是坐在了塔酷的小木屋,思考着如何将这种令人振奋的经历与其他残疾朋友分享。豪斯对罗斯说:"他们厌恶医生,他们想知道根据自己的情况如何活下去。"

这番谈话催生了"残疾人之家"——一个致力于帮助美国 5 千万残疾人和看护的快速增长的社交网站。在这个社交网站疲软的时

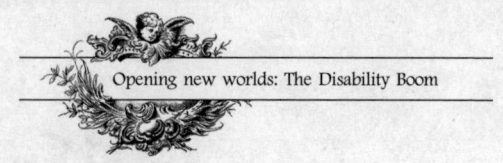

Opening new worlds: The Disability Boom

That chat led to the launch of Disaboom.com, a fast-growing social network aimed at the 50 million Americans with disabilities and their caregivers. In a time of social-network fatigue, as Facebook and MySpace have spawned hundreds of bland imitators, Denver-based Disaboom is unique. It focuses on a large, untapped audience eager to get answers and make connections, and one that advertisers had previously been unable to reach.

Like the entrepreneurs in the stories that follow, House demonstrates that disabilities are no obstacle in the brave new world of technology. If anything, the determination they engender provides a clear business advantage. According to the U.S. Census Bureau, the percentage of self-employed Americans with disabilities has grown from 12% to 15% since the dawn of the Web. For the rest of us, the figure has stayed static at 8%. Your next competitor may just zoom past you in a wheelchair.

When House wants to get somewhere, he goes fast. "That is how I ended up in the wheelchair," he says. During a ski vacation in Snowbird, Utah, House ignored the sign that read DANGER! ROCK! and at 20 became a quadriplegic① from the pectorals② down. But House lost no time pursuing his next goal: He began studying for medical school. His Disaboom colleagues all have stories of his dangerously fast driving; one had to pull him from his car when it skidded off the road into the Colorado snow.

House is the public face of Disaboom, writing most of the medical guides to the 40 disabilities the site covers and participating in its forums.

---

① quadriplegic [ˌkwɔdriˈpledʒik] n. 四肢瘫痪者
② pectoral [ˈpektərəl] adj. 胸的

"残疾人之家"开辟新商机

代,尽管脸书网和聚友网还在成批产出数以百计的乏味模仿者,但位于丹佛的"残疾人之家"仍然独具魅力。"残疾人之家"密切关注大量从未使用过网站的民众,他们迫切需要得到答复,对外联络,广告商也难以取得这样的效果。

就像下面这个故事讲述的企业家一样,豪斯证明了残疾人在伟大的科技新领域畅通无阻。如果有什么区别的话,那就是他们自身拥有的决心提供了一种明显的商业优势。美国人口调查局的数据显示:自网站开办以来,残疾人的自我雇佣率从12%上升到15%。而其他健康人的自我雇佣率仍然停留在8%。你未来的竞争者可能就是坐着轮椅急速驶过你身边的残疾人。

豪斯一旦定下目标,就会马不停蹄。他说:"这就是我现在为什么坐轮椅。"在犹他州雪鸟的一次滑雪休假期间,他忽视了写有"危险!石头!"的标志,20岁便成为一名胸部以下残疾的人。但豪斯争分夺秒地继续追求他的下一个目标:他开始上医学院。"残疾人之家"的同事都知道他飞车的危险故事,这次事故使他再也无法开车进入科罗拉多滑雪场。

豪斯是"残疾人之家"的公众人物,他在网页上为40名残疾人用户提供医疗指导,并且参与网络论坛活动。他和罗斯初建的公司就像福克斯剧院,略具格兰·豪斯这名残疾人医生的特点,并开始赢得评论家和观察家的关注,但这没有对他们造成伤害。尽管至少有一位病人坚持要得到他的亲笔签名,但格兰·豪斯却没有丝毫炫耀的意图。

Opening new worlds: The Disability Boom

It doesn't hurt that he and Roth founded the company just as the Fox drama House, which partially features a disabled doctor named Greg House, started winning over critics and viewers. Glen House was not the inspiration for the show, although at least one patient insisted on his autograph anyway.

It helped that Roth, one of the founders of biotech firm AspenBio, came aboard as CEO. Roth swiftly garnered $15 million in funding and began targeting advertisers. Since then, Disaboom had racked up $1 million in ad sales to corporate Godzillas such as Ford (F, Fortune 500), Avis (CAR, Fortune 500), Johnson & Johnson (JNJ, Fortune 500), and T-Mobile, and had served up 23 million online ads.

Roth launched a sister site, Disaboomjobs.com, in an effort to address the 60% unemployment rate among disabled Americans. He even bought a disabled-dating site called lovebyrd.com. "We don't want Disaboom to smell like a doctor's office," Roth says. "We want to deal with dating issues, sex issues, how to drive a fast car."

Disaboom officially launched since it started. The main site now boasts 90,000 registered users, and the rate at which new users sign up is growing by 500% a month. Presidential Barack Obama and John McCain both launched profiles on the site. Roth and House maintain folders full of thank-you e-mails, many from parents of disabled kids who didn't know where to turn until they found sympathy and suggestions from the Disaboom community.

The site is not without problems. Roth decided to take Disaboom (DSBO.OB) public before its launch; as of late August, the stock was trading at an anemic 50 cents a share, $1.30 off its 2007 high. One

"残疾人之家"开辟新商机

生物技术公司 AspenBio 的创始人之一、海外首席执行官罗斯助了公司一臂之力。罗斯很快以债券的方式投资 1 500 万美元,并开始锁定广告商。迄今为止,"残疾人之家"已经募集了百万美元的广告销售,与福特、艾维斯、强生等世界 500 强企业和德国电信等哥斯拉公司合作,提供了 2 300 万条在线广告。

罗斯还建立了"残疾人工作之家"的姊妹网站,处理美国残疾人 60% 的失业率问题。他甚至买下了残疾人约会网站——"爱伯德网站"。罗斯说:"我们不希望'残疾人之家'散发医生办公室的气味。我们还应该处理约会专题、性爱专题,以及如何飙车等问题。"

"残疾人之家"自成立以来就发起了正式活动。其主要网站现已有 9 万名注册用户,新用户的注册率以每月 500% 的速度增长。巴拉克·奥巴马总统和约翰·麦凯恩均在网站挂了网页。罗斯和豪斯保留了很多文件夹,里面全是表示感谢的电子邮件,其中很多来自残疾孩子的家长,他们曾经不知所措,后来在"残疾人之家"的网上社区找到了关怀和建议。

网站也遇到过很多困难。罗斯决定先公示再上市。八月底,股票以每股 50 美分的低价卖出,比 2007 年的高价低 1.3 美元。一名残疾人在 GearAbility.com 博客中抱怨,"残疾人工作之家"为残疾人提供的职位特别少,很多内容读起来像人力资源广告。华盛顿特区的一群游说人、美国残疾人协会科技政策高级总裁杰尼夫·西姆普生说:"闲言碎语很多。我们一直在谈论他们,但我认为他们

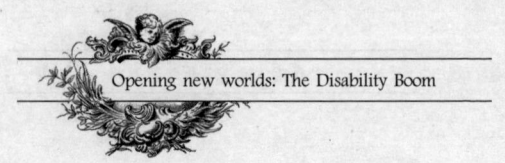
Opening new worlds: The Disability Boom

disabled blogger at GearAbility.com complained that Disaboom jobs listed too few positions specifically for the handicapped, and that much of the content read like PR blurbs. "There's a lot of buzz about them," says Jennifer Simpson, senior director of technology policy at the American Association of People with Disabilities, a lobbyinggroup in Washington, D. C. "We talk about them all the time, but I don't think they're where they want to be." House and Roth are working on that. They recently struck deals with the Mayo Clinic and Harvard Medical School to license a reliable range of medical content. With $ 4 million cash in hand, Disaboom's stock slump isn't going to bite anytime soon. The 39 employees on staff include three full-time "social marketers," who write blogs and help promote the site on a range of popular websites such as Digg and Twitter.

"This is the tip of the iceberg," says Roth at his conference table in a suburban Denver office park. He already has plans to launch other social networks for underserved markets. Neither he nor House will say more than that, but it seems likely that they'll soon be doing something they weren't supposed to do, one more time.

(933 words)

"残疾人之家"开辟新商机

并非应该如此。"豪斯和罗斯一直在为此努力,他们最近与梅奥诊所和哈佛医学院合作,获准使用一系列可靠的医学资源。"残疾人之家"拥有400万美元的现金,其股票价格任何时候都不会暴跌。网站有39名工作人员,包括3位全职"社会市场商人",他们写博客,并在"掘客"和"推特"等一系列流行网站上推广网站。

罗斯在丹佛郊区办公场所的会议桌前说:"事情初见端倪。"他已经计划建造其他的社会网络。他和豪斯都没有对此作详细解说,但他们将再次完成意料之外的事情,这一点似乎是有可能的。

知识链接

The American Association of People with Disabilities 美国残疾人协会拥有140 000多名独立成员,是美国最大的残疾人组织,成员包括各类残疾人、其家庭成员和支持者。

Disaboom.com "残疾人之家"是最大的残疾人在线社会网络工作和信息资源网站。自2008年上线以来,网站注册用户已超过9万人。用户通过博客、论坛、聊天室、视频、图片等分享信息和经历。此外,网站还有成千上万的生活模式、权威的治疗方案和医学类文章,帮助残疾人学习、生活和找工作的板块。

题 记

　　摩根士丹利经济学家理查德·伯纳把多面夹击美国的金融危机戏称为"完美风暴"。其实，处在风口上的美国大公司又何尝不是战战兢兢，在凛冽的寒风中瑟瑟发抖呢？雷曼公司倒闭、美林被收购、房地美、房利美和美国国际集团被国有化……金融系统的游戏规则被彻底改写。政府一方面试图压制投机和通货膨胀，一方面试图带领经济走出衰退，联邦储备委员会疯狂地使用各种货币政策工具，却收效甚微。从长期看，政策制定者的注意力必须转向，包括如何系统地管理重要的金融机构使之不至于产生权力过大的管理者，部分金融体系是否最好还是由公共部门控制。但从短期看，政府必须确保自己有能力、井然有序地清理当下搅得它烦躁不安的各类金融机构。美国政府在超出裁判的角色之后，到底还能走多远呢……

Changing the Rules of the Game

Just two days after allowing a large investment bank to fail as a stern statement of free market discipline, Ben Bernanke, chairman of the Federal Reserve Board, and Hank Paulson, Treasury secretary, in effect nationalized American International Group, the insurance giant. There was no alternative, but these dramatic steps show how finance will never be the same again.

By allowing Lehman Brothers to fall, the authorities demonstrated their reluctance① to save financial institutions with public money. Banks—even big, famous ones—would be allowed to fail if it were felt the system could handle it. But AIG was too important to go under. Default on its $441bn exposure to credit default swaps and other derivatives would have been a global financial catastrophe. Cancelling the insurance it underwrote would cause another wave of writedowns, further reduce lending and spread the crisis deeper and further. As with Freddie Mac and Fannie Mae, the nationalisation of AIG has caused problems for future policymakers, but future systemic moral hazard is of secondary importance

---

① reluctance [riˈlʌktəns] *n.* 不愿意

改写游戏规则

美联储主席本·伯南克和财政部长汉克·鲍尔森按照苛刻的自由市场运行规律，批准了一家大型投资银行的破产，而就在两天之后，他们却宣布了保险业巨头——美国国际集团的国有化生效。尽管别无选择，但这些戏剧性的步骤表明，金融业将发生根本性的变化。

官方承认了雷曼兄弟公司的倒闭，表明其不愿动用公共资金挽救金融机构。如果金融系统能够承受，即使是大型的知名银行也可任其倒闭。但美国国际集团的地位如此显赫，无论如何也不能破产。该公司在信用违约互换及其他金融衍生品上的4 410亿美元的敞口如果出现拖欠，一场全球性的金融灾难将无法避免。取消它对保单的担保责任将导致新一波的资产减记，进一步减少贷款并将危机扩散得更加深远。与房地美和房利美一样，对美国国际集团的国有化给未来的政策制定者带来一些问题，但当金融系统本身处于风险时，未来系统性的道德风险则处于次要地位。

救助美国国际集团的方案已在按部就班地良性运行。美联储交给保险公司一笔850亿美元的贷款，条件是用美国国际集团的顶级

Changing the Rules of the Game

when the system itself is at risk.

The AIG rescue package was well-designed. The Fed gave the insurer an $85bn loan, charged at punitive rates and secured against AIG's best assets, while replacing the management and taking a warrant for almost four-fifths of AIG's equity. This should allow the insurer to meet its obligations until it is able to sell off some of the assets on its $1,000bn balance sheet. The Fed's other actions were also well-judged. It was right to hold its fire by keeping interest rates at 2 per cent. With credit markets jammed up, an interest rate cut would, for the most part, only have delivered a psychological boost. Injecting liquidity, on the other hand, brought relief as banks scrambled① for short-term funding, and should be continued. After a year of what felt, at times, like a phoney② war, the past two weeks have seen unimaginable changes in the world financial system. The collapse of Lehman, the buy-up of Merrill Lynch and the nationalizations of Fannie, Freddie and AIG were obvious landmarks. Of potentially greater importance, however, the reach and power of the state has been greatly extended. The Bear Stearns bail-out involved the Fed moving to cover investment banks. With the AIG takeover, it has moved into insurance.

In the long run, policymakers must turn their minds to how systemically important institutions should be governed without creating over-powerful regulators, and whether any parts of the financial system might best be kept in the public sector. They also need an exit strategy for

---

① scramble ['skræmbl] vi. 争夺
② phoney ['fəuni] n. 骗人的东西

改写游戏规则

优质资产作为担保、并以惩罚性的利率记息,同时更换管理层、并有权获得美国国际集团近五分之四的股票。这将使保险公司履行义务,直至售出其一万亿美元资产负债表上的部分资产。美联储的其他举动也很明智,将利率始终控制在2%的基点上。随着信贷市场的拥堵,降息最多只能引起一种心理亢奋。另一方面,由于银行忙于争夺短期债券,注入资产折现力得到缓解,也应该持续放缓。经过一年偶尔有点像虚张声势的战争后,过去两周的世界金融体系出现了不可思议的变化。明显的转折点是雷曼公司倒闭,美林被收购,房地美、房利美和美国国际集团被国有化。而可能更重要的是,国家的手伸得更长、国家权力已大大延伸。贝尔斯登救助行动使美联储插手投资银行,而对美国国际集团的接管则使其进入保险行业。

如果从长计议,政策制定者的注意力必须转向,包括如何系统地管理重要的金融机构使之不至于产生权力过大的管理者,部分金融体系是否最好还是由公共部门控制。他们也需要制定从长期无所作为的领域退出的战略。但从短期看,政府必须确保自己有能力、井然有序地清理当下搅得它烦躁不安的各类金融机构。清债信托公司就是为储蓄和借贷危机期间处理此类事务而设立的。

目前的混乱还不止于此。对货币市场基金的担忧正在显现。货币基金作为极端安全、低回报的工具,投资于优质短期的公司债券。货币市场基金注销曾获高度评级的雷曼公司7.85亿美元的债务后,首次"跌破面值",即每股资产净值跌至1美元以下。只要

Changing the Rules of the Game

those areas in which it has no long-term role. In the short term, however, the government must make sure it has the ability to wind down, in an orderly fashion, the wide range of institutions that it is now worried about. The Resolution Trust Corporation was created to do this during the savings and loan crisis.

This is not the end of the current turmoil. Concerns are now being raised about money market funds. Designed as ultra-safe, low-return vehicles, they invest in top-rate short-term corporate bonds. Having written off $785m of once highly rated Lehman debt, Reserve Primary Fund "broke the buck" for the first time—its net asset value per share fell below its target of $1. Further losses will occur only if other big companies fail. But consumers may retreat from the funds. With dwindling assets, funds would buy fewer short-term bonds, further adding to the difficulty of obtaining short-term credit.

The rules of the game have been rewritten dramatically over this past fortnight but the game, at least, is still being played in some form. That is a victory of sorts. Governments are currently rightly preoccupied with crisis management. The next challenge will be to work out how far the state should stay as more than just an umpire①.

(636 words)

---

① umpire [ˈʌmpaiə] *n.* 仲裁人，裁判员

改写游戏规则

其他公司破产，进一步的损失还将出现。但消费者可以退出基金。由于资产减少，基金会减少短期债券的购买，这将进一步加大获取短期信贷的难度。

尽管游戏规则已经在过去两周被戏剧性地改写，但游戏至少还在以某种形式继续。这算得上是某种胜利。各国政府目前正忙于处理危机。但他们要解决的下一个挑战是：政府在超出裁判的角色之后，到底还能走多远。

知识链接

AIG 美国国际集团是世界保险和金融服务的领导者，也是全球首屈一指的国际性保险服务机构，业务遍及全球一百三十多个国家及地区，其成员公司通过世界保险业最为庞大的财产保险及人寿保险服务网络，竭诚为各商业、机构和个人客户提供服务。美国国际集团也是个人和大型企业投资管理市场中的翘楚，为客户提供专业的股票、定息证券、地产及其他投资管理服务。美国国际集团的股票在纽约证券交易所、美国 ArcaEx 电子证券交易市场、伦敦、巴黎、瑞士及东京的股票市场均有上市。

题 记

联想正式宣布完成收购美国国际商用机器公司的个人电脑业务，标志着这笔价值17.5亿美元的交易最终尘埃落定。这一消息震惊了整个世界。对于国际商用机器公司而言，转手个人电脑业务将推动其朝着软件以及服务等利润丰厚的方向发展，但它并不愿意把这部分业务出售给在服务器等盈利领域与自己展开激烈竞争的对手戴尔和惠普。更为重要的是，公司可以通过这项交易获得进军中国市场的通行证。对于目前在中国个人电脑市场占据三分之一市场份额的联想而言，本次收购业务标志着中国企业的海外扩张达到顶峰，联想将成为全球第三大个人电脑厂商，仅次于戴尔和惠普。本次收购抑或是国际商用机器公司的"瘦身药"，抑或是联想的"大补丸"，仁者见仁，智者见智，但双方的交易终究是顺理成章，各取所需。

A Bridge between Companies and Cultures

I.B.M. announced the sale of its personal computer business to Lenovo, China's largest personal computer maker, a deal that reflects the industrial and economic ambitions of not only the two companies but also their two nations. Under Lenovo's ownership, the I.B.M. personal computer business will continue to be based in the United States and run by its current management team. I.B.M. will take a stake of 18.9 percent in Lenovo, which is based in Beijing but plans to have headquarters in New York.

The significance of the deal may exceed the relatively modest amount that Lenovo is paying: a total of $ 1.75 billion in cash, stock and debt. The transaction points to the rising global aspirations of corporate China as it strives to become a trusted supplier to Western companies and consumers. The sale also signals recognition by I.B.M., the prototypical American multinational, that its own future lies even farther up the economic ladder, in technology services and consulting, in software and in the larger computers that power corporate networks and the Internet. All are businesses far more profitable for I.B.M. than its personal computer unit.

But the move signals an acknowledgment by I.B.M. that its future in China may be best served by a close partnership with a local market leader—particularly one, as in Lenovo's case. The chief executive of Lenovo

企业和文化之间的桥梁

美国国际商用机器公司宣布,将自己的个人电脑业务出售给中国最大的个人电脑制造商联想,这项交易不仅是两家公司在产业和经济野心上的对话,也是两个国家之间的对话。 国际商用机器公司的个人电脑业务将会在联想的所有权下以现在的管理团队继续在美国运营。 国际商用机器公司将持有联想18.9%的股份。 联想的基地在北京,计划在纽约设立总部。

本次收购的重要性可能超出了联想支付的相对微薄的17.5亿美元的现金、股票和债券。 这项交易说明,日益增长的全球化目标激励中国公司努力成为西方企业和消费者值得信赖的供应商。 本次销售也标志着国际商用机器公司的共识:典型美国跨国公司的未来应该立足于更高的经济阶梯,即提供技术服务和咨询、软件或公司局域网和互联网的大型计算机。 对国际商用机器公司来说,所有这些都比做个人电脑业务更加有利可图。

但是此举意味着国际商用机器公司的认同,即它在中国的未来最好是与中国本地市场的领导企业密切合作——特别是像联想那样的企业。 现任国际商用机器公司的高级副总裁、负责个人电脑业务

A Bridge between Companies and Cultures

will be Stephen M. Ward Jr., currently an I.B.M. senior vice president in charge of the PC business. Lenovo's current chief and president, Yang Yuanqing, will become Lenovo's chairman.

American companies, in one industry after another, are scrambling to take advantage of the vast potential of the Chinese market. Chinese companies like Lenovo, meanwhile, are increasingly seeking to tap into overseas markets, management expertise and technological skills. "This is an encouraging sign of the increasingly sophisticated trans-Pacific ties between the United States and China," said Timothy F. Bresnahan, an economist at Stanford University. "Seeing the Chinese seeking these kinds of economic links can only be a good thing."

The complex transaction is meant to serve as a bridge between very different companies from different cultures, by seeking to ensure that I.B.M. has a stake in the Chinese company's success. Whether in the United States, in China or anywhere else in the world, such a stake would be in I.B.M.'s self-interest; a messy exit from the personal computer industry could rankle corporate customers, hurting I.B.M.'s other businesses, and tarnish① its stellar brand name.

I.B.M. has agreed to hold onto its stake in Lenovo for three years, with an option of extending it. I.B.M.'s financial commitment to Lenovo could help open doors for its efforts to win other business in China. Besides management expertise, Lenovo would be acquiring five-year brand-licensing rights to a computer business best known for its I.B.M. Thinkpad notebooks, its sleek black desktops and the product line's distinctive tricolor I.B.M. logo.

While Lenovo will have its headquarters in New York, the hub of the

---

① tarnish ['tɑːnɪʃ] vt. 使暗淡

企业和文化之间的桥梁

的史蒂芬·沃德,将担任联想的首席执行官。 联想的现任总裁兼首席执行官杨元庆将担任联想的董事长。

美国一个又一个行业的企业纷至沓来,抢夺潜力巨大的中国市场。 而联想之类的中国企业也同时越来越多地寻求挤进海外市场,学习管理经验和技术技能。 斯坦福大学的经济学家蒂莫斯·布莱斯纳罕认为:"这是一个令人鼓舞的标志,美国和中国跨太平洋的纽带越来越紧密。 见证中国人积极寻求这种经济联系是件好事。"

这项复杂的交易意味着通过寻求确保国际商用机器公司在中国公司的股份,从不同的文化角度搭建不同公司之间的桥梁。 无论是在美国、中国或者世界其他地方,这种股份与国际商用机器公司的自身利益密切相关。 杂乱无章地退出个人电脑行业可能会激怒全体顾客,损害公司的其他业务,并玷污其一流的品牌。

公司同意三年内持有联想股份,三年后选择是否扩大。 公司对联想的财政承诺可以助其打开大门,在中国开拓其他业务。 除了管理技术,联想还将获得为期五年的商标使用权,如最出名的 Thinkpad 笔记本电脑、时尚黑色台式机,以及生产线上独特的三色 IBM 标识。

联想计划在纽约设立总部,但国际商用机器公司的个人电脑业务中心在北卡的罗利,那里是设计和开发部门的大本营。 公司在世界范围内雇佣了 1 万名员工,专营个人电脑,但在美国工作的人不到四分之一。 事实上,40%的人已经在中国工作。 根据双方达成的协议,公司将继续提供技术支持、融资,以及在全球范围内为之前

A Bridge between Companies and Cultures

I.B.M. PC business is in Raleigh, N.C., where its design and development operations are based. I.B.M. employs about 10,000 people worldwide in its PC business, although fewer than a quarter of those workers are in the United States. In fact, 40 percent already work in China. Under the agreement, I.B.M. will continue to handle technical support, financing and warranty coverage globally for its former personal computer division. Those tend to be steady and profitable cash-generating businesses, even as the PC business itself has been only intermittently① profitable for I.B.M. lately.

It was I.B.M. that moved the personal computer industry from a hobbyist market into the corporate and consumer mainstream with its first PC in 1981. Today, I.B.M. is a distant third in worldwide PC market share, behind Dell and Hewlett-Packard. I.B.M.'s personal computer sales are about $10 billion a year, or about 11 percent of its $89 billion in revenue, but it has hovered between slight profits and losses in recent years. In its hasty entry into the PC business in the early 1980's, I.B.M. made what turned out to be a strategic mistake: it chose outside suppliers for the crucial technologies of the microprocessor and the software operating system, helping Intel and Microsoft become two of the most profitable companies in the world.

For nearly a decade, executives have debated dropping out of the personal computer business. Samuel J. Palmisano, who became I.B.M.'s chief executive in 2002, finally made the move. He decided that the company's management and investment resources would be better used in its other businesses like software and services to help customers use information technology to help automate business tasks from product

---

① intermittently [intə'mitəntli] adv. 间歇性地

企业和文化之间的桥梁

的个人电脑业务实施担保。这些往往是稳定和现金收益颇丰的业务,即使个人电脑业务近期只是间歇性地为公司盈利。

这是国际商用机器公司自1981年涉及个人电脑业务以来第一次将个人电脑业务的重心从个人消费者市场转向公司市场。公司目前的个人电脑全球市场份额排名第三,远远落后于戴尔和惠普。公司的个人电脑销售额每年大约100亿美元,抑或890亿美元收入的11%左右,但最近几年一直在盈利甚微和亏损之间徘徊。在匆忙进入个人电脑业务的20世纪80年代初,公司做出了一个被证明是错误的战略:选择做微处理器和软件操作系统这两个核心技术的外部供应商,帮助英特尔和微软成为了世界上最盈利的两家公司。

近十年来,高层们一直就是否退出个人电脑市场争论不休。直到2002年塞缪尔·帕米萨诺接任首席执行官,才最终尘埃落定。他认为公司的管理和投资资源可以更好地用于其他业务,如软件或服务,帮助顾客利用信息技术,让企业实现从产品设计到生产的自动化交易流程。斯坦福C.伯恩斯坦公司的分析师A. M.萨克纳吉认为,"从战略角度看,个人电脑业务对国际商用机器公司不再重要。帕米萨诺决定把业务重点放在更加有利可图、更有增长潜力的部门"。帕米萨诺在一份声明中表示,个人电脑业务"依然以家庭和消费电子行业为特征,热衷于巨大的经济规模,以个人用户和买家为轴心",但公司将在企业市场投放更多的精力。

高德纳咨询公司的分析师莱斯利·菲尔琳认为:"联想志在成为主要的国际玩家和知名品牌,并具备跨国公司的销售和盈利能力。

A Bridge between Companies and Cultures

design to procurement①. "The PC business is just not that important anymore to I.B.M. strategically," said A.M. Sacconaghi, an analyst at Sanford C. Bernstein & Company. "Palmisano has decided to focus instead on businesses that are more profitable for I.B.M. and promise higher growth." In a statement, Mr. Palmisano said the PC industry "continues to take on the characteristics of the home and consumer electronics industry which favors enormous economies of scale and a focus on individual users and buyers," while I.B.M. will focus more on the corporate market.

"Lenovo aspires to become a major international player and a recognized brand, a company with the ability to sell into multinational corporations and be profitable," said Leslie Fiering, an analyst for Gartner. "This deal improves its chances, but the business is only going to get tougher over the next few years." The personal computer industry, like most technology businesses, is not one in which low labor costs—one of China's advantages in competing with Western rivals—are much of an edge. The big winner in the business, Dell Computer, is mainly a master of ultra-efficient management of its suppliers, assembly and distribution.

I.B.M.'s rivals said the Lenovo purchase would create uncertainty among customers and provide opportunity for them. "It's hard to think back on a successful large merger in the computer industry, and I don't see this one being different," Michael S. Dell, chairman of Dell Computer said. "We like to acquire our competitors one customer at a time."

(1,020 words)

---

① procurement [prəˈkjuəmənt] n. 获得

企业和文化之间的桥梁

本次收购将助其成功,但个人电脑业务在今后几年会更加艰难。"个人电脑行业和大部分的技术行业一样,是一个夕阳行业,它不能仅靠廉价的劳动成本,尽管这是中国和西方对手竞争时的一大优势。行业的大赢家"戴尔电脑"主要是在供应商、组装和销售方面具备超高效的管理能力。

国际商用机器公司的竞争对手表示,联想的本次收购将会造成客户的不确定性,这让他们有机可乘。 戴尔电脑的董事长迈克尔·戴尔说:"难以回想计算机行业的大型成功并购案例,我不认为本次的收购有什么不同。 我们希望一次俘获竞争对手的一个客户。"

知识链接

Gartner 高德纳咨询公司是全球最具权威的 IT 研究与顾问咨询公司,成立于 1979 年,总部设在美国康涅狄克州斯坦福。其研究范围覆盖全部 IT 产业,就 IT 的研究、发展、评估、应用、市场等领域,为客户提供客观、公正的论证报告及市场调研报告,协助客户进行市场分析、技术选择、项目论证、投资决策。为决策者在投资风险和管理、营销策略、发展方向等重大问题上提供重要咨询建议,帮助决策者作出正确抉择。公司拥有 1 200 多位世界级分析专家,在全球设有 80 多个分支机构,客户几乎囊括了绝大部分世界级大公司。

题　记

　　苹果首席执行官的继位人能与手机 iPhone、平板电脑 iPad 在全球市场的无限风光相媲美吗？离开乔布斯后的苹果是否能再造辉煌？也许苹果公司可参阅伯克希尔·哈撒韦公司和通用电气公司的案例。尽管巴菲特先生高超的投资能力使伯克希尔的股东们赚得盆满钵满，但公司已经确定了三名杰出的内部候选人，其中之一将会在巴菲特永久离开时接替他担任首席执行官。通用电气是一家非常注重继承人计划编制的公司。杰克·韦尔奇在辞去首席执行官的几年前，就和通用电气的主管们确定了三名候选继承人。自从乔布斯被查出患胰腺癌后，外界一直期待他能公布接班人计划，而他迟迟未对外表态。乔布斯的健康已成苹果发展的不确定性。能够继承乔布斯的独特视野、创新能力和激励能力，继续为苹果服务的人选，成为公众关注的普遍话题。

The Seamless Handover

Steve Jobs and the case for succession planning have already drawn the attention of the world: Is he sick, or isn't he? And if he is sick, just how serious is his condition? Ever since an emaciated① Steve Jobs appeared on stage at a conference to introduce Apple's new generation of iPhone, rumors have been flying about the state of his health. Various non-committal statements from Apple executives have thickened the fog surrounding the issue.

Only a few days Apple's stock slipped from $166.29 to $154.40. That partly reflects the firm's prediction that sales will grow slower than it initially expected in the next quarter, as the global economy slows. But it also shows that investors are worried about both the health of Mr. Jobs, who underwent successful surgery to tackle pancreatic cancer in 2004, and about Apple's lack of an explicit plan to replace him should become incapacitated. Apple's experience is a wake-up call to board directors everywhere, who need to sharpen their thinking on executive succession, especially given the febrile state of today's financial markets. As companies' profits fall, demands for a firm and possibly new hand on the leadership tiller will grow. Confusion at the top may be exploited by short-sellers, who will dump a firm's shares and buy them back on the cheap after bad news

---

① emaciate [iˈmeisieit] *vt.* 使憔悴

权力移交天衣无缝

史蒂夫·乔布斯及其继任计划引起了全球的关注：他究竟病了还是没病？ 如果他生病了，情况有多严重？ 自从面容憔悴的史蒂夫·乔布斯出席会议介绍苹果的新一代产品 iPhone 以来，关于他健康状况的传闻从未间断。 来自于苹果管理层的各种各样非正式声明又加深了笼罩在这个事件上的迷雾。

几天之间，苹果的股票从 166.29 美元下跌至 154.40 美元。 这部分反映了公司的预测：由于全球经济增长放缓，销售量的增长将慢于最初对下一季度的预测。 但这也显示，投资者不仅担心乔布斯先生的健康状况，也担心苹果公司因为没有明确替换乔布斯的计划而失去适应能力，尽管乔布斯 2004 年做手术成功地战胜了胰腺癌。苹果公司的经历对董事会的每个股东来说都是一个警告，特别是在金融市场目前所处的狂躁期，每个人都需要对行政继承加深思考。由于公司的利润下降，人们增加了对有铁腕手段或新的领导者的需求。 短期卖家可能会利用领导层的困惑，高价抛售公司股份，然后在坏消息使股价下跌时以低价回购。 市场规范者近期已经抑制了金融股票市场上的短期操作，他们正在寻找新的目标。

这一切引发了两个重要问题：第一，公司对首席执行官的健康情况会泄露多少消息？ 第二，公司对外界宣传的继承计划应该有多

The Seamless Handover

has driven down the share price. Regulators have recently crimped the shorts' activity in financial stocks; they are looking for new targets.

All this raises two important questions: first, how much should a company divulge① about its CEO's health? And second, how explicit should it be to the outside world about its succession plans? The by-the-corporate-governance-book answer to the first question is that so long as directors are kept informed of a CEO's health and the boss is still capable of performing his or her duties, there is no obligation to make any public statement. This seems to be Apple's approach: it considers Mr. Jobs's health a private matter. But when investors believe that a company's fortunes are intimately tied to a visionary leader—as is the case with Apple—speculation about that leader's longevity② can have a direct impact on the share price. If, on the other hand, a firm convinces investors it has strong successors-in-waiting, then rumors that the boss has the sniffles③ (or worse) are less likely to set its stock price aflutter④.

So the answers to the two questions posed are linked: a company with a strong succession plan in place is less likely to have to broadcast its leader's vital signs to the world. To see how this can be done, consider the case of Berkshire Hathaway, the holding company run by the legendary Warren Buffett. Mr. Buffett's famed investment prowess has helped make Berkshire's shareholders rich, and, at 77, he shows no signs of flagging. Still, he stresses regularly that Berkshire is prepared for a post-Buffett

---

① divulge [dai'vʌldʒ] vi. 泄露
② longevity [lɔn'dʒeviti] n. 生命
③ sniffle ['snifl] n. 抽噎
④ aflutter [ə'flʌtə] adj. 惊慌的

权力移交天衣无缝

明确？ 公司管理手册对第一个问题的回答是：只要董事会了解首席执行官健康状况的信息，而且老板仍然有能力履行他/她的职责，就没有必要做任何公开的声明。 这似乎就是苹果的行事方式：认为乔布斯先生的健康状况是私人问题。 然而，当投资者相信公司的财富与一个具有远见卓识的领导者紧密相关时（如苹果公司），对领导人寿命的预测可能对公司股价产生直接影响。 另一方面，如果公司能使投资者确信，他们有实力很强的接班人，那么有关老板病危的谣言就不会导致股价波动。

因此，以上提到的两个问题的答案其实是相互联系的：一个有着完备的继承者计划的公司不大可能向世界公布其领导者的关键信息。 要了解这种传承如何完成，可参阅伯克希尔·哈撒韦公司的案例，这是一家由传奇人物巴菲特控股的公司。 巴菲特先生高超的投资能力使伯克希尔的股东们赚得盆满钵满，77岁高龄之际，仍然没有丝毫松懈的迹象。 并且，他还在定期强调，伯克希尔正在为后巴菲特时代做准备。 在伯克希尔2007年度会议上，巴菲特先生一语双关："我极不情愿抛弃死后仍然继续掌控投资组合的想法，即放弃我的希望，给'跳脱思考的框架'注入新的含义。"报告指出，公司已经确定了三名杰出的内部候选人，其中之一将会在巴菲特永久离开时接替他担任首席执行官。

巴菲特先生是一位谦虚、逍遥自在且超级富有的人。 而只有巨额财富这个形容词才适用于乔布斯先生。 作为具有紧迫感的企业创建人，乔布斯可能不太愿意支持放弃苹果公司领导权的想法或公开宣布继承人才的储备。 但是，最近一轮关于他健康状况的猜测使之变得比任何时候都更为重要。 也许，苹果的下一项产品应该由一位

The Seamless Handover

future. "I've reluctantly discarded the notion of my continuing to manage the portfolio after my death—abandoning my hope to give new meaning to the term 'thinking outside the box'," quippedMr. Buffett in Berkshire's 2007 annual report. The report stated that the firm has identified three outstanding internal candidates who could replace Mr. Buffett as CEO if he becomes permanently indisposed①.

Mr. Buffett is a modest, laid-back and fabulously wealthy guy. Only the last of those adjectives can be applied to Mr. Jobs. A driven business-builder, he may be reluctant to countenance the idea of giving up leadership of Apple or of having a publicly announced succession pool below him. But the latest round of speculation over his health makes the case for such a pool stronger than ever. Perhaps Apple's next gizmo launch should even be fronted by a potential successor, rather than Mr. Jobs, clad in his trademark black garb. Some boards fret that setting up a formal horserace may be counterproductive. Divisive rival camps may form. But speculation about succession to the corner office will occur anyway, and a formal plan both makes the process more transparent and allows the CEO and directors to manage any internal tensions more easily.

One company that has placed great emphasis on succession planning is General Electric (GE). Several years before standing down as CEO, Jack Welch and GE's directors identified three potential successors: James McNerney, Robert Nardelli and Jeffrey Immelt. All three were put through their paces in a high-pressure process that one of the candidates likened to "playing in the last two minutes of the Super Bowl, but for two years." In the end, GE chose Mr. Immelt. The handover was seamless and for several

---

① indisposed [ˌindisˈpəuzd] *adj.* 有病的

权力移交天衣无缝

潜在的继承人来发布,而不是身穿黑色招牌高领衫的乔布斯先生。有些董事会成员感到烦恼,认为开展正式的竞争可能会产生相反的效果。 可能会出现四分五裂的敌对阵营。 但是,对进入角落办公室的继承人的猜测无论如何都会存在,而一个正式的计划不仅使过程更加透明,也使首席执行官和高管们更容易掌控所有的内部紧张状态。

通用电气(GE)是一家非常注重继承人计划编制的公司。 杰克·韦尔奇在辞去首席执行官的几年前,就和通用电气的主管们确定了三名候选继承人:詹姆斯·麦克纳尼、罗伯特·纳德利和杰夫瑞·伊梅尔特。 三人都接受了高压考察,其中一位候选人将其比喻为"在超级杯的最后两分钟上场,却为此准备了两年"。 最后,通用选择了伊梅尔特先生。 权力移交天衣无缝,在接下来的几年,通用电气以持续增长的销售量和利润让投资者兴高采烈。 但是,伊梅尔特先生的幸运星在近几个月却黯然失色。 公司宣布重组,在竞标过程中业务部门从6个减少到4个,以简化管理和提高利润。 公司还廉价抛售了几项业务。

尽管无法评判通用电气公司的董事们是否做出了正确的选择,但他们的继任规划仍然可以很好地为他们服务。 苹果公司的董事们也应该很好地向他们学习。

知识链接

Berkshire Hathaway 伯克希尔·哈撒韦公司由沃伦·巴菲特创建于1956年,是一家世界著名的保险和多元化投资集团,总部在美国。该公司主要通过

The Seamless Handover

years GE continued to delight investors with increased sales and profits. But in recent months its fortunes—and Mr. Immelt's star—have faded. The company announced reorganization, reducing its number of business units from six to four in a bid to simplify its management and boost profits. It is also selling off several activities.

Although the jury remains out on whether GE's directors made the right choice, their approach to succession planning served them well. Apple's directors would do well to follow it.

(857 words)

权力移交天衣无缝

国民保障公司和 GEICO 以及再保险巨头通用科隆再保险公司等附属机构从事财产/伤亡保险、再保险业务。伯克希尔·哈撒韦公司不仅在珠宝经销连锁店 Helzberb Diamonds、糖果公司 See's Candies, Inc.、从事飞行培训业务的飞安国际公司、鞋业公司(H.H.Brown and Dexter)等拥有股份,还持有美国运通、可口可乐、吉列、华盛顿邮报、富国银行以及中美洲能源公司的部分股权。

题 记

安然公司的沉浮是资本主义史册上最具传奇色彩的事件之一。安然公司通过创造性地将期货、期权等金融工具引入能源交易，迅速成为世界上最大的能源交易和其他商品交易商。但安然将公司收入和业务稳定与自己的股票价格绑在一起，实行泡沫化经营，利用会计审计制度中的缺陷隐瞒债务，导致其快速崩溃。人们普遍认为，安然公司高调的狂妄自大与人类的愚蠢和贪婪相辅相成，而"安然"一词早已俨然成为"贪婪、自傲、欺诈和华尔街不公正"的代名词。更让人不安的是，华尔街的金融分析专家们长期以来为安然公司摇旗呐喊，即便在公司股票市值已经缩水时还鼓励人们不要出售，这种做法不禁让人们对被华尔街奉为金科玉律的诚信客观打上了问号。资本主义不再风度优雅。现代金融运作、公司管理和公司兴衰透过安然公司的沉浮，向世人掀开了新的一页。

The Rise and Fall of Enron

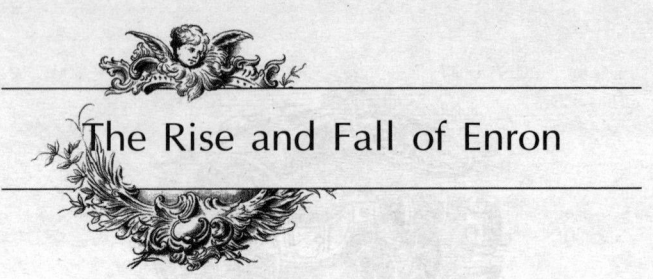

The rise and fall of Enron is an instant classic in the annals of capitalism because, in one calamitous① stroke, it wipes out so many sanctified illusions that rule in the magic marketplace. Enron embodies Nobel-class hubris like that of the market sophisticates who brought Long-Term Capital Management to ruin. It also smells of the raw monopolistic greed common a century ago. An energy-trading company that Wall Street had valued at $80 billion ten months ago is a penny stock affter ten months. Meanwhile, California consumers and businesses are stuck with the ruinously② inflated electricity prices that Enron rode to brief financial glory. The firm's gullible creditors include some of the best gilt-edged names in American banking—J. P. Morgan Chase, Citigroup—whose ancestral houses were big players during the first Gilded Age too. Unfortunately, then and now, these venerable③ financial institutions lured millions of innocents to the slaughter, unwitting shareholders who bought

---

① calamitous [kəˈlæmitəs] *adj.* 多灾难的，不幸的
② ruinously [ˈruinəsli] *adv.* 毁灭地，败坏地
③ venerable [ˈvenərəbl] *adj.* 值得尊重的

安然公司的浮沉

安然公司的浮沉是资本主义史册上的瞬时经典，因为一次不幸的打击竟毁灭了众多统治不可思议的市场的神圣幻想。安然事件体现了诺贝尔阶层的傲慢，如同久经世故的市场老手把长期资本管理领向了毁灭。它也带着一个世纪前原始垄断者共有的贪婪气息。10个月前还被华尔街估值达800亿美元的能源贸易公司，10个月后的股价只有1美分。同时，安然公司驾驭的短期金融繁荣造成了毁灭性的高电价，加州的消费者和企业深受其害。安然公司受骗的债权人包括J. P. 摩根、花旗集团等美国银行最有信誉的名字，它们的祖辈曾是第一个镀金时代地位显赫的弄潮儿。不幸的是，这些受到尊重的金融机构在当时和现在引诱数百万无辜的人成为替罪羔羊，而那些被华而不实的诺言贿赂的股东却毫不知情。

在本案例中，被宰割的羔羊包括安然自己的员工，他们中成千上万的人突然失业，当高层管理者巧妙地阻止员工从直线下降的安然公司股票中卖掉401（k）账户之时，这些大佬们却在抛售自己的股票。如果银行的金融损失足够严重（目前我们对全部真相不得而知），也会殃及美国的纳税人，他们的钱将再次以"拯救金融体系"

The Rise and Fall of Enron

the exuberant① promises.

In this case, the lambs include Enron's own employees, thousands of whom are abruptly out of work, because top management cleverly prohibited their 401(k) accounts from selling Enron's plummeting stock while the big boys were dumping theirs. If the financial losses to banks are severe enough—we don't yet know the full truth—then US taxpayers may be burned too, their money used once again to rescue delinquent financiers from their just deserts in the name of "saving the system." Nobody ever said capitalism was pretty.

Markets are imperfectible human artifacts and always subject to gross error, not to mention high-stakes fraud, because the transactions are always the work of human beings. Computerization and esoteric mathematical formulations do not change that humble fact; neither does the Internet. This same lesson was learned from great pain and loss in the early twentieth century and led eventually to the political understanding that markets without governors and regulators will repeatedly throw off disastrous consequences—extreme price swings, occasional busts and clever larcenies—so stabilizing rules and limits were imposed. That knowledge was pushed aside by the modern era's deregulation.

Enron was a massive experiment in e-commerce—a commodity-trading firm that used the Internet to connect distant buyers and sellers of everything from electricity and natural gas, steel and newsprint to pollution

---

① exuberant [igˈzjuːbərənt] *adj.* (语言等)华而不实的

安然公司的浮沉

的名义援助正在沙漠中拖欠债务的金融家。当然,从未有人谈论过资本主义的风度优雅。

市场是人类不完美的产物,它经常会出现一些严重的错误,更别说出现高风险的骗子,因为交易总是人类的作品。计算机的使用和深奥的数学公式也无法改变这种卑劣的事实,因特网也不能改变这种事实。人们正是在20世纪初从巨大的痛苦和损失中得到了同样的教训,最终才导致了政治上的理解,即没有管理者和规范者的市场将重复灾难性的后果——极端的价格波动、不时的破产和狡猾的盗窃,所以人们才实行了稳定市场的规则和限制。这些知识已被当今时代的反规则化搁置一边了。

安然公司是电子商务领域的一次大型试验。电子商务是一个商品贸易公司,使用互联网连接远程的买者和卖者,销售各种商品:从电力到天然气、钢铁和新闻用纸到污染借贷、保值的利率或气候等金融衍生品。尽管安然已经破产,网站上的言辞仍然盛气凌人。公司的网站仍旧在向公众发问:"为什么选择安然?我们擅长风险调停技术,我们有良好控制风险的系统……我们已经成功地为所有的潜在投资筹集了资金。"结果显示,这些恰好是它所缺失的品质,"新经济"的狂妄自大使之毁于一旦。如果你要宣泄人类的愚蠢和贪婪,安然公司的高调似乎合情合理。安然解释道:违反规定、利用互联网销售、老牌的公司参与激烈、持续的价格竞争,所有这一切迫使他们消除低效或是退出。消费者从更低的批发价中获益,"软能源"替代品制造商,如风力、太阳能制造商也能获益。安然

The Rise and Fall of Enron

credits and financial derivatives hedging against interest rates or the weather. On Enron Online, the hubris① was still on display, despite the bankruptcy. "Why Enron?" the company's website asks. "We have strong skills in risk intermediation and good systems to control risk.... We have successfully sourced capital for all potential investments." As it turns out, these are the very qualities that were missing, the "new economy" conceits that brought it down. Enron's siren song was plausible enough if you left out the human folly and greed. Deregulation, combined with Internet trading, exposed the old-line utilities to fierce, continuous price competition, the firm explained, forcing them to eliminate inefficiencies or get out. Consumers would win from the lower wholesale prices; so would producers of "soft energy" alternatives, like wind or solar. Enron would preside like a wise monarch.

But while Enron promised to scrutinize the soundness of buyers and sellers, nobody was scrutinizing the trader king. The middleman is unregulated in this brave new world. When Enron management made a series of outrageous and self-interested off-the-books deals to raise capital, its auditor, Arthur Andersen, gave approval. The credit-rating agencies still remained mute. Enron's bankers were busy touting the stock as on its way to the moon. Enron and chairman Kenneth Lay, meanwhile, pumped nearly $2 million into the election of George W. Bush, who returned the favor by letting Enron pick federal regulatory appointments. Lay and his agents were all over Vice President Cheney's secretive energy task force, and White

---

① hubris [ˈhjuːbris] *n.* 骄傲，傲慢

安然公司的浮沉

公司能像明智的君主那样主宰一切。

但就在安然承诺仔细审查买者和卖者的信誉稳固性之时，却无人审查这个贸易国王的信誉。中间人在这个勇敢的新世界被放任自流。当安然的管理者做出一系列蛮横和利己主义的账外交易以增加资产的时候，其审计员亚瑟·安德森却获得授权。信用评级机构仍然保持沉默。在它穷途末路之时，安然的银行家们却正在忙于兜售股票。同时，安然及其总裁肯尼思·雷对乔治·W. 布什的竞选注入近两百万美元，后者作为回报给予安然联邦规制职位。雷与其代理人的职权均超越了副总统切尼的秘密能源特别工作组，而白宫经济顾问劳伦斯·林德赛作为安然的"顾问"得到5万美元。

加州照明不足的灾难和不断高涨的电费账单是一个初步证据确凿的垄断价格欺诈案件（同时通过多种途径为"修理"切断电流输出而导致的人为稀缺），迫切需要刑事调查。合谋尚未得到证实，安然公司是否参与也没有结果，但公司创下的利润却颇为壮观。虽然加州仍在喘息，但安然公司的股票价格却已经翻了一倍多。安然其后使用新的魅力身份更多地举债经营，扩大在全世界覆盖面，开辟了更多的贸易平台——精明的分析师甚至也无法理解所有的融资方式。这是典型的不受约束的海盗行为，并以熟悉的方式结束。

我们了解些什么？首先，大规模的违规造成普通公民的道德堕落，同时为大型操纵敞开大门。其次，纽约时报的弗洛伊德·诺里斯指出，安然从根本上讲不是一家能源公司，而是交易各种金融工具的金融机构，完全不受规范的限制。安然公司就像一家银行，必

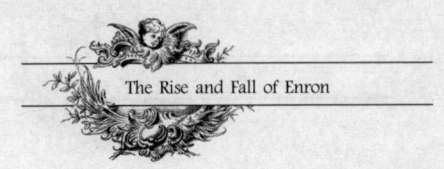

The Rise and Fall of Enron

House economic adviser Lawrence Lindsey received $50,000 as an Enron "adviser".

The disaster of California's blackouts and soaring electric bills was a prima facie case of monopoly price-gouging—artificial scarcity induced by utilities simultaneously shutting down electricity generation for "repairs"—that cries out for criminal investigation. Collusion① has not yet been proved nor Enron's involvement, but the firm profited spectacularly. While California groaned, Enron's share price more than doubled. Enron then used its new glamour status to leverage still more debt, expanding its reach worldwide and opening more trading tables—financing it all in ways even savvy analysts couldn't understand. It was the classic behavior of unfettered freebooters, and it ended in the familiar way.

What did we learn? First, wholesale deregulation has a vicious downside for ordinary citizens and is open to gross manipulation. Second, as Floyd Norris of the New York Times pointed out, Enron is essentially not an energy company but a financial institution that trades various financial instruments, utterly free of regulating limits. Like a bank, it must raise huge capital flows to maintain liquidity to underwrite the transactions, but unlike a bank or a financial market, it operates without oversight. Third, nearly every party to this debacle—Enron itself, its auditor, the bankers and brokerages—is guilty of profound conflicts of interest. They do not tell the truth to retail customers like small-scale investors for fear of offending their big investment clients. Enron, it seems, didn't tell the truth to its

---

① collusion[kəˈluʒən] n. 勾结；共谋

安然公司的浮沉

须筹集庞大的资金流来维持流动性,以承担交易,但它又不同于银行或金融市场,在运行时无需监督。 第三,这次崩盘的每一方——安然公司本身、其审计师、银行家和经纪公司——几乎都无条件地背负利益冲突罪。 他们没有对零售客户说实话,与小规模投资者担心得罪他们的大型投资客户如出一辙。 安然似乎也没有对它的银行家讲真话,当然他们并没有要求它这么做。

我们了解得越多,就越可将安然的倒塌看做废除《格拉斯·斯蒂格尔法案》的合乎逻辑的结果,该法案禁止商业银行兼并投资公司。 补救议程应该从对银行和金融重新实施管制开始,以恢复谨慎和诚实交易的环境。 能源、电信和航空公司等其他部门首当其冲。

令人欣慰的是,安然事件将扭转政治策略,同时刺激一下我们的立法者。 当然,许多州政府已经从加州承受的痛苦中吸取了教训。 但是,不要指望华盛顿。 即使安然公司彻底崩溃之后,民主党的领袖们还是会继续设置更多的违规骗局,如果他们重新开启如何在神奇的市场创造财富的基本审查制度,就会意识到他们的资金赞助人陷入极度心烦意乱的困境。 精英舆论领袖可能会坚持放任主义的教条,随它继续分崩离析,直到血腥的损失也淹没过他们的鞋。

知识链接

401(k) 401(k)计划指美国1978年《国内税收法》新增的第401条k项条款

bankers either, and they didn't ask.

As we learn more, the fall of Enron may be seen as the logical result of repealing the Glass-Steagall Act, which prohibited commercial banks from merging with investment houses. The remedial agenda would start with the reregulation of banking and finance, in order to restore a milieu of prudence and honest dealings. Other sectors should follow: energy, telecommunications and airlines, for starters.

It would be comforting to think this event will turn politics around and put a little spine in our legislators. Certainly many state governments have learned from California's pain. But don't count on Washington. Even after Enron's meltdown, leading Democrats continue to shill for more deregulation, aware that their money patrons will be most upset if they reopen fundamental scrutiny of how wealth is created in the magic market. Elite opinion leaders will probably stick with the laissez-faire[①] dogma, as it continues to fall apart, until the bloody losses lap over their shoes too.

(1,028 words)

---

① laissez-faire [leiseiˈfeə(r)] n. 放任政策(尤指资本主义国家的政府对工商业者的自由)

的规定。401(k)计划是一种缴费确定型(DC)计划,实行个人账户积累制,适用于私人盈利性公司。该计划由雇员和雇主共同缴费,缴费和投资收益免税,只在领取时征收个人所得税。雇员退休后养老金的领取金额取决于缴费的多少和投资收益状况。

The Glass-Steagall Act 作为《1933年银行法案》修订条款的《格拉斯·斯蒂格尔法案》,其核心有二:建立联邦存款保险公司(FDIC),要求吸收存款的商业银行和储蓄机构参与存款保险;对商业银行和投资银行实行分业经营,禁止银行包销和经营公司证券,只能购买由美联储批准的债券。

题 记

　　剥离雷曼架构，一个悲哀的话题。雷曼兄弟本是一个由遍布世界的几百个法律实体组成的金融帝国，当它宣布破产的那一刻，引起了资本市场的极度恐慌，全球交易几乎冻结。雷曼骤然而至的灭顶之灾，不仅创造了美国历史上最大的企业破产案，更被铭刻在了金融界的集体记忆之中。启动这家昔日全球投行巨擘的破产程序关系到各国债权人的切身利益：美国财富管理行纽伯格·伯尔曼仍在寻找买主；巴克莱银行以极低的价格拿走了雷曼兄弟的核心业务；野村证券收购雷曼兄弟后已决定整合日本和亚洲除日本以外地区的股票业务，创建一个真正的泛亚太商业模式；通过雷曼兄弟投资石油集团的客户还无法退出已经开放的交易。与其说雷曼兄弟在繁荣时期拼命追逐利润和隐瞒亏损的做法导致了这场危机，还不如说美国打着"更好地保护债权人利益"的《破产法》大旗，按照本国利益诉求对剥离雷曼架构做出最妥善的安排。

Unravel Lehman Structure

In the two weeks since Lehman Brothers' dramatic collapses, almost all of its operating businesses have been sold off and thousands of jobs have been saved. To the casual observer, Lehman's demise no longer looks so catastrophic①.

But the rushed sale of Lehman's US investment banking business and the subsequent sale of most of its European and Asian businesses are a sideshow to the real task of repaying the failed bank's thousands of creditors by liquidating② its highly complex financial assets. No previous bankruptcy or insolvency③ situation comes close to the challenge that faces the administrators and lawyers trying to salvage value from Lehman. They have prioritized the sale of Lehman's operating business units, because the prospects for achieving any such sale were diminishing rapidly as rival banks targeted clients and staff.

Now only Neuberger Berman, Lehman's prestigious US wealth management business, the UK asset management unit and the Capstone Mortgage Services businesses, also based in the UK, have yet to find buyers.

---

① catastrophic [ˌkætəˈstrɔfik] *adj.* 悲惨的
② liquidate [ˈlikwideit] *vt.* 清偿
③ insolvency [inˈsɔlvənsi] *n.* 无力偿还

剥离雷曼架构

　　自雷曼兄弟戏剧性地崩溃两周以来，几乎所有的经营业务都已廉价售出，数以千计的工作职位得以拯救。对那些悠闲的观察员来说，雷曼的转让看起来不再如此悲天悯人。

　　但是，匆忙地贱卖雷曼兄弟在美国投资银行的业务和随后出售其大部分欧洲和亚洲的业务，运用清偿其高度复杂的金融资产的手段偿还银行数千债权的不动产，这些都是次要事件。以前从来没有因破产或无力偿债的情况而近距离面临挑战：管理人员和律师试图挽留雷曼公司的残余财产价值。由于竞争银行把客户和职员作为目标，实现此类销售的前景正在迅速消失，所以他们优先考虑出售雷曼兄弟的经营业务。

　　目前只有雷曼兄弟享有声望的美国财富管理行、英国资产管理部门、总部也设在英国的开普斯顿债权服务公司纽伯格·伯尔曼，仍在寻找买主。这些交易预计在今后的四周内进行。到目前为止，已经面世的交易只是普通人和基础设施受益。唯一真正受益的是工作人员，因为买家只支付名义金额，使其进入基金总额来支付债权人。

　　资产剥离倒计时。

　　星期日，9月14日：雷曼兄弟在美国宣布破产。

Unravel Lehman Structure

Deals for these are expected in the next four weeks. The transactions seen so far have been for people and infrastructure. They only really benefited staff, with the buyers paying only nominal sums that will go into the pot to pay creditors.

Countdown

Sunday, September 14: Lehman Brothers declared bankrupt in the US.

Wednesday, September 17: Barclays agrees purchase of Lehman's US broker-dealer business and real estate assets including Times Square headquarters. 10,000 jobs involved.

Monday, September 22: Nomura agrees purchase of Lehman's Asian business. Barclays withdraws from talks to buy Lehman's European business.

Tuesday, September 23: Nomura agrees purchase of Lehman's European corporate finance and equities businesses, safeguarding 2,500 jobs.

Friday, September 26: Talks with Nomura on deal to buy Lehman's European fixed income business stall.

Nomura's deal to buy Lehman's European equities and corporate finance business involved no client assets or trading inventory. Barclays' agreement to buy Lehman's US investment banking operations saw the UK bank take on just $47bn of trading assets and a similar size portfolio of liabilities—a fraction of Lehman's overall trading and banking books. That leaves a mammoth task ahead, and visibility over recovery rates for creditors remains poor.

"I'm interested the debt is being priced at 19 cents in the dollar. The fact that someone is putting a price on it is a spectacular gamble," says

剥离雷曼架构

星期三，9月17日：巴克莱银行同意购买雷曼兄弟的美国经纪人业务和房地产资产，包括时代广场总部。涉及10 000个职位。

星期一，9月22日：野村证券同意购买雷曼兄弟的亚洲业务。巴克莱银行退出购买雷曼兄弟欧洲业务的谈判。

星期二，9月23日：野村证券同意购买雷曼兄弟的欧洲企业融资和股票业务，保留2 500个就业岗位。

星期五，9月26日：野村证券收购雷曼兄弟欧洲固定收益业务的会谈陷入困局。

野村证券收购雷曼兄弟的欧洲股市和公司金融业务的交易不涉及客户资产或贸易清单。巴克莱银行收购雷曼兄弟美国投资银行业务的协议，见证了英国银行将470亿美元的营业资产和类似规模的投资组合负债纳为己有：少部分雷曼兄弟的总体交易和银行账簿。这给未来留下了艰巨的任务，债权人回收率的能见度非常渺茫。

普华永道的合伙人以及雷曼兄弟欧洲业务的行政官托尼·洛马斯说："债务目前售价19美分，我对此很感兴趣。事实上，有人正在提价，这是一次场面壮观的赌博。"新的优先任务就是发售持有雷曼兄弟的欧洲主要经纪业务客户的套头基金资产。管理人员预计这还需要几个星期，因为不是所有的客户账户都被隔离，有些资产作为抵押品，为举债经营而提高债务。

此外，有些对冲基金的头寸情况与雷曼帝国的其他部分相关，一旦雷曼倒闭就会被分裂为个体法人实体。所以，英国石油公司认为，尽管雷曼兄弟可能持有几百万份股票，但如何在一组对冲基金的客户之间进行分配，却远非条理清晰，客户们声称，他们是通过雷曼兄弟投资的石油集团。不仅仅是对冲基金，雷曼兄弟崩溃之

Unravel Lehman Structure

Tony Lomas, partner at PwC, administrator to Lehman's European business. The new priority is to release assets belonging to hedge funds that were clients of Lehman's European prime brokerage operations. Administrators expect this to take weeks, as not all client accounts were segregated, and some assets were used as security to raise debt for applying leverage.

Moreover, some hedge fund positions were linked to other parts of the Lehman empire, which was broken up into its individual legal entities the moment it went bankrupt. So while Lehman may hold several million shares in say BP, it is far from clear how to divide them between a group of hedge fund clients claiming to have invested in the oil group through Lehman. It is not just hedge funds; many conventional long-only clients have also been unable to close trades that were open with Lehman at the time of its collapse.

These investment clients are not guaranteed to recover the full value of their portfolios on the Friday night prior to Lehman's collapse on Sunday. Providers of leverage may have a prior claim on the assets. And portfolio values could have been hit by market movements in the past two weeks, when hedge funds have been unable to trade.

The biggest challenge then begins in earnest: liquidating Lehman's gigantic portfolio of derivatives contracts, securities holdings, warehoused mortgages and real estate assets. At its last quarterly results, posted days before it went under, Lehman reported total assets of $ 600bn. But it is hard to know yet what Lehman's real assets and liabilities are because of the scale of its involvement in derivatives. The gross value of its interest rate swaps book is more than $ 10 trillion, according to one insider. Unwinding it all will require the assistance of existing staff, which could

剥离雷曼架构

时,许多因循守旧、仅做长期投资的客户还无法退出已经开放的交易。

在雷曼帝国倒塌的周日之前的周五晚上,这些投资的客户仍然无法保证收回投资总存量的全部价值。举债经营的供应商可能对资产有优先索赔权。当对冲基金一直不能交易之时,市场波动在过去两周可能已经对投资业务形成冲击。

然而,最大的挑战才真正开始:清算雷曼兄弟衍生工具合约的庞大投资业务、证券控股、仓库抵押贷款和房地产资产。根据倒闭前颁布的上季度业绩,雷曼总资产为6 000亿美元。但由于其参与衍生产品的规模庞大,很难分辨雷曼兄弟的实际资产和负债资产。据知情人士透露,利率互惠信贷的总值超过了10万亿美元。需要现有工作人员的帮助才能了解一切,而这又可能是引起紧张局势的根源。

没有人期待资产剥离过程会很快结束。大多数观察家预计至少需要两年时间。雷曼兄弟的很多员工可能会高兴地发现,他们已经在巴克莱银行或野村证券找到新老板,但倒闭公司的债权人仍然需要漫长的等待,才知道他们将获得什么样的补偿——如果有的话。

知识链接

Neuberger Berman 纽伯格·伯尔曼是一家国际资产管理公司。服务项目涉及全球各企业和个人的资产管理,包括基金、信托、资产净值,固定收入和交替资产层等。完整的共有基金信息包括控股、发行、情况说明书和内容说明书。个人可以设立账户。

Unravel Lehman Structure

be a source of tension.

No one expects the process to be rapid. Most observers expect this all to take two years at the very least. Many of Lehman's staff may be glad to have found a new parent in Barclays or Nomura, but creditors to the failed firm have a long wait before they know what—if anything—they will receive.

(750 words)

剥离雷曼架构

Nomura 野村证券是日本第一大券商,也是最早拓展中国金融和投资业务的境外机构之一。1925年成立的野村证券目前在全球28个国家和地区设有办事机构,业务范围涵盖证券经纪业务、投资金融、投资信托、离岸金融业务,以及金融服务。

BP 英国石油集团公司(British Petroleum)是世界上最大的石油和石化集团公司之一,总部设在英国伦敦,目前的资产市值约为2 000亿美元,拥有逾百万股东、近11万名员工遍布全世界,在百余个国家拥有生产和经营活动。公司的主要业务是油气勘探开发、炼油、天然气销售和发电、油品零售和运输,以及石油化工产品生产和销售。

题 记

  银行业在市场的检验中确立了自己的从业理念和价值取向，从而形成了银行业的核心价值观：水善利万物而不争，居善地，言善信，心善渊。但安然大厦的倒塌和世通公司的陨落却将银行业的掠夺本性赤裸裸地暴露在大庭广众之下。多家银行在这两家企业穷途末路的过程中推波助澜、追逐暴利。花旗银行将大笔资金暗中转移到一个秘密的离岸公司，这个公司假装要从安然购买汽油，安然接着就将这笔"现金"收入账户。另一笔虚假交易随后接踵而至，将本金和利息交付花旗银行。世通公司聘用银行的"明星"分析员，撰写所谓"公正的"研究报告，坚持不懈地乐观评述，运作股票价格的大幅上扬，促使世通公司的股票在三年里翻了四倍。尽管这些银行都不同程度地受到了惩罚，但银行的公信力和形象却从此不再如日中天。

The Banks that Robbed the World

In a Money Program special investigation, a team of lawyers investigate the rise and fall of the bosses of Enron and WorldCom and look at the financiers who bankrolled the companies' activities. They were once celebrated as two of the world's most successful companies. But in 2002 Enron and WorldCom were exposed as corrupt organizations, run by fraudsters that had lined their pockets with tens of millions of dollars and destroyed $ 240bn worth of investor's money. America's biggest banks helped them at every stage. The moneymen devised one trick after another to conceal the true state of the companies' finances. In return, these Wall Street firms earned hundreds of millions in fees and loan interest. Ken Lay and Bernie Ebbers are under investigation for the two biggest financial scandals ever, but until last year they were business heroes.

How it began

In the mid 1980's they were corporate small fry, but over the next fifteen years they would build the companies that spawned① the frauds that shook the world. Ebbers and Lay's first incentive to bend the rules

---

① spawn [spɔːn] vt. 大量生产

掠夺世界的银行

一个律师团队在货币项目的特殊调查中，研究了安然公司和美国世界通信公司老板们的崛起和陨落，并采访了为公司的活动提供融资的金融家们。这两个公司曾经是全球最成功的公司之一。2002年，安然和世通却被爆出腐败的丑闻，由赚大钱的骗子操纵，数以百万计的美元直落他们的腰包，吞噬了投资人价值2400亿美元的财富。美国最大的银行帮助他们一步步实施计划。金融家们设计了一个又一个的骗局，掩盖公司的金融真实状况。作为回报，这些华尔街的公司赚取了数以千万美元的小费和贷款利息。肯·莱和伯尼·埃伯斯正在为迄今为止的两桩最大的金融丑闻接受调查，但直到去年为止，他们都还是商界的英雄。

事情的发生

20世纪80年代中期，他们还是无足轻重的小公司，但在接下来的15年中，他们所建的公司却发生了震惊世界的欺诈案。埃伯斯和莱触犯规章的初始动机来自于提高他们的股票期权。为了让期权价值扶摇直上，老板们只需要让他们的公司表现得更加有利可图。这就给了埃伯斯和莱虚增账面价值的巨大动机。在花旗银行的帮助下，正是莱的安然公司首先开始行动。1993年，花旗银行将1.25亿美元暗中转移到一个秘密的离岸公司，这个公司假装要从安然购

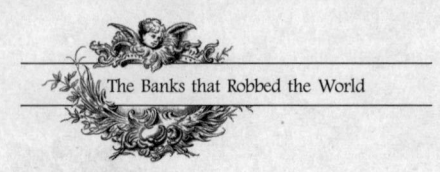

The Banks that Robbed the World

came out of a desire to boost the value of their share options. Bosses only had to make their companies appear more profitable for their options to soar in value. This gave Ebbers and Lay plenty of incentive to cook the books. It was Lay's Enron that started first, with the help of Citibank. In 1993 Citibank funneled① $125m dollars into a secret offshore company that pretended to buy gas from Enron, which then logged this "cash" as income on its accounts. No gas ever changed hands in fact and later another fake deal was set up so that Citibank would get all its money back—plus interest. Over the years, Citibank would secretly lend almost $5bn, with other banks like JP Morgan lending another $4bn.

Scam after scam

Enron's share price rose as investors were duped, and Ken's options were rising in value. At around the same time, WorldCom's Ebbers was working with Citibank subsidiary, Salomon, on another scam. Eager to grab lucrative work on WorldCom's aggressive strategy of takeovers, Salomon was giving Ebbers a parcel of shares in many of the new share flotation or 'initial public offerings' (IPOs) that it was organizing. The shares soared giving Ebbers instant profits. And within a year, Salomon was asked to handle WorldCom's record-breaking $37bn takeover of MCI, earning $33m for this job alone.

The next big scam was for the banks to employ "star" analysts—meant to write unbiased research to help investors decide what shares to buy—to help boost the WorldCom share price. Salomon's star telecoms

---

① funnel ['fʌnəl] vt. 使汇集,使集中

掠夺世界的银行

买汽油,安然接着就将这笔"现金"收入账户。而实际上根本没有汽油转手,另一个虚假交易随后接踵而至,这样花旗银行既收回了本金,又得到了利息。多年来,花旗银行秘密转借将近50亿美元,其他如JP摩根等银行转借了另外的40亿美元。

一个又一个诡计

安然股价随着投资者的受骗上当而上升,肯的期权价值也一路飙升。几乎就在同时,美国世界通信公司的埃伯斯正在与花旗银行的子公司所罗门设计另一场骗局。所罗门急于从世通公司野心勃勃的收购战略中获取利润丰厚的机会,正在向埃伯斯交付很多刚上市的新股权出售或正在组织之中的"初始公开销售证券"(首次公开募股)。飙升的股票迅速给埃伯斯带来利润。不到一年,所罗门就被要求处理世通公司收购微波通信公司的交易,仅在这次破纪录的370亿美元收购案中,所罗门公司就赚了3 300万美元。

对银行来说,另一个巨大阴谋就是聘用"明星"分析员,即撰写公正的研究报告,帮助投资者决定购买哪种股票——帮助世通公司大幅提高股票价格。所罗门的明星电信分析员杰克·格鲁曼和埃伯斯交往甚密,非同寻常,他在埃伯斯的游轮上度周末,参加他的婚宴,出席世通公司的董事会。由于他坚持不懈的乐观评述,世通公司的股票在三年里翻了四倍。

末日即将来临

安然公司也备受银行的青睐,但是直到1999年的早期,它的财务总监安德鲁·法斯托还在孤注一掷地掩藏公司的债务,并大量虚构公司的利润。美林公司帮他设计了使人眼花缭乱的、复杂的秘密公司的网络,以使安然公司能够稍微支撑得更久一些。美林得到了

The Banks that Robbed the World

analyst, Jack Grubman was unusually close to Ebbers—he spent weekends on his yacht, went to his wedding and attended WorldCom board meetings. Helped by his relentlessly optimistic reviews, WorldCom's share price quadrupled① in three years.

The end is nigh

The banks also loved Enron, but by early 1999, its chief financial officer, Andrew Fastow, was desperate to conceal the company's debts and pump up its profits. Merrill Lynch helped him set up a dizzyingly complex network of secret companies which would prop up Enron a while longer. Merrill's got the lucrative job of raising the finance for LJM2, one of the shell companies designed to cover up Enron's debts. Wall Street investors were offered fabulous rates of return for investing. Because of the scam, Enron claimed profits of a $1bn in 2000. In fact it had none.

In March 2000 the stock market collapsed and things were getting bad for WorldCom, where costs were rocketing out of control. To cover it up, Scott Sullivan, the company's chief financial officer, began the world's biggest fraud. WorldCom executives began to record the spiraling day-to-day costs as spending on assets. This meant that they could account for them over the long term and so boost short-term profits. Nine billion dollars would be misstated in this way.

Back at Enron, Citibank was persuading outside punters② to invest in a new shell company—Yosemite, which would lend cash to Enron. This time, when Enron got the cash it paid off its previous loans from Citibank.

---

① quadruple [ˈkwɔdrupl] *adj.* 四倍的
② punter [ˈpʌntə] *n.* 船夫

掠夺世界的银行

为 LJM2 融资的肥缺,而 LJM2 是事先设计好的空壳公司之一,用来掩盖安然的债务。 华尔街的投资者们得到了令人难以置信的投资回报率。 因为这场作假,安然声称在 2000 年盈利 10 亿美元。 实际上,它一分钱也没有赚。

2000 年 3 月,股票市场暴跌,世通公司陷入困境,成本失控,急骤飙升。 公司财务总监斯科特·沙利文为了掩盖事实,开始运作世界上最大的一起欺诈案。 世通公司的经理主管人员开始将每天螺旋式上升的开销计入资产。 这就意味着他们能够将这些费用长期摊销,从而提高短期利润。 公司以此种方式虚报了 90 亿美元。

回到安然公司。 花旗银行正在劝说外界的投资者买进一个新空壳公司——约塞米蒂的股票,该公司借钱给安然。 这次,安然一拿到现金,首先偿付了早前从花旗银行借的贷款。 所以,即使安然现在崩盘,花旗银行仍旧安然无恙,而约塞米蒂的投资者则一无所有。

倒塌

安然靠做假账而生存,最后毁于做假账。 审计公司亚瑟·安达信发现了一个导致股东资产净值巨额减少的会计差错。 这就是安然崩溃的第一步:接受调查、股价暴跌、最后破产。 安然大厦的倒塌开启了泛滥的闸门,市场陷入混乱,接着一系列新的丑闻被曝光,最后一个就是世通公司。 世通公司和安然公司的经理主管人员晚些时候注定要接受审查,联邦调查局正在设法寻找控告埃伯斯和莱的证据。

余波

但是,造成这些事件的银行家们又怎么样呢? 分析师杰克·格

The Banks that Robbed the World

So now if Enron collapsed, Citibank would be alright but the Yosemite investors would lose everything.

The collapse

Enron was living by the pen, and would die by the pen. Auditors Arthur Andersen discovered an accounting error that led to a huge reduction in stockholder equity. This was the first step in an avalanche① that led to the investigations, the stock price collapse and finally the bankruptcy. Enron's collapse opened the floodgates and the markets went into a tailspin as a rash of new scandals was exposed, the last of which was at WorldCom. Executives at both WorldCom and Enron are due to be tried later and the Feds are still trying to build a case against Ebbers and Lay.

Aftermath

But what about the bankers who made it all possible? Analyst Jack Grubman was sacked, but got a payoff of over $30m. Merrill Lynch has been fined $100m and CSFB $150m. The biggest fine, $300m, was levied on Citigroup. But it can afford it, with estimated profits of $16bn this year.

(859 words)

---

① avalanche [ˈævəlɑːnʃ] n. 崩溃

掠夺世界的银行

鲁曼被解雇,但却得到了 3000 万美元的辞退工资。 美林证券公司被罚款 1 亿美元,瑞士信贷第一波士顿银行被罚款 1.5 亿美元。 受罚最多的是花旗银行,累计征收 3 亿美元。 但花旗银行能够承受,因为它今年的预期利润已达 160 亿美元。

知识链接

Citigroup 花旗银行是花旗集团属下的一家零售银行,其主要前身是 1812 年 6 月 16 日成立的"纽约城市银行"(City Bank of New York),经过近两个世纪的发展、并购,已成为美国最大的银行,也是一间在全球近五十个国家及地区设有分支机构的国际大银行,总部位于纽约市公园大道 399 号。

CSFB 瑞士信贷第一波士顿银行(Credit Suisse First Boston)是一个全球领导级的银行投顾公司,提供各式金融产品,以及综合性的财经顾问、资本筹募、行销与贸易等项服务,据点遍布超过 37 个国家,并拥有超过 15 000 名的员工。

题　记

　　面对全球经济可能的"最糟糕表现",全球性的应对之举,将是遏制国际金融危机蔓延的应急良策。美联储、欧洲央行、英国英格兰银行以及加拿大、瑞士和瑞典等国的央行联手降息;美国出台了新一轮的救市方案;英国宣布了对其主要银行注资的计划,寻求更大范围的国际援助。此前更多是在各自为战的大国,终于摆出团结一致的姿态,紧急出面"止血",共同应对金融危机。世界各国的政策制定者们重新开始制定更有效的系统应对金融危机管理,重新审视随心所欲的自由市场模式,即法国人喜欢称之为的"盎格鲁-撒克逊资本主义",正是这种模式导致了危机的发生。尽管市场能否回来,现在下结论还为时过早,但国际协调的结果使人们充满期待:市场活力有重新焕发的机会。

The Global Concerted Action

The action was carefully coordinated for maximum effect around the world. First came an early-morning announcement by the British government that it had crafted a $ 90 billion rescue package for its banks. Then five central banks from around the world, including the two big ones—the U. S. Federal Reserve and the European Central Bank—announced a cut in interest rates. Jean-Claude Trichet, president of the European Central Bank, described the cuts as an "important mark of confidence" that showed an "intimate cooperation" among monetary authorities around the world. Under normal circumstances, such measures would have bucked up moods and stock prices in financial centers across the globe.

Instead, the big concerted action with barely a shrug from Wall Street. Stock markets worldwide continued to roil, and banks everywhere remained in the firing line. "Confidence has completely crashed, and it will take a while to rebuild it," says Craig Wright, chief economist at the Royal Bank of Canada, who is nonetheless hopeful that these and other measures will eventually start to work. "But it's hard to hear positives in a thunderstorm of gloom."

The mess caused by fast-and-loose mortgage lending in the U.S. has

全球协同行动

全球对此次行动尽最大努力进行了谨慎的协调。英国政府率先在清晨宣布,已经起草了一份900亿美元拯救银行业的提议。随后,世界五家中央银行宣布降息,其中包括最大的两个央行——美联储和欧洲中央银行。欧洲央行主席吉恩·克劳德·特里谢视此次降息为"提振信心的重要标志",并表明了世界各国货币当局的亲密合作。通常情况下,如此这般的举措会在全世界范围内起到提振信心、提升股价的作用。

但华尔街对这次大型的协同行动却不屑一顾。全球股市继续下跌,各地银行首当其冲。加拿大皇家银行的首席经济学家克雷格·怀特认为,"信心已经完全崩溃,这需要相当的时间来恢复"。虽然如此,他对这些行动和其他举措终将奏效还是充满希望:"但在乌云密布的暴风骤雨之中,很难听到积极的信息。"

美国彻底放松信贷抵押市场引起的混乱已经引发了全球的严重危机,并彰显出对全球化规模和局限的信心缺失。金融建立在信任的基础之上,但这种信任突然被恐惧取代:从马德里到澳门,对存款安全系数的焦虑在储户之间蔓延;全球银行业对相互拆借的恐惧

The Global Concerted Action

blown into a perilous① global crisis of confidence that has revealed both the scale and the limitations of globalization. Finance is built on trust, and suddenly that trust has been replaced by fear: fear among depositors from Madrid to Macao over the safety of their money; fear among banks worldwide about lending to one another; and fear among politicians, central bankers and regulators that they don't have adequate tools to fix the problem.

At the root of the troubles are the "toxic assets"—the highly leveraged securities mainly linked to U.S. mortgages—that banks around the world still have on their books. In its latest estimate, the International Monetary Fund (IMF) calculated that losses on these virtually worthless securities could amount to $1.4 trillion. So far, banks have written off less than half that. Concern about who is still holding dud paper has gummed up credit markets, with banks refusing to lend to one another for fear that the borrowers may default or may have themselves lent to other banks that could default. That in turn is causing solvency problems for some financial institutions that rely on short-term borrowing to fund their operations.

In its latest economic outlook, the IMF predicted that the U.S. economy will grow just 0.1% next year, its worst showing in 18 years. Europe is expected to fare no better, and China, India and other emerging economies that have been critical drivers of global economic growth over the past five years are also expected to slow markedly. That means nobody will be able to take over for the U.S. as the locomotive of the world economy, and everyone will drag down everyone else. Overall, the IMF expects world economic growth to slow down, and it warns, "The world

---

① perilous [ˈperiləs] *adj.* 危险的

全球协同行动

与日俱增;政治家、中央银行家和调节员们也在担心,他们难以找到有效的方法来解决问题。

问题的根源就是那些"有毒资产"——主要是与美国抵押贷款相关联、高度杠杆化的证券,它们仍然在世界银行的账簿上赫然在目。据国际货币基金组织的最新估算,这些垃圾债券所导致的损失高达14万亿美元。但迄今为止,银行业的账面减计还不到上述金额的一半。银行对仍然持有的垃圾债券的恐惧搅乱了信贷市场,不愿互相拆借,担心借贷人违约或转手借给其他银行,造成拖欠。这又引起了一些依赖短期借贷支撑其运行的金融机构的融资问题。

国际货币基金组织在最新一期的《世界经济展望》中预测:美国下一年度的经济增长将仅为0.1%,是近18年来最糟糕的表现。欧洲的经济状况也不容乐观,中国、印度以及其他一些新兴经济体曾在过去5年一直主导着全球经济的增长,他们目前也面临增速显著放缓的迹象。这就意味着没有国家能取代美国作为世界经济火车头的地位,而国家和地区之间还可能相互拖累。就整体而言,国际货币基金组织预测全球经济增速会放缓,同时发出警告:"全球经济正步入大面积的衰退期,面临全球成熟的金融市场自20世纪30年代以来最危险的动荡。"加拿大皇家银行的总裁赖特预测:"美国将进入缓慢衰退期,经济复苏也不幸放缓。"

在严峻的经济低迷时期,美国和其他国家一样,发现全球出口商品和服务越来越困难。根据美国商会提供的数据,美国1 200万的工作岗位依赖贸易,占工厂岗位的五分之一。美国农场三分之一

The Global Concerted Action

economy is now entering a major downturn in the face of the most dangerous shock in mature financial markets since the 1930s." Wright, CEO of the Royal Bank of Canada predicts, "The U.S. will go into a shallow recession, unfortunately followed by a shallow recovery."

In the event of a severe economic downturn, the U.S.—like other countries—would find it much harder to export its goods and services around the world. According to the U.S. Chamber of Commerce, 12 million American jobs depend on trade, including 1 in 5 factory jobs. 1 in 3 acres of U.S. farmland is planted for export, and many of the nation's biggest corporations, from Coca-Cola to Microsoft and Google, depend on substantial revenues from overseas.

Beyond the immediate economic impact, there are already signs that this meltdown will have longer-term repercussions①. One is that policymakers everywhere will have to go back to the drawing board to figure out a more effective system of financial-crisis management. "Governments are making the same mistake over and over again. They're trying to deal with the crisis on a piecemeal basis," says Dennis J. Snower, president of Germany's Kiel Institute for the World Economy. He advocates a far more ambitious solution, including the creation of a new international agency that can act as a lender of last resort to stricken banks. In Washington, Robert B. Zoellick, president of the World Bank, concurs that only a multinational solution can really work. "While American eyes are on the intersection of Wall and Main streets, there is much more to the story," he says. "The response to these crises will have to be larger and global."

---

① repercussion [ˌriːpəˈkʌʃən] n. 后果

全球协同行动

的土地种植的农产品用于出口,可口可乐、微软、谷歌等很多国家最大型的企业,也依赖于海外市场的大额收入。

除了直接的经济影响,已有迹象表明,这次经济崩溃还具有较长期的效应。其一是世界各国的政策制定者们需要重新开始制定更有效的系统应对金融危机管理。德国基尔市全球经济研究院的院长丹尼斯·J.斯诺尔说:"政府一而再、再而三地犯同样的错误。他们正尝试在一个支离破碎的基础上处理危机。"他提出一个更具挑战性的解决方案,包括创建新的国际机构,担当饱受打击的银行的最后贷款人。在华盛顿,世界银行行长罗伯特·B.佐利克也指出,只有多国的共同努力才能真正奏效。他说:"当美国的目光停留在华尔街和主街的交叉路口之时,其实还有更多的危机处理方案。对这些危机的反应将会更大和全球化。"

另一个可能的反应是重新审视随心所欲的自由市场模式,即法国人喜欢称之为的"盎格鲁-撒克逊资本主义",正是这种模式导致了危机的发生。华尔街的雷曼兄弟破产后、美国国会初次讨论救市时,法国总统尼古拉斯·萨科奇掀起了一场辩论。他在土伦市演讲时,将这次危机形容为"建立在柏林墙的倒塌和冷战结束基础之上的世界末日——自由和繁荣的伟大梦想"。就资本主义而言,他倡导市场和国家之间的"新平衡","市场永远正确的想法是胡扯"。

目前,首当其冲的是要努力维持已经变得焦躁不安、反复无常的全球金融体系的稳定。英国宣布了对其主要银行注资的计划,寻求更广范围的国际援助,首相戈登·布朗直言不讳:"现在不是墨守

The Global Concerted Action

Another possible repercussion: a reexamination of the freewheeling, free-market practices—what the French like to call "Anglo-Saxon capitalism"—that led to this crisis. French President Nicolas Sarkozy kicked off that debate as Wall Street was reeling from the collapse of Lehman Brothers and Congress was first debating the bailout package. In a speech in Toulon, he said the crisis marked "the end of a world that was built on the fall of the Berlin Wall and the end of the Cold War—a big dream of liberty and prosperity." As for capitalism, he called for a "new balance" between the market and the state and added, "The idea that markets are always right was a mad idea."

For the moment, the priority remains trying to stabilize a global financial system that has become worryingly volatile①. Announcing Britain's plans to recapitalize its major banks and reach out for a broader international solution, Prime Minister Gordon Brown didn't mince words. "This is not a time for conventional thinking or outdated dogma but for the fresh and innovative intervention that gets to the heart of the problem," he said. The big yawn with which global stock markets greeted the move said it all: given the beaten-down state of the financial system and the questions that continue to swirl around it, far more concerted action is needed if confidence is to be restored.

(994 words)

---

① volatile ['vɔlətail] *adj.* 反复无常的

全球协同行动

陈规的时候,而是需要直达问题核心的新方法和创新。"全球股市对此次举措显示出的巨大疲软说明了一切:考虑到金融体系备受打压的状态和持续困扰金融体系的问题,如果要重拾信心,还需要采取更多的协同行动。

知识链接

The World Bank Group 世界银行集团是联合国系统下的多边发展机构,它包括五个机构:国际复兴开发银行、国际开发协会、国际金融公司、多边投资担保机构和国际投资争端解决中心。这些机构联合向发展中国家提供低息贷款、无息信贷和赠款,资助它们克服穷困,在减轻贫困和提高生活水平的使命中发挥着独特的作用。

题 记

就在安然财务丑闻爆发，美国证监会宣布对安然进行调查之时，安达信的休斯敦事务所在两周内销毁了数千页安然公司的文件，从而开创了美国历史上第一起大型会计行受到刑事调查的先河。曾经独步天下的安达信会计师事务所一夜之间陷入全面崩溃的境地。然而在3年之后，峰回路转。美国最高法院推翻了地方法院对"安然倒闭事件"中的安达信公司所作的有罪判决。更有些律师露骨地认为，法庭判决显示了对美国企业观的同情，即企业对损毁日常文件拥有较大的自由权。还有不少商业利益集团为之欣喜若狂，期待政府和舆论施加在他们头上的"紧箍咒"松绑，盼望战战兢兢的华尔街走出"信誉危机"的困扰。然而，尽管最高法院推翻了判决，安达信也无望复活。因为对于一家靠信誉吃饭的会计师事务所而言，安然丑闻已经使其品牌价值荡然无存。

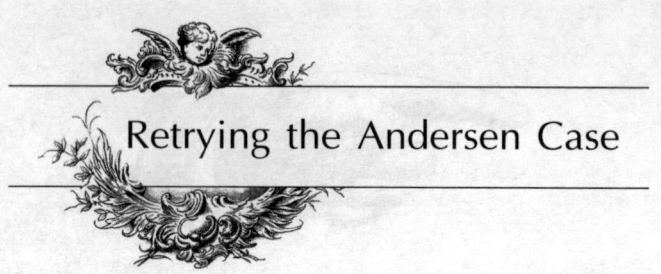

Retrying the Andersen Case

The Supreme Court overturned the criminal conviction of Enron Corp.'s accounting firm recently, nullifying① with a single stroke one of the government's biggest victories in the corporate scandals that climaxed the bull market of the 1990s. Advice to Enron jury on accountants' intent is faulted. The court ruled unanimously that the Houston jury that found Arthur Andersen LLP guilty of obstruction of justice was given overly broad instructions by the federal judge who presided at the trial.

As a result of the faulty instructions, the justices ruled, the firm was convicted without proof that its shredding of documents was deliberately intended to undermine a looming Securities and Exchange Commission inquiry. U.S. District Judge Melinda Harmon should have instructed the jury that the law required the government to prove that Andersen knew it was breaking the law, the court ruled. "Indeed, it is striking how little culpability② the judge's instructions required," Chief Justice William H. Rehnquist wrote in the opinion for the court. "For example, the jury was told that, even if Andersen honestly and sincerely believed that its conduct was lawful, you may find it guilty." Legal analysts said the decision was a

---

① nullify [ˈnʌlifai] vt. 使无效
② culpability [kʌlpəˈbiləti] n. 有过失

安达信案件重审

最高法院近日推翻了为安然做审计的会计公司的犯罪判决,一次性地宣布政府在企业丑闻中的最大胜利之一无效,这场丑闻曾在20世纪90年代的牛市达到顶点。 安然陪审团关于会计犯罪行为的申辩被判违法。 法庭一致裁定,主持审判的联邦法官对发现安达信会计师事务所妨碍司法罪的休斯敦陪审团的指示模糊不清。

  法庭根据错误的指令,裁决公司在没有证据的情况下被判有罪,即证明安达信故意损毁文件,妨碍潜在的证券交易会调查。 法庭认定,美联邦区法官梅琳达·哈蒙应该让陪审团知道,法律要求政府证明安达信知法犯法。 主审法官威廉姆·H·雷恩奎斯特在给法庭的意见书上写道:"确实,很明显,法官的指令几乎不需要担当过失。 比如,陪审团被告知,即使安达信诚心诚意地相信他们的行为是合法的,你也可以裁决他们有罪。"法律分析人士认为,这个裁决是起诉律政司合谋犯罪的主要障碍。 律政司防企业欺诈行为特别工作组的前任官员威廉姆·B·玛塔娅说:"输掉此类官司的案例太多了。 安达信会计师事务所只不过是所有企业欺诈案件中的一个典范。"

  有些律师更露骨地认为,法庭判决显示了对美国企业观的同情,即企业对损毁日常文件拥有较大的自由权,这种行为通常被冠

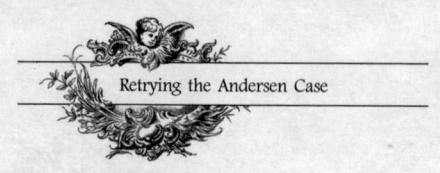

Retrying the Andersen Case

major setback to the Justice Department's corporate crime prosecutions. "To lose a case like this is huge," said William B. Mateja, a former official of the Justice Department's corporate fraud task force. "Arthur Andersen was the poster-child case of all the corporate fraud cases."

More broadly, some lawyers said the court's decision shows its sympathy for corporate America's view that companies should be freer to engage in routine document destruction—often under the ironic title of "document retention policy". That is even more important because the statute under which the Justice Department prosecuted Andersen was amended by Congress Sarbanes-Oxley law to make it easier for the government to prosecute wrongful document destruction. "The Supreme Court may be using this as a vehicle to signal some concern" about Sarbanes-Oxley, said Henry T.C. Hu, a professor of corporate and securities law at the University of Texas. But Mateja, in private practice, said that Congress's intent to prevent improper document destruction was clear. "I'm still going to counsel clients to be extremely careful if and when they dust off document-retention policies," he said.

Although a rebuke to the government, the court's decision is little comfort for Andersen and its former employees. The Chicago-based firm has a staff of only 200 left out of the 28,000 people who once worked there. But the company said the ruling may help the firm in its main remaining task: fighting shareholder lawsuits related to its work for Enron, Global Crossing Ltd. and other clients. "We pursued an appeal of this case not because we believed Arthur Andersen could be restored to its previous position, but because we had an obligation to set the record straight and clear the good name of the 28,000 innocent people who lost their jobs at

安达信案件重审

以"文件保存政策"的讽刺称号。由于国会萨班斯-奥克斯利法修正了律政司起诉安达信的法规,使政府起诉文件销毁不当的借口更加容易,这种行为就更为重要。德州大学企业与证券法律教授亨利·TC.胡认为,关于萨班斯-奥克斯利法,"最高法院可能正利用它作为传递某种利害关系的工具"。但私人企业家玛塔亚认为,国会阻止不当的文件损毁行为的意图很明显。他说:"我仍打算劝告客户,在万一不遵守文件保管政策的时候要极其谨慎。"

尽管对政府有所指责,但法庭的审判并未对安达信和它的前雇员造成困扰。曾拥有28 000人之众的芝加哥公司仅余200名员工。而且公司方面认为,裁决有助于完成剩余的主要任务:应付股东的相关诉讼,包括为安然、环球电讯和其他客户的服务。公司发言人帕特里克·多顿在声明中说:"我们继续上诉不是因为我们相信安达信能够重回原来的地位,而是因为我们有责任以正视听,为28 000名在这场诉讼中丢掉工作的无辜的人们和千分之十的安达信同仁恢复名誉,还要帮助确保公民的公正决议,创造直面公司的记录。"

代理助理总检察长约翰·C·瑞希特尔在一份声明中说,律政司已经以"抢在证券会调查前损毁大量文件的决定违反法律"的罪名对安达信实施罚款。瑞希特尔指出,原告继续审查裁决,将"决定案件是否再审"。但是法律分析家却认为这是不可能的,因为宪法禁止双边危害和裁决需要更艰难的取证标准。支持安达信案件的华盛顿法律基金会的一名高级行政法律顾问保罗·卡门那说:"当陪审团要求你展示邪恶的意图时,这将难上10倍。"前投资银行家弗兰克·P.夸冲是一名可能的裁决受益者,他因指令损毁文件以阻碍调查的类似指控被定罪。这也将对大卫·B.邓肯的判决产生影响,

Retrying the Andersen Case

the time of the indictment and tens of thousands of Andersen alumni, as well as to help secure a fair resolution of the civil set the record straight facing the firm," company spokesman Patrick Dorton said in a statement.

Acting Assistant Attorney General John C. Richter said in a statement that the Justice Department had charged Andersen because of its "determination that the substantial destruction of documents in anticipation of an investigation by the Securities and Exchange Commission violated the law." Richter said prosecutors continue to examine the decision and will "determine whether to retry the case." But legal analysts said that is unlikely, given the constitutional prohibition against double jeopardy① and the tougher standard of proof required by the decision. "It would be 10 times harder with a jury instruction that you must show evil intent," said Paul Kamenar, senior executive counsel for the conservative Washington Legal Foundation, which supported Andersen in the case. One possible beneficiary of the decision is former investment banker Frank P. Quattrone, who was convicted on similar charges of ordering document destruction to thwart② investigations. It may also affect the conviction of David B. Duncan, the Andersen partner who pleaded guilty to a single count of obstructing justice, under the government's interpretation of the law, then testified against his former firm. Duncan is a likely witness in upcoming Enron criminal trials, and he will not be sentenced until his government cooperation has ended.

Andersen was in charge of auditing the books at Enron, the high-

---

① jeopardy [ˈdʒepədi] *n.* 危害
② thwart [θwɔːt] *vt.* 阻碍

安达信案件重审

他是安达信的合作伙伴,按照政府对法律的解释,他因阻碍司法的单一罪名而服罪,然后作证指控他的前公司。邓肯可能是即将来临的安然刑事审判的见证者,除非他与政府的合作终止,否则会被判刑。

安达信会计师事务所受雇于安然,审计它的账簿。财政崩溃、野心勃勃的休斯敦能源巨头安然公司耗尽了几千雇员和其他投资者的存款,在政治上伤害了安然主席肯尼斯·L.莱一向亲近的布什政府。安然倒闭事件公开后,安达信的律师南希·坦布尔发了一封电子邮件,提醒雇员公司要求销毁日常文件的政策。证券交易委员会正式通知安达信接受调查时,重达两吨的文件已被销毁。在起诉安达信的过程中,政府认为,损毁文件的行为是为了防止证监会发现安达信的某些行为,如在帮助安然粉饰"资产负债表外"的活动公布收益。因此,政府认为该公司触犯了联邦法律,"不道德地劝告"他人掩盖证据,构成犯罪。在最高法院的口头辩论中,一名律政司的律师把安达信比作擦掉犯罪现场指纹的罪犯。

但雷恩奎斯特认为,该公司更像"一位建议儿子用自己的权利挣脱强迫自证其罪法网的母亲"。它"不是天生邪恶",说服某人扣留来自政府的文件,是政府针对安达信的行为做出的断言。

知识链接

Arthur Andersen 安达信会计师事务所由美国芝加哥大学教授阿瑟·安达信先生于1913年创建,曾以其稳健诚信的形象被公认为同行业中的"最佳精英",与普华永道(PWC)、毕马威(KPMG)、安永(E. Y)、德勤(D. T)

Retrying the Andersen Case

flying Houston energy conglomerate① whose financial meltdown wiped out the savings of thousands of employees and other small investors—and politically damaged the Bush administration, with which Enron Chairman Kenneth L. Lay had been close. As Enron's collapse became public, Nancy Temple, a lawyer for Andersen, sent an e-mail, reminding employees of the company's policy of routine document shredding. Two tons of documents were destroyed until the SEC formally notified Andersen that it was under investigation. In prosecuting Andersen, the government argued that the shredding was done to prevent the SEC from finding out about such matters as Andersen's role in helping Enron puff up the reported returns of "off balance sheet" activities. Thus, the government argued, the firm violated a federal law that made it a crime to "corruptly persuade" anyone to cover up evidence. At oral argument in the Supreme Court, a Justice Department lawyer likened Andersen to a felon② wiping his fingerprints at a crime scene.

But in his opinion, Rehnquist suggested that the company was more akin to "a mother who suggests to her son that he invoke his right against compelled self-incrimination." It "is not inherently malign" to persuade someone to withhold documents from the government, but that is what the government asserted with respect to Andersen's conduct.

(955 words)

---

① conglomerate [kən'glɔmərət] n. 集成物
② felon ['felən] n. 重罪人

安达信案件重审

一道成为全球五大会计师事务所。安达信在鼎盛时期拥有85 000多名员工，遍布全球84个国家。2002年，安达信公司因安然事件倒闭。

SEC 美国证券交易委员会（the U. S. Securities and Exchange Commission）是直属美国联邦的独立准司法机构，负责美国的证券监督和管理工作，也是美国证券行业的最高机构，具有准立法权、准司法权、独立执法权。证券交易委员会的总部在华盛顿特区，拥有4个部，18个办公室，3 100多名职员。

题　记

　　拥有85年历史的美国第五大投资银行贝尔斯登被摩根大通接管，成为华尔街信贷危机中最大的一家倒闭公司。这次收购要么是摩根大通历史上最棒的交易，要么就是最终发现贝尔斯登的资产负债表上"地雷"太多，实际上却是一钱不值的交易。一段历史的终结留给人们心中的酸楚真是五味杂陈。星期一，掺杂着谣言的各种传闻铺天盖地，恐慌如约而至。星期二，高盛宣布不再介入贝尔斯登衍生品交易，银行拒绝给贝尔斯登的债务提供任何保护。星期三，高盛等券商已经开始做贝尔斯登的对家，现金如溪水般流出。星期四，对冲基金的大批离场终于抽干了贝尔斯登的最后一滴血，它如同一个奄奄一息、但五脏俱全的空壳巨人。星期五，这个世界上貌似最强大的投资银行的心脏停止了跳动。这或许就是现代金融市场的效率：铰链上最薄弱的一环在瞬间被摘除，资源被重新分割，整个系统继续前行。

The Last Days of Bear Stearns

You could detect a trace of fear in his voice. Mostly he seemed stunned. One of Bear Stearns's top bond executives had dialed me up unprompted. The executive had dished about competitors in the past, but he had never initiated a discussion, much less one about his own firm. Now he explained that financial institutions that he dealt with—firms he had traded with for years—were suddenly asking him whether Bear had the cash to execute their trades. Such news had yet to surface in the press, but the investment bank's shares had dropped nearly 20% in the previous ten days, and there were murmurs that short-sellers were circling. The executive asked whether I'd heard rumors of trouble, and he tried to preempt① them. "We're making money," he said. "Our counterparties are getting paid, trades are clearing, business is picking up. It doesn't seem to be the likely scenariofor an investment bank's collapse."

Several days later Bear Stearns was swallowed by J.P. Morgan Chase. But all the brouhaha② over the deal—were the shares worth $2 or $10? Should the Federal Reserve have intervened? —has obscured how

---

① preempt [pri(ː)'empt] vt. 优先购买
② brouhaha [bruː'hɑːhɑː] n. 骚动

贝尔斯登最后的日子

你能觉察出他声音中的恐惧感,似乎主要还是震惊。贝尔斯登一位高级证券主管主动给我打来电话。这位主管挖苦了过去的竞争者,但他从未参与任何讨论,更不用说提及自己的公司。现在,他解释说,自己效力多年的金融机构突然问他,贝尔斯登是否有资金完成交易。这些新闻已通过媒体浮出水面,投资银行的股票在过去10天下降了将近20%,做空者正在私下绕圈进场。主管问我是否听到了这些惹是生非的谣言,试图抢购先买权。他说:"我们正在赚钱。我们的对手正在获利,交易明朗,生意上扬。似乎不可能出现投资银行倒闭的局面。"

几天后,贝尔斯登就被摩根大通收购。但整个交易的争议是:股票是值2美元还是10美元?美联储是否应该介入?这些骚动掩盖了人们对贝尔斯登倒闭的震惊。这也在提醒人们:对于一个建立在信誉之上的公司来说,当信誉消失时,公司也随之倒闭。从贝尔斯登同意换股、进而被摩根大通收购的前一星期看来,公司重组揭示了贝尔斯登的长期客户和生意伙伴对这家投资银行失去信心的速度之快,这也削弱了贝尔斯登继续生存的能力。

不管贝尔斯登见证自身应对挑战的能力有多么坚强,客户却另

astonishing Bear's collapse is. It's a reminder that in a business based on confidence, when that confidence evaporates, so does the business. A reconstruction of the week before Bear Stearns agreed to be funded, and then acquired, by J.P. Morgan Chase, reveals the speed at which Bear's longtime customers and counterparties lost their faith in the investment bank and undermined its ability to continue.

However much Bear Stearns saw itself as strengthened by its struggles, customers thought otherwise, and that hastened Bear's fall. Molinaro's comments notwithstanding, some had begun inching away months earlier. Bob Sloan says he counseled clients to seek other prime brokers because he saw a "30% to 35% chance" that Bear would collapse. Sloan's clients had pulled out $ 25 billion in assets. Others, of course, would desert only when the panic hit. And a few days would be all it took to show just how shallow the reservoir of trust for the firm was.

MONDAY: WE DON'T COMMENT ON RUMORS

If there's one thing that companies hate to do, it's comment on rumors. Such statements, the thinking goes, only confer legitimacy on unfounded gossip. But there it was in a Bear press release: "There is absolutely no truth to the rumors of liquidity problems that circulated in the market." At that moment, it appeared to be true. The firm had some $ 17 billion in cash. Of course, Bear was noted for its addiction to leverage even at a time when Wall Street, which runs on debt, was drunk on the stuff. Bear had $ 11.1 billion in tangible equity capital supporting $ 395 billion in assets, a leverage ratio of more than 35 to one. And its assets were less liquid than those of many of its competitors.

贝尔斯登最后的日子

有想法,而这又加速了贝尔斯登的破产。 好在有些客户听信了莫利纳多的评论,早在几个月前就开始撤资。 鲍勃·斯隆说,他曾劝说客户去寻找其他的资深经纪人,因为他认为贝尔斯登倒闭的概率达"30%至35%"。 斯隆的客户撤出了250亿美元的资产。 当然,其他人只有等到恐慌来临时才放弃。 短短的几日足以看出,社会对公司的公信存储是多么的浅薄。

星期一:我们对谣言不做评论

如果公司有一件最不愿意做的事的话,那就是对谣言做出评论。 人们认为,这些说法只是在毫无根据的闲谈中交换合理的意见。 但是贝尔斯登曾在新闻发布会上说:"市场上流传的资产流动性问题的谣言毫无根据。"这在当时似乎不置可否。 公司大约有170亿美元的现金。 即使负债累累的华尔街被债务搞得晕头转向之时,贝尔斯登就以致力于资产平衡而出名。 贝尔斯登拥有111亿美元的有形股权资本,支持3950亿美元的资产,财务杠杆率超过35比1。 其资产流动性小于它的许多竞争者。

但是到了周一,这个问题变得比谣言更可怕。 前一个周五的晚些时候,一家言行不一致的大型银行断然拒绝了贝尔斯登20亿美元短期贷款的要求。 依靠证券的回购贷款对投资银行至关重要,因为它要靠上亿美元的借入借出为日常业务提供资金。 发生在华尔街的此类拒贷如同好友在发薪日的前一天拒绝借给你5美元。 贝尔斯登的执行官们举步维艰,只好到别处筹钱。 但是这种征兆却明确无误:信誉正在逐步衰竭。

The Last Days of Bear Stearns

But by Monday, the problem had metastasized① into something more dire than a rumor. Late the preceding Friday, a major bank—accounts differ on which—had rebuffed② Bear's request for a short-term $2 billion loan. Such securities-backed repurchase loans are crucial for investment banks, which borrow and lend billions to fund their daily business. Being denied such a loan is the Wall Street equivalent of having your buddy refuse to front you $5 the day before payday. Bear executives scrambled③ and raised the money elsewhere. But the sign was unmistakable: Credit was drying up.

TUESDAY: IF I KNEW WHY, I WOULD DO SOMETHING

Confidence continued to ebb, and Bear again tried to reassure investors. "Why is this happening?" CFO Molinaro asked rhetorically on CNBC. "If I knew why it was happening, I would do something to address it." The rumors were "false," he said. "There is no liquidity crisis. No margin calls. It's nonsense."

Still, momentum was turning against the firm. That morning Goldman Sachs's credit derivatives group sent its hedge fund clients an e-mail announcing another blow. In previous weeks, banks such as Goldman had done a brisk business agreeing to stand in for institutions nervous, say, that Bear wouldn't be able to cough up its obligations on an interest rate swap. But on Tuesday, Goldman told clients it would no longer step in for them on Bear derivatives deals.

---

① metastasize [məˈtæstəsaiz] vi. 转移
② rebuff [riˈbʌf] vt. 严厉拒绝
③ scramble [ˈskræmbl] vt. 仓促行动

贝尔斯登最后的日子

星期二:如果我知道为什么,我会采取措施

当信心继续下滑时,贝尔斯登试图再次安抚投资者。首席财务官山姆·莫利罗纳在美国全国广播公司财经频道斟词酌句:"为什么会发生这种情况?如果我了解原因,我一定会设法应对。"他认为谣言是"假"的,"不存在清偿危机,不会增收保证金,这是胡说八道"。

但冲击公司的势头仍然存在。那天早上,高盛信用衍生品集团向它的对冲基金客户发了一封电子邮件,宣布另一个打击的到来。前几周,高盛之类的银行业务繁忙,允诺缓解机构的紧张局面,即贝尔斯登不会在利率交换期勉强交出债务。但在周二,高盛通知客户,它不再为他们介入贝尔斯登衍生品做任何交易。

这种预兆是不祥的,但这还没有结束。贝尔斯登仍在不断地遭受打击。借助信用违约掉期1000万美元的保险成本,前一个月前还在35万美元之间徘徊,现在已超过百万美元大关。银行拒绝对贝尔斯登的债务承担任何进一步的信用保护。

星期三:贝尔斯登的流动资产怎么样了?

高盛邮件的信息泄露之后,缺口就此打开。最终,数以百计的对冲基金和其他客户,开始急速地撤出资金。

小型研究机构信用展望公司的分析师大卫·亨德勒与贝尔斯登取得联系,试图找出到底发生了什么。但是接触后发现一切良好。然后亨德勒询问4月底到期的40多亿美元的信贷服务。亨德勒估计,如果贝尔斯登需要现金,这些将绰绰有余。然而,亨德勒被告

The Last Days of Bear Stearns

It was ominous①, but it wasn't yet the end. Bear continued absorbing blows. The cost of insuring $10 million in Bear debt via credit default swaps, which had hovered near $350,000 in the month before, shot past $1 million. Banks refused to issue any further credit protection on Bear's debt.

WEDNESDAY: HOW LIQUID IS BEAR?

When word of the Goldman e-mail leaked out, the floodgates opened. Hedge funds and other clients, eventually running into the hundreds, began yanking their funds.

Dave Hendler, an analyst at research boutique CreditSights, called a Bear contact to find out what was going on. The contact said that all was fine. But then Hendler asked about a $4 billion credit facility due to expire in April. If Bear needed cash, Hendler reckoned, that was probably more than enough. Hendler says he was told that the facility had actually expired in February and several banks had backed out, reducing the credit line to $2.8 billion. Bear, he was told, was waiting until the release of its quarterly earnings to reveal the status of the loan. Neither Bear's liquidity nor its lenders' confidence, it appeared, was what it had seemed.

THURSDAY: CALL JAMIE DIMON

The gravity of the situation had finally registered at Bear. Schwartz returned to New York and convened② a meeting of the top leadership. Liquidity was plummeting; according to published reports, it had fallen to

---

① ominous [ˈɔminəs] adj. 预兆不祥的
② convene [kənˈviːn] vt. 聚集

贝尔斯登最后的日子

知,这笔业务实际上在 2 月份就已到期,几家银行已经停止贷款,信贷额度降至 28 亿美元。他被告知,贝尔斯登一直在等待公司公布季度收入,以便显示贷款状况,贝尔斯登的流动性资产和借贷者的信心似乎与表现不一致。

星期四:求助杰米·戴蒙

严峻的形势终于在贝尔斯登出现。施瓦兹返回纽约,旋即召开了高层会议。但流动资产仍在大幅下跌。据报道,周末降至 20 亿美元。施瓦兹当晚孤注一掷地向摩根大通首席执行官杰米·戴蒙求助。

即使在公司歇斯底里地商议救助方案之时,贝尔斯登的执行官们仍然试图让世界相信一切尽在掌控之中。施瓦兹当晚接见了一位著名的纽约对冲基金经理,他是贝尔斯登的长期主要经纪客户。施瓦兹恳求这位经理现身第二天早上的美国全国广播公司财经频道,表达他对贝尔斯登的信心。这位对冲基金经理对此婉言谢绝,并对贝尔斯登需要客户向世界证明它的兴旺发达感到困惑。他很快就明白了其中的原委。

星期五:现在一切都完了

早上 9 点,贝尔斯登宣布接受摩根大通 300 亿美元的注入资金,而且这一举措得到了政府的支持。在电话会议上,施瓦兹听起来似乎仍在与现实作斗争。他解释说:"贝尔斯登遭受了太多谣言的重创。我们试图向时局提供一些事实,但是……谣言还在不断加剧。"他说,客户要求兑现"加速了昨天的流通……局势正在按部就

The Last Days of Bear Stearns

$ 2 billion at week's end. Desperate, Schwartz contacted J.P. Morgan CEO Jamie Dimon that evening.

Even as the firm frantically negotiated a rescue package, Bear executives continued to try to convince the world that everything was under control. That evening Schwartz contacted a well-known New York hedge fund manager (a longtime Bear prime brokerage client). He pleaded with the manager to appear on CNBC the next morning and express his confidence in Bear. The hedge fund manager declined politely but wondered why Bear needed a client to convince the world of its health. He wouldn't wonder long.

FRIDAY: IT'S ALL GONE NOW

AT 9 A.M., Bear announced $ 30 billion in funding provided by J.P. Morgan and backstopped by the government. In a conference call Schwartz sounded as if he was still fighting reality. "Bear Stearns has been subject to a significant amount of rumor," he explained. "We attempted to try to provide some facts to the situation, but ... the rumors intensified." He said customer requests to cash out "accelerated yesterday ... and at the pace things were going, there could be continued liquidity demands that would outstrip our liquidity resources." The new loan facility, he said, would restore calm.

Of course, that didn't pan out. Bear's stock dropped nearly 40% in the first half-hour of trading. Within days, Bear's 85 years as an independent entity were at an end.

(1,170 words)

贝尔斯登最后的日子

班地发展,持续的资产折现需求将会超出我们的资金流动储备"。他认为,新的贷款融通将会使局面恢复平静。

当然,这种预期并没有奏效。 贝尔斯登的股票在交易的前半小时几乎下降了40%。 就在这几天,贝尔斯登85年的独立实体机制告终。

知识链接

CNBC 消费者新闻与商业频道(Consumer News and Business Channel)是美国全国广播公司环球集团所持有的全球性财经有线电视卫星新闻台、全球财经媒体中公认的佼佼者,其深入的分析和实时报导赢得了全球企业界的信任。消费者新闻与商业频道遍布全球89个国家,设有129个记者站,拥有1 700名新闻采编人员,主要报道各地财经头条新闻以及金融市场的即时动态。

题 记

  随着美国房地产市场的不断下滑,房地美和房利美两家公司面临对越来越多无法偿还的担保贷款赔偿,而投资者担心还会有更多的损失出现。让其自行倒闭还是政府出手援救?美国政府陷入进退两难的尴尬困境。一方面,房利美和房地美的关键事实证明,他们在美国房地产金融界占有举足轻重的地位,如果让其倒闭,美国经营几十年的住房金融体系将要面临重建,那么美国房地产市场将在二三十年内都无法发展。另一方面,如果为了避免两家公司破产,出现全面的政府接管,就意味着纳税人将不得不负担房地美和房利美所有的贷款和担保出现的巨大损失。然而,次贷危机造成的信贷紧缩引发了持续的市场恐慌,两家房贷抵押机构资不抵债,濒临破产。没有人确切地知道问题所在,只有曾经促使贝尔斯登破产的恐慌再次弥漫华尔街。

Key Facts on Fannie Mae and Freddie Mac

The U.S. government plans to takeover Fannie Mae and Freddie Mac, and all shareholders of the two mortgage giants will take a hit, an influential lawmaker said on Saturday. The move to take control of the two companies, which may be announced Sunday, could amount to the largest financial bailout in the nation's history, and is a bid to ward off further damage to the U.S. housing market which is in its deepest downturn since the Great Depression.

Here are some key facts about the two companies.

FANNIE MAE's formal name is Federal National Mortgage Association, which was created in 1938 by Congress as part of a campaign aimed at expanding the secondary U. S. mortgage market and increasing home ownership and rental housing.

FREDDIE MAC's formal name is Federal Home Loan Mortgage Corp, which was created in 1970 by Congress as part of a campaign aimed at expanding the secondary U. S. mortgage market and increasing home ownership and rental housing.

WHAT DO THE COMPANIES DO?

Fannie Mae and smaller Freddie Mac are shareholder-owned

房利美和房地美的关键事实

一位有影响力的立法者周六表示,美国政府计划收购房利美和房地美,两家抵押贷款巨头的所有股东将遭受打击。控制两家公司的举动可能在周日宣布,这将成为这个国家历史上最大的一次金融援助,这样做是为了抵御自大萧条以来处于最低谷的美国住房市场的进一步损失。

以下是两家公司的一些关键事实。

房利美的正式名称是联邦全国抵押协会,它由国会于1938年创建,是旨在扩大美国住房抵押贷款二级市场、增加自置居所和租赁房屋的部分计划。

房地美的正式名称是联邦住房贷款抵押公司,它由国会于1970年创建,是旨在扩大美国住房抵押贷款二级市场、增加自置居所和租赁房屋的部分计划。

公司做什么?

房利美和较小的房地美是由国会管理的股份制公司,他们在抵押贷款市场维持住房资金流动以支持房地产。根据国会的章程,这两个公司常常被称为政府赞助企业,或 GSEs。它们受惠于政府主导的隐含担保,能够通过对投资者出售债务的方式,以相对廉价的

Key Facts on Fannie Mae and Freddie Mac

companies charged by Congress with supporting housing by keeping money flowing in the mortgage market. Due to the congressional charter, the two are often referred to as government-sponsored enterprises, or GSEs. Due largely to an implied government guarantee, they are able to raise funds relatively cheaply by selling debt to investors. The funds they raise are then used to purchase home loans from mortgage originators such as banks, allowing the lenders to make fresh home loans. While the collapse of the subprime mortgage market, which caters to borrowers with poor credit histories, has contributed significantly to the U.S. housing slump, the vast majority of mortgages purchased by Fannie Mae and Freddie Mac are prime, fixed-rate loans on which borrowers are current. Fannie Mae and Freddie Mac bundle the loans they purchase into securities which are sold, with a guarantee of payment, to investors worldwide. In addition, the two companies also guarantee mortgages and pay owners of the loans when there is a default①.

SIZE OF INVESTMENTS

The two companies hold some of the loans they purchase and securities they bundle in their investment portfolios. Fannie Mae said its portfolio was $758.1 billion, while Freddie Mac said its portfolio was a record $798.2 billion. Including investments and guarantees, Fannie Mae's total book of business topped $3 trillion for the first time, twice its size at the beginning of 2002. With Freddie Mac's $2.2 trillion in investments and guarantees, the two have a hand in nearly half of the

---

① default [di'fɔːlt] *n.* 违约

房利美和房地美的关键事实

债务成本筹集资金。然后,他们用筹集到的资金用于从银行之类的抵押贷款原始人处购买住房贷款,允许放款者出台新的住房贷款。尽管次级抵押贷款市场的崩溃,迎合了借款人不良的信用记录,成为美国房地产不景气的显著原因,但房利美和房地美购买的绝大多数抵押贷款是最好的固定利率贷款,成为贷款人手中的流通币。房利美和房地美把它们购买的贷款与证券捆绑在一起,以付款保证的方式出售给世界各地的投资者。此外,两家公司还保证在违约时抵押贷款和向贷款者支付贷款。

投资规模

这两家公司持有的一些它们所购买的贷款和证券,捆绑在其投资组合中。房利美表示,其投资组合达7 581亿美元,而房地美表示,其投资组合已达到创纪录的7 982亿美元。包括投资和担保在内,房利美的账面业务总额首次突破3万亿美元,规模是2002年初的两倍。如果算上房地美2.2万亿美元投资和担保,这两个集团的资金占整个12万亿美元国家抵押贷款市场的将近一半。

它们为什么遇到麻烦?

随着住房市场继续恶化,赎回权的丧失已扩散到除次级抵押贷款以外更高质量的抵押贷款。两家公司已被要求签署它们用于投资的贷款,支付违约保障贷款消耗的资本。据报道,自住房市场泡沫破裂以来,房利美和房地美已损失近140亿美元。与许多其他的金融机构不同的是,房利美和房地美从未被要求持有与它们的资产相应的资金。这使得它们只有较少的缓冲资金来吸收损失。资金缺口表明,它们无法从贷方回购抵押贷款。

Key Facts on Fannie Mae and Freddie Mac

entire, $ 12 trillion national mortgage market.

WHY ARE THEY IN TROUBLE?

As the housing market continues to deteriorate, foreclosures① have spread beyond subprime loans to higher-quality mortgages. The two companies have been required to write down their loans held for investment and pay out on guaranteed mortgages that default, depleting their capital. Fannie Mae and Freddie Mac have reported nearly $ 14 billion in losses since the housing market bubble burst. Contrary to many other financial institutions, Fannie Mae and Freddie Mac have never been required to hold much capital relative to their assets. That leaves them with a smaller cushion for absorbing losses. A lack of capital also indicates they are unable to buy mortgages from lenders.

THE SOLUTION?

Analysts and investors had expected the two companies to raise capital, but their falling share prices made that increasingly difficult. Fannie Mae raised $ 7.4 billion of capital by selling common and preferred shares. Freddie Mac has announced plans to raise $ 5.5 billion but its ability to do that by selling shares will be difficult given the sharp drop in its stock price.

WHY DOES IT MATTER IF THEY REMAIN SOLVENT?

The two companies' presence in the struggling housing market is widely considered to be critical. They help keep mortgage rates low for many consumers, but the companies are struggling to balance growth

---

① foreclosure [fɔːˈkləuʒə] n. 丧失抵押品赎回权

房利美和房地美的关键事实

解决办法?

分析师和投资者期待两家公司筹集资金,但它们下滑的股票价格使资金的筹集越来越困难。房利美通过销售普通股和优先股筹集了74亿美元的资金。房地美宣布计划筹集55亿美元,但考虑到其急剧下降的股票价格,它通过销售股票达到目标的能力将遇到困难。

为什么它们保持偿债能力很重要?

人们普遍认为,在风雨飘摇的住房市场,两家公司的存在举足轻重。它们帮助许多消费者保持低位抵押贷款利率,但两家公司都在艰难地维持平衡增长,通过买入贷款来抵御不断上升的逾期债款。两家公司的债务证券都具有高位信用评级,世界各地的银行和机构投资者广泛持有他们的债务证券。所以,一次信用危机不仅会给公司带来损害,还会增加借贷成本。

有没有先例?

1979年,房利美曾因其负债市值超过资产市值而无力偿付债务。随着市场因素最终朝着对公司有利的方向发展而扭转局势。美国政府并没有介入。

谁监督这两家公司?

美国联邦住房企业监督办公室成立于1992年,曾是两房公司的监管者,但最近被更为强势的联邦住房金融机构正式接管。联邦住屋企业督察办公室被普遍认为缺乏监管公司的关键能力,从而根据刚刚通过的立法由较强势的监管者取而代之。

Key Facts on Fannie Mae and Freddie Mac

through buying loans against rising delinquencies①. The companies' debt instruments, which have a high credit rating, are widely held by banks and institutional investors around the world. A crisis in confidence could not only damage the companies but increase the cost of borrowing.

IS THERE A PRECEDENT②?

In 1979, Fannie Mae became insolvent③ as the market value of its liabilities④ exceeded the market value of its assets. This turned around as market factors eventually worked in the company's favor. The U. S. government did not get involved.

WHO OVERSEES THE TWO COMPANIES?

The Office of Federal Housing Enterprise Oversight, created in 1992 was the companies' regulator until it was officially replaced by the stronger Federal Housing Finance Agency recently. OFHEO was widely considered to lack crucial powers to oversee the companies and was replaced by the stronger regulator under the just-passed legislation.

(782 words)

---

① delinquency [di'liŋkwənsi] *n.* 不法行为
② precedent ['presidənt] *n.* 先例
③ insolvent [in'sɔlvənt] *adj.* 无力偿付债务的
④ liability [laiə'biliti] *n.* 债务;责任

房利美和房地美的关键事实

知识链接

The Office of Federal Housing Enterprise Oversight 美国联邦住房企业监督办公室(OFHEO)是住房和城市发展部的一个内部机构,1992年根据联邦住房企业财务安全和稳健法成立,由总统任命、并经参议院批准的一名董事管理。它的主要职责是确保两个政府资助的企业——联邦国民抵押贷款协会(房利美)和联邦住宅贷款抵押公司(房地美)——资本充足以及金融安全和稳健。

Federal Housing Finance Agency 美国联邦住房金融局(FHFA)是联邦住房企业监督办公室(OFHEO)的继任者,独立的联邦法定监管机构,由美国能源部住房和城市发展机构与联邦住房金融委员会合并而成。它的主要职责是监管房利美、房地美以及12个联邦住宅贷款银行系统。

题　记

　　在伦敦金融城这块占地仅2.6平方公里的弹丸之地，云集着包括英格兰银行总部在内的世界主要的金融机构，拥有独立的司法系统，18世纪以来一直是英国、乃至世界的金融中心。但是，随着次贷危机的扩散，渗透力和破坏力不断加大，伦敦金融城的"蝴蝶效应"随着金融危机在华尔街的肆虐跌宕起伏。危机已经在伦敦金融城的模式中产生了三种主要反应：一种是"受惊的兔子"模式，这种方法牵涉避免在尘埃落定前作出任何决定。另一种是"尼克·李森"效应，用房屋下赌注，认为正在经历的极端波动可能会带来丰厚的利润。第三种是"拉小提琴的尼禄"策略，为讨好老板而做出孤注一掷的努力。金融城才华横溢的金融人士，在希望与失望太多次交替上演之后，可能会被迫重新考虑他们的生活选择。但塞翁失马，焉知非福？伦敦金融城既因感染次贷病毒而日渐式微，也因纽约的衰败影响力日渐上升，声名鹊起。

Panic in the Financial City of London

Absolute panic interspersed with deep, dark depression seems to be the order of the day in the City of London.

After many conversations in the past day or two with my former clients and colleagues in financial services, I can say that never during my own 12-year City career at four investment banks did I ever witness such a horrifying air of despondency. No one seems to believe that things could have got so out of control so quickly, especially when in the past months there appeared to be some "green shoots of recovery". I have listened as one equity salesman talked of "the system potentially grinding to a halt over the next couple of weeks". A former colleague spoke of a potential "total meltdown of the system". Fear is overpowering greed with consummate① ease and the herd mentality proves as strong as ever. Previous "masters of the universe" look on bewildered and powerless while former "big swinging dicks" appear to have been plunged in cold water.

---

① consummate [ˈkɔnsəmeit] adj. 完美的,圆满的

伦敦金融城陷入恐慌

当天的伦敦金融城似乎完全陷入恐慌，弥散着深深的、忧郁的萧条氛围。

过去的一到两天中，我与金融行业的前客户和同事多次交谈，可以说，我在四家投资银行任职 12 年的金融城生涯中，从未目睹如此可怕的沮丧气氛。尤其是当过去几个月浮现了一些"经济复苏的苗头"之时，似乎没有人相信局势会如此之快地失控。我听一位股票推销员说，"接下来的几周金融系统可能慢慢停止"。一位前同事谈到了潜在的"系统整体崩溃"。令人担忧的是无法抵抗的贪婪竟然无懈可击，从众心理如从前一样强烈。早先的"宇宙主宰"看起来不知所措和无能为力，而以前的"大型摇摆迪克斯"似乎已经被打入冷宫。

今天，我坐在家里，将那个世界抛诸脑后，带着模棱两可的情感观察这一切。我知道，某些贪婪的"城市男孩"的行为引发了这场大灾难，他们多年来不计后果地用他人的钱财赌博。在某种程度上，这次金融风暴就属于作恶者自毙。我也意识到，我们正在华尔街和伦敦金融城观看一场真正的人间悲剧，它将对世界各地的家庭

Panic in the Financial City of London

Today, having left that world behind me, I sit at home and observe all this with equivocal① feelings. I know the actions of certain greedy "Cityboys" brought this catastrophe about by years of reckless gambling with other people's money. To some extent this financial turmoil is just chickens coming home to roost. I am also aware that what we are seeing on Wall Street and in the City of London is a genuine human tragedy that will have lasting implications for families around the world.

Discussions with former peers suggest that the crisis has engendered three main reactions in those City types who have been fortunate enough not yet to have lost their jobs. There is the "Startled Rabbit" approach. This involves avoiding making any decisions until the dust settles. I spoke to a middle-ranking hedge fund manager who told me quite simply that he was going to sit on his hands and take neither any long positions nor any short ones. He felt that the uncertainty was so massive he could not make informed decisions and that investing now would therefore be "like entering a casino and putting all my chips on black".

Then there is the "Nick Leeson" response. This involves betting the house in the belief that the extreme volatility② we are experiencing can result in massive profits. Some people, if they are unsure whether they will have a job next year—or indeed that capitalism will still be functioning— are inclined to double up while they can. Few former colleagues I have spoken to have admitted doing this themselves, but many of them have told

---

① equivocal [iˈkwivəkl] *adj.* 模棱两可的
② volatility [vɔləˈtiləti] *n.* 挥发性

伦敦金融城陷入恐慌

产生持久的影响。

那些足够幸运、还没有丢工作的前同行通过讨论得出结论,危机已经在这些金融城的模式中产生了三种主要反应:一种是"受惊的兔子"模式。这种方法牵涉避免在尘埃落定前作出任何决定。我与一位中级对冲基金经理交谈时,他很简洁地告诉我,他打算守住手头的资金,既不做多头,也不卖空。他认为,不确定性是如此之大,以至于他无法作出明智的决定,目前的投资"就像进入赌场,所有的赌注付之东流"。

其次是"尼克·李森"效应。这种方法指用房屋下赌注,认为我们正在经历的极端波动可能会带来丰厚的利润。有些人即使无法确定下一年度是否有工作,或者资本主义确实仍在运行,只要力所能及就有意屈从。我提到的几位前同事,几乎没有人承认自己如此行事,然而他们中的很多人却告诉我那些私有业主和对冲基金经理的故事,他们目前就显示出不顾一切的倾向。

最后的反应是我称之为"拉小提琴的尼禄"策略。潜在的就业损失可能使办公室的某些自动装置消耗额外的时间,如他们外出时外套还留在椅子上,这是为了讨好老板做出的孤注一掷的努力。但更多相信宿命的员工认为,如果失业的末路已经无可更改,酒吧则是观望混乱和埋葬悲伤的最好去处。一天,我在下午 5 点 30 分来到金融城的一家酒吧,里面几乎爆满。我偶然了解到,酒吧里几个喝得醉醺醺的人来自一家目前正参与合并的银行。他们告诉我,既然解雇似乎不可避免,佯装努力工作毫无意义。但是,我还发现,许

Panic in the Financial City of London

me stories about proprietary① traders and hedge fund managers who are currently exhibiting this devil-may-care tendency.

The final response is what I call the "Fiddling Nero" strategy. Potential job losses may make certain automata spend extra hours in the office—and still leave their jacket over their chair when they do go out—in a desperate attempt to curry favor with their bosses. But more fatalistic workers think that, if the writing is on the wall, the pub is the best place to observe the chaos and drown their sorrows. I was in a certain City bar one day at 5.30pm and it was almost completely full. I happened to know that several of the hard-drinking folk inside were from a bank that is currently involved in a merger. They told me they saw no point in pretending to work hard when the sack seemed inevitable. However, I also found that many City workers were there to attend a leaving do of a senior salesman—and hoped to find a job at their former colleague's new employer. As one broker commented drily: "For some reason, this is the best attended leaving drinks I've ever been to."

So, after speaking to my more level-headed former friends and colleagues, what can I suggest that worried financial services employees do as banks crash, merge and rein in spending? First, ring that headhunter immediately. They may be inundated② with calls but it is better to be on their lists than not. Second, network like it's going out of fashion. Obviously, suck up to the boss even more than normal, but also think of all

---

① proprietary [prə'praiətəri] *adj.* 私有的
② inundate ['inʌndeit] *vi.* 充满

伦敦金融城陷入恐慌

多金融城的工作人员在那里参加一个高级业务员的欢送会,希望在他们前同事的新雇主那里找到一份工作。 正如一位经纪人冷冰冰地评论的:"出于某种原因,这是我去过的最好的告别酒会。"

因此,与头脑更冷静的前朋友和同事谈话后,,当银行破产、并购和支出受控时,我该建议焦虑的金融服务人员做什么呢? 第一,立即打电话给猎头公司。 他们可能会被潮水般的电话淹没,但在他们的名单上登记总比不登好。 第二,网络好像正在过时。 很显然,不仅要超乎常规地巴结老板,还要考虑所有的朋友、客户和前同事,了解他们的公司是否有机会。 第三,削减开支,让你的配偶也这么做。 即使你有工作,今年的奖金至少低百分之三十。 这不仅仅是因为利润下降太多,而是因为老板付给你的酬劳少到他们可以忽略不计,当金融城找工作的人供过于求时,威胁换到其他公司的旧把戏显然无足轻重。

然而,我的主要结论是:这可能是因祸得福。 对真正热爱紧张、有竞争力的工作以及骇人听闻地长时间工作的金融城人士,我了解得并不是太多。 金融城吸收了非常有才华的人,与它提供的巨大报酬是如此的不成比例。 也许其中的一些聪明人可能会被迫重新考虑他们的生活选择,我敢说,他们会最终选择运用自己的聪明才智,做一些更令人愉快、更令人满意、更有价值的事情。

知识链接

Nick Leeson 尼克·李森是巴林银行的交易员,在衍生性金融商品的超额交

Panic in the Financial City of London

your friends, clients and former colleagues and whether there are opportunities at their firms. Third, reduce your spending and make your spouse do the same. Even if you keep your job, bonuses will be at least 30 per cent lower this year. This is not just because profits will be down by so much but because your bosses will pay you as little as they can get away with and the old trick of threatening to move to a different firm won't cut the mustard when there is a glut of City people seeking jobs.

My main conclusion, however, is that this could be a blessing in disguise. I don't know many City workers who really love their stressful, competitive jobs and the hideously long hours. The City sucks up very talented people, such are the disproportionately massive rewards that it offers. Perhaps some of these smart cookies may be forced to review their life choice and end up choosing to use their talents to do something more enjoyable, fulfilling and, dare I say it, worthwhile.

(882 words)

伦敦金融城陷入恐慌

易中投机失败,造成 14 亿美元的损失,导致巴林银行在 1995 年 2 月 26 日倒闭。

Fiddling Nero 拉小提琴的尼禄。据说公元 64 年,一场持续 5 天的大火烧毁了大半个古罗马,皇帝尼禄在大火中拉小提琴,一边拉,一边高歌《特洛伊覆亡曲》。其实小提琴当时根本还没发明,他拉的是七弦琴。这个故事暗喻是尼禄自己纵火,目的是建造一个新的罗马城。

题 记

　　迪士尼主题公园的发展轨迹描绘了缔造商业帝国的独特风景。"制造一个产品"的经营梦想赋予公园在虚幻背景下展示迪士尼人物和角色的"主题"。"塑造一个品牌"的经营策略使公园形成了产品多元化或产业多元化的经营格局。迪士尼乐园不仅因创造米老鼠、白雪公主和小鹿斑比等角色而享誉全球,还与影视媒体企业、玩具商、服装商等合作开发了一系列拥有固定主题的产品。"拥有一批客户"的经营目标增强了消费者对迪士尼乐园的认知度,产生了广泛的客源聚集效应。"与媒体融合"形成了迪士尼主题公园快捷、健康发展之路,推动迪士尼从一个以主题公园和娱乐为主的美国本土公司发展成为以媒体经营为主的全球化集团。迪士尼主题公园赋予的创意出奇制胜,它将现代文明的产物培育成无尽的宝藏,然后将这些宝藏转变为庞大的经济成果并持续发展。

Walt Disney's "Theme Park" Development

Disneyland's origins had deep roots in Walt Disney's past. He later told inquirers that he first had the idea for a new kind of amusement park when he took his two young daughters out for fun on weekends and found that, "…existing kids' parks and fairs were often dirty, sleazy①, money-grubbing places." In spite of the fact he had never developed real estate or managed a large-scale construction project, Disney nourished his notions of a new kind of amusement park throughout the late 1940s and early 1950s. His idea for displaying Disney characters in a fantasy setting was a bold departure from present-day amusement parks and carnivals that offered rides, games, and inexpensive food. Instead Disneyland was conceived as an extension of the Disney brand, and would be the first "theme park" built in the United States, signaling a major shift in amusement park construction and, equally as importantly, in real estate development surrounding major attractions.

As his ideas for the development began to expand and take shape, Walt found little enthusiasm for the project within his own company. His brother Roy, the financial director of the studio, strongly opposed it, believing that this "fanciful, expensive amusement park would lead to

---

① sleazy [ˈsliːzi] *adj.* 破烂的

迪士尼"主题公园"的发展

　　迪士尼乐园的原型很久以来就已经深深植根于沃尔特·迪士尼的心中。日后，他告诉询问者，当他带着两个小女儿愉快地外出度周末的时候，第一次产生了建一座新型游乐园的想法。他发现，"已有的儿童乐园和博览会通常是很脏、低俗和乱收费的地方"。尽管实际上他从未做过房地产开发或管理大规模的建筑项目，迪士尼却在19世纪40年代末至50年代初滋生了建立新型游乐园的想法。他在虚幻的背景下展示迪士尼人物和角色的想法，大胆地与当时游乐场和嘉年华的模式分道扬镳，那种模式只提供骑乘、游戏和廉价食物。而迪士尼乐园被认为是迪士尼品牌的延伸，并且可能是美国建立的首家"主题公园"，它标志着游乐园主流风格的转变，对周边主要景点的房地产开发也同样重要。

　　当沃尔特对迪士尼乐园的想法日益详细和具体化时，他发现自己对公司里的其他项目几乎失去了热情。作为迪士尼工作室的财务总监，他的兄弟罗伊极力反对，认为建这种"虚幻、昂贵的游乐园将导致经济损失"。许多银行家、投资者也认为，迪士尼缺乏房地产开发与建造经验，根本无法克服如此大的跨越。但是沃尔特对自己的设想信心十足，他避开了迪士尼公司的阻挠，开始通过自己的人寿保险借贷和出售位于南加利福尼亚的度假村来筹集资金。他组

financial ruin." Most bankers and investors agreed, feeling that Disney's lack of real estate development and construction experience was too large a hurdle to overcome. But Walt, confident of his own vision, sidestepped the studio and began to gather funds by borrowing on his life insurance and selling vacation property in southern California. He assembled a staff of designers, planners, and artists and formed WED Enterprises—the letters were his initials—as a personal corporation to house them.

Operating out of a small building on the Disney Burbank lot, the WED group began a long process of creative brainstorming. Its members conceptualized, designed, and reworked Walt's broad ideas. They visited other amusement attractions around the country to gather data and impressions and flesh out development plans, and with the help of commercial contractors created a rough construction timetable. But major large hurdles—obtaining financing and securing a location—still blocked the launching of the park's construction. Walt recognized his need to seek real estate development expertise and solicited a pair of marketing studies from the Stanford Research Institute: one would examine the economic prospects of developing Disneyland, and the other the ideal location for construction.

After determining the facility could be profitable, the Stanford group closely examined a host of factors—demographic statistics, urban growth trends, population concentrations, traffic patterns, freeway construction, availability of experienced commercial contractors, weather conditions—before recommending a sight in Anaheim, a rapidly growing town just southeast of Los Angeles. The study eventually led to the purchase of a 160-acre orange grove alongside the new Santa Ana freeway; its proximity to a major freeway meant the park was a short 27-minute drive from downtown Los Angeles.

迪士尼"主题公园"的发展

建了一个由设计者、规划者和艺术家组成的团队,并成立了以他的首字母命名的 WED 公司,作为私人公司来管理他们。

WED 集团经历了长期的集思广益,在迪士尼伯班克的一块地上的一座小型建筑物中开始运营。其成员对沃尔特无拘无束的想法进行构思、设计和改造。他们参观了国内其他久负盛名的游乐园,收集数据和观感,充实开发计划,并在商业承包商的帮助下制定出粗略的建造时间规划表。但是,主要的大障碍——筹集资金和找块地——依旧困扰着迪士尼乐园项目的正式实施。沃尔特意识到,他需要去斯坦福研究院学习房地产开发技术和招标两项营销研究,即检验开发迪士尼乐园的经济前景和找到理想的建设地点。

斯坦福研究团队在验证迪士尼乐园的可盈利性后,严谨细致地考察了一系列的因素,如人口统计数据、城市发展趋势、人口密度、交通结构、高速公路建设、获取有经验的商业承包商的可能性、天气情况等,然后推荐了位于洛杉矶市东南部快速发展的小镇阿纳海姆的一片风景区。公司最终根据研究报告买下了圣安娜高速公路旁一块大约 160 英亩的橘林。如果主题公园靠近高速公路,那么从洛杉矶市中心驱车只需 27 分钟即可到达。

根据沃尔特后来的回忆,他曾饱受资金匮乏的困扰。银行家们跟他说:"户外娱乐行业是文化的时代错误,已经老态龙钟,摇摇欲坠。"几个月后,他与美国广播公司达成一项长期协议,美国广播公司作为主要投资者,提供电视网络,他走出了资金短缺的困境。随着资金的到位和选址的确定,迪士尼乐园于 1953 年夏天正式开工。工程师和前海军上将乔·福勒担任建筑总监,全盘指挥管理商业承包商和建筑公司,他后来在迪士尼乐园管理长达 10 年之久。

Walt Disney's "Theme Park" Development

Disney had struggled to find additional financing; as he later recalled, he was told by bankers that "the outdoor amusement business was a cultural anachronism that had already declined into senility." A few months later, the financial breakthrough came with a long-term agreement with ABC which brought the television network in as a major investor. With financing in place and a location secured, construction began in the summer of 1953. Commercial contractors and construction companies fell under the overall leadership of Joe Fowler, an engineer and retired navy admiral① who became construction supervisor, and later park manager for ten years.

Disneyland was formally opened a year later to glowing reviews. Unlike other amusement parks of the day, Disneyland was developed and constructed to be instantly recognizable as an extension of the Disney brand and the Disney philosophy. The rides used an array of Disney motifs②, costumed Disney characters roamed the park, and Sleeping Beauty Castle, the looming attraction at the heart of the park, was instantly recognizable to millions of people since it was seen every Sunday night on ABC television. Disneyland became, in a sense, the capstone of Walt Disney's career.

The capstone of his career also quickly became the cornerstone of an empire. In its first six months, one million people visited the park; in its first full year, three million people passed through its gates. The park quickly generated capital to finance a vast expansion, and in subsequent years, each time the park expanded its capacity, revenues increased more than proportionately to the added capital. In spite of his lack of real estate

---

① admiral [ˈædmərəl] n. 海军上将
② motif [məuˈtiːf] n. 基调

迪士尼"主题公园"的发展

迪士尼乐园一年后正式对外开放时好评如潮。迪士尼乐园有别于当时的其他游乐场,它的开发和建造立即被认为是迪士尼品牌和迪士尼企业文化的延伸。游乐场的乘坐装置运用了一系列的迪士尼主题,身穿迪士尼服装的人物漫步公园,数以百万计的人立刻认出了光彩照人地耸立在公园中心的睡美人城堡,因为每周日晚他们都会在美国广播公司的电视台与之邂逅。在某种意义上,建造迪士尼乐园是沃尔特·迪士尼职业生涯的顶峰。

沃尔特·迪士尼职业生涯的顶峰也很快成为迪士尼商业帝国的基石。头六个月,100万游客造访了迪士尼乐园;一年整,游客人数已达300万。迪士尼乐园产生的流动资金又资助其大面积扩张,在随后的岁月里,迪士尼乐园的容量每扩张一倍,增加的收益比例就多于新投入的资金比例。尽管迪士尼缺乏房地产开发经验,他开创了扩张公园规模的同时不影响公园正常运营的模式。

迪士尼也认识到,迪士尼乐园应该成为度假者的旅游胜地,所以他计划在公园周围留出空间建造旅馆和饭店,这种设计后来用在了迪士尼世界的建筑中,旅馆和饭店与游乐园成为一个整体。迪士尼世界的特色在于其资产超过20个自有场所,从露营地到高级别墅。巴黎和日本的迪士尼主题公园进一步复制了迪士尼模式。迪士尼从动画和电影到度假旅游的多样化经营方式中,还包括迪士尼航线。

事实上,迪士尼乐园象征着娱乐和主题公园发展与建设中的大转变。今天,几乎所有的美国大型娱乐场所都奉行了迪士尼的衍生模式和追求目标:集中的便利设施,优越的客户体验,轻松和无缝扩张的发展规划,最重要的是,给予公园身份和独特性意义的"主

Walt Disney's "Theme Park" Development

development experience, Disney had created park plans that allowed for expansion and resulting construction that would not interfere with ongoing park operations.

Disney also recognized that Disneyland would become a destination for vacationers, and his plans left room for hotels and restaurants to be built surrounding the park—a model that later was used in the construction of Disney World, where hotels and restaurants are an integral part of the amusement park; Disney World features more than 20 Disney-owned resorts on its property, ranging from campsites to deluxe villas. The Disney model has been further replicated in Disney theme parks in Paris and Tokyo as well; Disney's diversification from cartoons and movies into vacation environments includes a Disney cruise line as well.

In fact, Disneyland signaled a major shift in amusement and theme park development and construction. Almost every major amusement park in the U.S. today is a descendant of and aspires to the Disney model: a focus on convenience, a superior guest experience, development planning allowing easy and seamless expansion, and most importantly a "theme" that gives a park a sense of identity and uniqueness.

By developing Disneyland, Walt Disney not only changed the fortunes of the Disney Company; he also revived the dying American amusement park business and made it a multi-billion dollar industry entertaining millions of people every year. Disney is justifiably celebrated for creating characters like Mickey Mouse, Snow White and Bambi, but his effect on real estate development and theme park construction is no less significant.

(1,001 words)

迪士尼"主题公园"的发展

题"。

通过建设迪士尼乐园,沃尔特·迪士尼不仅改变了迪士尼公司的财富,还复苏了惨淡的美国娱乐公园行业,使之成为每年拥有数百万计游客、产出数 10 亿美元的公司。尽管迪士尼因创造米老鼠、白雪公主和小鹿斑比等角色而举世闻名,但他在地产开发和主题公园建设方面所起的作用也不容小觑。

知识链接

The Stanford Research Institute　斯坦福研究院(SRI)多年来在众多的研究与发展领域为政府、商业机构和其他客户提供服务,以专业精湛的研究人员和职业技术(包括各种学科的研究团队)享誉全美。

ABC　美国广播公司(American Broadcasting Company)是美国传统三大广播电视公司之一,创立于 1943 年。目前的最大股东是沃尔特·迪士尼公司,为迪士尼-ABC 电视集团的成员。集团总部在纽约市曼哈顿,节目制作总部在加利福尼亚的伯班克市,与迪士尼公司的总部和迪士尼摄影棚由人行天桥相连。

题　记

苹果公司运用固定价格在线音乐下载服务的理念不仅为其赢得了大量的客户，也随着苹果iTunes的普及成长为数字音乐领域无可争辩的王者。尽管唱片公司也获得了丰厚的收入，弥补了CD销售滑坡带来的损失，但是，一些唱片公司认为，苹果公司坚持每首歌曲99美分的下载价格影响了它们的财路。在与唱片公司的较量中，苹果在数字音乐市场上的主导地位使它具有更多的筹码。苹果坚决抵制了音乐公司要求增加音乐下载费用的"贪婪"欲望，甚至威胁关闭iTunes网上音乐商店。美国版权委员会最终驳回了美国音乐出版商协会等提出的提高数字音乐下载版税分成的要求。不过，委员会也没有同意苹果提出的降低版税标准的要求。当这场较量的天平偏向了苹果公司的时候，唱片公司能够承担与苹果分道扬镳的代价吗？

Apple Defeats Music Rate Hike

It looks like Apple won't be closing the iTunes store because of a dispute with music publishers over royalties on downloaded songs. The Copyright Royalty Board in Washington, D.C., today declined a request by the National Music Publishers Association to increase royalties from 9 cents to 15 cents on songs purchased from online music stores like iTunes. Apple adamantly① opposed the proposed 66% increase and threatened to shutter iTunes if it was approved.

In a statement submitted to the board, iTunes vice president Eddy Cue said Apple didn't want to raise its 99 cents a song price or absorb the higher royalty costs itself. Cue's statement was first reported by Fortune. PricewaterhouseCoopers estimates that Apple only makes about 10 cents a song in profit. Apple spokesman Tom Neumayr said the company was happy with the ruling. "We're pleased with the CRB's decision to keep royalty rates stable," he said.

---

① adamantly [ˈædəməntli] adv. 坚决地

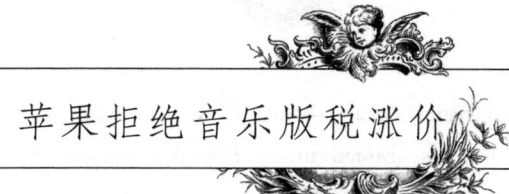

苹果拒绝音乐版税涨价

苹果公司似乎不会因为与音乐出版商对下载歌曲的版税争端关闭 iTunes 商店。 位于华盛顿特区的版税委员会拒绝了全美音乐出版商协会的请求，他们要求对 iTunes 之类的网上音乐商店增收版权使用费，从 9 美分涨至 15 美分。 苹果公司坚决反对将版税提升 66% 的建议，并威胁称，如果该提议被通过，将关闭 iTunes 商店。

在提交给版税委员会的一份报告中，iTunes 的副主席埃迪·克鲁声称，苹果公司不愿对售价 99 美分的单曲提价，也不想独自消化较高的税收成本。 财富杂志首次报道了克鲁的报告。 普华永道会计师事务所估计，苹果公司的单曲仅有约 10 美分的利润。 苹果发言人汤姆·纽曼尔表示，苹果公司很高兴这样的裁决。 他说："我们很乐意接受版税委员会做出维持版税利率稳定的决定。"

版税委员会是一个由 3 名法官组成的小组，他们负责在联邦版权法许可内监督和授权，包括设定音乐销售专利的使用费率。 当前的使用费率是 1997 年制定的法规，监管 CD 光盘等实体音乐产品近

Apple Defeats Music Rate Hike

    The Copyright Royalty Board is a three-judge panel that oversees statutory① licenses granted under federal copyright law. That includes royalty rates for music sales. The current case followed the expiration last year of a 1997 decision that had governed sales of so-called physical music products like CDs for a decade. CRB's decision will set royalty rates for the next five years. This is the board's first ruling on the digital sale of music.

    Cue's threat was greeted with disbelief by many people in the technology world. Apple has artfully used the iTunes store to spur demand for iPods, its most popular product. Before Apple opened the store in 2003, there was virtually no place for iPod owners to purchase music online. And so iTunes helped grow the market for the gadget by appealing to people who didn't want to patronize② illegal file-sharing services and risk a music industry lawsuit. iTunes ended up as the largest music retailer on the Internet. Piper Jaffray estimates that Apple will sell 2.4 billion songs this year, giving it an 85% share of the digital music market.

    But the company's aggressive position in this case illustrates the challenges faced by the nascent③ digital music industry. The Recording Industry Association of America says sales of digital songs and albums rose 46% last year, to $1.2 billion. Apple laments that its profits are still slim. Therefore, Apple argues, it would be dangerous to raise its 99-cents-a-song price. Apple pays an estimated 70 cents on the sale of every dollar it collects per song to the record companies responsible for each track. The

---

① statutory [ˈstætjutəri] *adj*. 法定的
② patronize [ˈpætrənaiz] *vt*. 光顾
③ nascent [ˈnæsənt] *adj*. 新生的

苹果拒绝音乐版税涨价

10 年的销售，去年已经终止。 版税委员会的裁决将为未来 5 年设置专利使用费率。 这是委员会第一次对数字音乐销售做出裁决。

　　克鲁的威胁受到许多技术界人士的怀疑。 苹果巧妙地使用 iTunes 商店，刺激对其最流行的产品 iPod 的需求。 苹果公司在 2003 年首开音乐商店之前，iPod 用户事实上无处购买在线音乐。 这样 iTunes 通过用这种小配件吸引不想使用非法文件共享服务和冒险触犯音乐行业诉讼的人，助其拓展 iPod 的销售市场。 iTunes 最终作为最大的音乐零售商出现在互联网。 派佩·贾弗雷估计，苹果公司今年将出售 24 亿首歌曲，占有数字音乐市场 85% 的份额。

　　但苹果公司在这件事上采取的侵略性立场说明，新生的数字音乐产业面临严峻挑战。 美国唱片行业协会指出，去年的数字歌曲和专辑销售上涨了 46% ，达到 12 亿美元。 但苹果公司仍然非常遗憾，认为它的利润不足挂齿。 因此，苹果表示，如果 99 美分一首的歌曲价格上升将会危机四伏。 苹果公司收集的每首歌曲销售达到一美元，必须向负责音轨的唱片公司支付大约 70 美分。 唱片公司则要支付 9 美分给音乐出版商，他们控制这些歌曲的版权。 唱片公司根本不愿从口袋里掏钱支付被提议的附加版税。 更不用说在他们曾经的摇钱树——CD 销量下降 20%、至 74 亿美元之时。 他们要求版税委员会放弃每首歌曲的固定收费，按整体销售收入的 8% 收税。

　　美国唱片行业协会主席米奇在一份声明中声称："我们很高兴，

Apple Defeats Music Rate Hike

record companies turn over 9 cents to the music publishers who control the copyrights to these tunes. The record companies were in no mood to pay the proposed royalty increase out of their pockets. Not when CD sales, their one-time cash cow, fell by 20%, to $7.4 billion. They asked the Copyright Royalty Board to abandon the fixed per-song payment in favor of 8% of wholesales revenues.

"We're pleased that this decision freezes the current rate for CDs and digital downloads for the five-year term," said RIAA chairman Mitch Bainwol in a statement. "No party got everything it wanted, yet at the end of the day, the certainty provided by this ruling is beneficial." The Digital Media Association, which represents Apple and other online music services, sought an even lower rate of 4.8 cents a track, or 6% of "applicable revenues". They didn't get what they wanted. But executive director Jonathan Potter also sounded relieved. "During this challenging time for the music industry and digital stores and services, we are pleased with the CRB's decision to keep royalty rates stable for the next five years," he said in a statement.

The music publishers had argued that Apple was selling songs at a low price to sell iPods, which didn't benefit them. Even so, they, too sounded a conciliatory① note in a statement released after the ruling was announced. "These events will bring clarity and order to an environment that for the past decade has been hampered by litigation② and uncertainty on all sides," said David Israelite, CEO of the National Music Publishers

---

① conciliatory [kənˈsiliətəri] adj. 和解的
② litigation [litiˈgeiʃən] n. 诉讼

苹果拒绝音乐版税涨价

这一裁决冻结了未来5年CD和数字下载的通用收费比率。任何一方都没有得到他想要的全部,但到了最后,这项裁决提供的必然性肯定有益。"代表苹果公司和其他在线音乐服务的数字媒体协会甚至寻求单曲收费比率低于4.8美分,或可用税收的6%。他们没有得到他们所想要的。但是执行董事乔纳森·波特似乎也缓和了态度。他在一份声明中宣称:"在这个对音乐行业、数字商店和服务充满挑战的时代,我们对版税委员会做出保持今后5年版税率不变的决定感到高兴。"

音乐出版商认为,苹果公司以低价出售歌曲以促进iPods的销量,这并不能使他们获益。即便如此,他们在裁决宣布之后也发出了和解声明。全国音乐出版商协会的首席执行官戴伟·以色列说:"这些事件将带来透明和有序的环境,在过去10年中,各方的诉讼和不确定性一直对他们造成阻碍。"世界领先的音乐出版商之一、百代唱片音乐出版公司的首席执行官罗杰·法克森说:"总之,我认为这里面没有太多的戏剧性,只不过是一组良好的比率设置,他们为歌曲作者提供良好的服务,为数字音乐传播者尽心尽力。"

知识链接

RIAA 美国唱片业协会(Recording Industry Association of America)是一个

Apple Defeats Music Rate Hike

Association.

"I think, all in all, there's not a lot of drama here, just a good set of rates that will serve songwriters well and work well for the purveyors[①] of digital music," said Roger Faxon, CEO of EMI Music Publishing, one of the world's leading music publishers.

(733 words)

---

① purveyor [pə'veiə(r)] n. 传播者；承办商

苹果拒绝音乐版税涨价

代表美国唱片业的贸易团体,成员由多家制作与发行约90%美国音乐唱片的私有公司实体如唱片公司与分销商组成。

EMI Music Publishing　百代唱片音乐出版公司成立于1897年,是全球历史最悠久的唱片公司之一。它的前身是英国留声机公司和英国哥伦比亚唱片公司。1955年,百代唱片音乐出版公司收购了美国Capital唱片公司,1957年在英国正式成立了百代唱片音乐出版公司。总部设在伦敦,在全世界146个国家和地区设有分支机构。目前百代唱片音乐出版公司拥有Captial,Apple,Virigin,Parlophone等多个唱片品牌,是英国唱片业的龙头公司。

题 记

全球最大的搜索引擎谷歌与全球第一家提供互联网导航服务网站的雅虎,签署了一项非排他性搜索广告合作协议,允许谷歌在雅虎网站上放置广告,此举每年有望为雅虎创造8亿美元的营收。一石激起千层浪。一些主要行业协会和广告商们对谷歌实力的怨恨和畏惧心理犬牙交错,如火山般爆发,纷纷要求美国司法部以及欧洲和加拿大的监管者动用否决权。他们联手抵制这笔交易,对谷歌竞价系统的公正性产生了质疑,担心此举将拉动价格的提升,影响报纸和其他网站的广告营收,并使谷歌在快速增长的网络广告市场拥有绝对的控制权。谷歌和雅虎交易面临着越来越严格的反垄断审查,业界的反对声也一浪高过一浪。但是各个企业却又不得不对谷歌投入更多的资金,毕竟它们要对自己的投资回报负责。

Google Dealing with Yahoo Draws Opposition

The Justice Department's antitrust① of the advertising partnership between Google and Yahoo has revealed the growing resentment and fear of Google's power among some of the biggest players in the advertising industry—the very customers that Google needs to keep expanding its business.

Some of the leading industry associations and advertising agencies that have come out against the deal have raised concerns that prices will rise. Their anxiety over Google's increasing dominance of the lucrative and fast-growing search advertising business, and the very fairness of Google's auction system for pricing search ads, could lead to growing confrontations. "Google and Yahoo claim these are auctions," said Robert D. Liodice, chief executive of the Association of National Advertisers. "Many of our marketers don't necessarily believe that these are real auctions." The association, which represents many of the largest advertisers in the United States, as well as its Canadian counterpart and a group representing

---

① antitrust [ˌænti'trʌst] n. 反垄断

谷歌雅虎交易遭到反对

司法部门对谷歌和雅虎广告合作的反托拉斯调查显示，广告行业的最大玩家们对谷歌实力的憎恨和畏惧心理正在蔓延，而他们正是谷歌拓展业务必须维护的消费者。

一些主要行业协会和广告商联手抵制这笔交易，他们担心此举将拉动价格的提升。谷歌对利润丰厚、高速增长的搜索广告业务的优势持续增长，谷歌的价格搜索广告拍卖系统非常公平，他们对此的焦虑可能导致日益加大的冲突。美国广告协会的首席执行官罗伯特·里奥迪斯表示："谷歌和雅虎声称要求拍卖。但我们的很多市场商人并不一定相信真有拍卖。"协会代表了美国的很多大广告商、加拿大广告商和全球报业集团，他们提请司法部、欧洲协调人和加拿大共同拦截这起交易。其他的几个工业团体批评了这起交易，但突然停止了阻拦请求。

司法部的复核预计大概在月底前完成。与此同时，支持谷歌的分析人士担心，这项决议使公司与政府管理者之间的冲突更为频

Google Dealing with Yahoo Draws Opposition

newspapers worldwide, has asked the Justice Department and regulators in Europe and Canada to block the deal. Several other industry groups have criticized the deal but have stopped short of asking it be blocked.

The Justice Department's review is expected to conclude perhaps before the end of the month. Meanwhile, analysts who follow Google worry that the agreement puts the company on a course to more frequent collisions with government regulators. That could slow its growth prospects, much as Microsoft's clashes with the government damped its ability to innovate. "All of this government and legislative friction is our biggest concern with Google moving forward with its business," said Christa Quarles, an analyst with Thomas Weisel Partners.

The sentiment in the advertising world is not unanimous. Some advertisers and agencies have said the deal could benefit them and their customers and could turn Yahoo, the No. 2 company in search advertising, into a stronger competitor to Google, the market leader. But even some of the deal's defenders said they were uneasy about Google's growing power and what they described as its inscrutable① auction for pricing ads. "What I like about this deal is that it makes Yahoo more viable," said David Kenny, managing partner of VivaKi, the digital and media division of the Publicis Groupe. "We absolutely want competition. But we are also pretty clear with Google that we want their algorithms to be more transparent."

Google and Yahoo have vigorously defended the deal, saying it would benefit users and advertisers. They have said that the agreement, under which Yahoo can choose to place ads sold by Google on some of its search

---

① inscrutable [inˈskruːtəbl] *adj.* 不可理解的

谷歌雅虎交易遭到反对

繁。这种冲突会慢慢显现,如微软和美国政府的摩擦就使它的创新能力受限。一位托马斯·韦塞尔合作投行的分析师克里斯塔·卡瓦勒斯表示:"所有这些政府和立法机构的摩擦是我们最大的担心,因为他们与谷歌的业务发展息息相关。"

广告界的感受各不相同。有些广告商和代理商认为,这笔交易可能让他们和他们的消费者受益,他们可能转投在搜索广告行业排名第二的雅虎,使其成为市场老大谷歌的强有力竞争对手。甚至有些交易的辩护者也声称,他们对谷歌的增长实力表示担忧,他们将此描述为定价广告难以预测的拍卖。公共社团数码和媒体部的维沃基管理合伙人大卫·肯尼表示:"我喜欢这笔交易因为它使雅虎更具可行性。我们绝对希望这种竞争。但我们也非常清楚,希望谷歌的算法更加透明。"

谷歌和雅虎奋力捍卫这场交易,声称它将有益于用户和广告商。他们指出,根据协议,雅虎可以在美国和加拿大选定谷歌运用搜索查询售出的广告,使雅虎的业务更加灵活。雅虎与微软谈判破裂之后即签约了这笔交易。谷歌的首席执行官埃里克·E.施密特声称,谷歌曾预测过大量的反对意见,但决定无论如何也要坚持这笔交易。他在一次媒体见面会上表示:"这笔交易策划精准,符合美国反垄断法条款。"他表示,当一家大公司设法创新时,有些改革

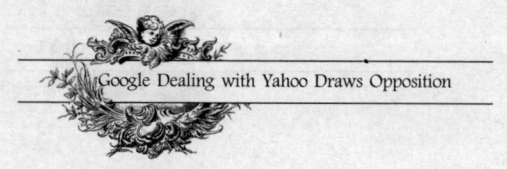
Google Dealing with Yahoo Draws Opposition

queries in the United States and Canada, would make Yahoo more viable. Yahoo signed the deal after merger talks with Microsoft broke off. Eric E. Schmidt, Google's chief executive, said Google had anticipated many of the objections but decided to pursue the agreement anyway. "The deal was designed precisely to meet the terms of antitrust law in the U.S.," he said during a meeting with reporters. When a large company tries to innovate, some of the initiatives it takes on will be unpopular or lead to criticism, he said. "The guidance that we use is: what is going to be beneficial to the end user? To sit there and say, because we anticipate stress, we are not going to do what we think is the right thing, that is not a good way to run the business." Google and Yahoo have created Web sites intended to answer concerns raised by marketers and regulators. Their executives have also met with marketers to seek their support.

The Association of National Advertisers said it had not found the companies' arguments persuasive. "We have not changed our opinion," Mr. Liodice said in an e-mail. He said that only one member of the association's board, which includes executives from nearly 30 major advertisers like Procter & Gamble, McDonald's, Wal-Mart Stores and Bank of America, was "uncertain" about whether the group should oppose the deal. He declined to name that member. Some large online advertisers like the Avis Budget Group and Buy.com said they support the agreement.

The diverging opinions among advertisers hinge to a great extent on whether they think the partnership with Google will strengthen or weaken Yahoo. One argument, put forward by Yahoo and some of its supporters, is that Yahoo will use Google ads mostly on relatively obscure queries in which Yahoo does not currently have any ads. Yahoo will continue to show its own ads on more popular search terms and reinvest any extra dollars in

谷歌雅虎交易遭到反对

提案也许不受欢迎,或引起非议。"我们运用的指导方针是:怎样做才能使终端用户受益? 难道就坐在那儿说,因为我们预料到有压力,就不打算做我们认为正确的事,这不是经营企业的好方法。"谷歌和雅虎已经创建了网站,有意回答市场商人和管理者的疑问。 管理层也在会见市场商人,极力寻求支持者。

美国广告主协会声称,它认为两家公司的辩解难以令人信服。里昂迪斯先生在邮件里说:"我们依然保留原来的观点。"他认为,董事会成员中,包括宝洁、麦当劳、沃尔玛和美国银行等将近30个主要广告商的主管,只有一位"不确定"集团是否反对这宗交易。他拒绝透露该公司的名字。 而艾维斯预算集团和易趣等一些大型网络广告商,则声明支持这项交易。

广告商之间存在着各种意见分歧,他们在很大程度上集中于与谷歌合作对雅虎的力量是加强还是削弱这一问题。 一种由雅虎及其一些支持者提出的观点认为,雅虎将主要在相对复杂难懂的查询领域利用谷歌的广告资源,因为雅虎目前还没有投放任何广告。 雅虎将使用更多流行的搜索词持续展示自己的广告,然后再投资额外的费用改善广告系统,这样就可以在一段时间之后不再依赖谷歌。 雅虎声称,这笔交易第一年就可带来2.5亿到4.5亿的额外运作现金流。 雅虎主席苏珊·L.戴克在公司博客上写道:"雅虎将利用这次

Google Dealing with Yahoo Draws Opposition

improving its advertising system so it can wean itself from Google over time. Yahoo has said the deal will bring it $250 million to $450 million in additional operating cash flow in the first year. "Yahoo will use this agreement to help us become a stronger competitor in all aspects of online advertising," Susan L. Decker, Yahoo's president, wrote on a corporate blog.

But others believe that once Yahoo begins enjoying the extra revenue from Google, it will want to increase the percentage of its ads that come from Google to further increase its revenue. "Over time, Yahoo will seek to outsource more and more of its stuff to Google, and this will mean the eventual atrophy① of Yahoo," said Rob Norman, chief executive of GroupM Interaction Worldwide, a unit of the advertising giant the WPP Group. Some analysts have suggested that the Justice Department could try to address this concern by putting a cap on the percentage of ads that Yahoo could use from Google. Gina Talamona, a Justice Department spokeswoman, declined to comment. The companies said they had agreed to delay the planned start of the deal to give regulators time to complete the investigation.

Another source of concern is whether the deal amounts to an attempt by the No. 1 and No. 2 competitors in the search market to fix prices for ads. The two companies reject that notion. "We keep hearing this argument that Google is going to somehow raise prices by doing this," Larry Page, a Google co-founder, said. "But we don't set the prices." Major advertisers, however, say Google sets minimum bids and controls other elements that affect the price advertisers pay. "The statement that it is an

---

① atrophy [ˈætrəfi] *n.* 萎缩

谷歌雅虎交易遭到反对

合作,帮助我们全面提升在线广告领域的竞争力。"

但是也有人认为,一旦雅虎开始享受谷歌带来的额外收益,就会渴望提升来自谷歌的广告比率,进一步增加收入。广告业巨头WPP集团旗下的一个部门、群邑全球互动首席执行官罗布·诺曼认为:"随着时间的推移,雅虎广告越来越多地外包给谷歌,这将意味着雅虎最终的萎缩。"有些分析师建议,司法部门应该介入,界定雅虎使用谷歌资源的比例。司法部发言人吉娜·塔拉摩娜对此保持缄默。两家公司表示,他们同意推迟启动已经计划好的交易,让管理当局有时间完成调查。

人们关注的另一个焦点在于,搜索市场排行第一和第二的竞争对手之间的交易能否达到控制广告价格的意图。两家公司对此拒绝表态。谷歌的共同创办人拉里·佩奇说:"我们一直听到这样的声音,谷歌打算以某种方式提高价格。实际上,我们并不定价。"但是,一些主要的广告商声称,谷歌设置最低标价,控制影响广告商付费的价格等其他要素。诺曼先生认为,"宣称这是一场拍卖、市场决定价格是不真实的"。

尽管主要的广告商抱怨谷歌持续增长的权势,他们仍然将网上开支越来越多地转向谷歌,因为市场营销人员能够从谷歌系统得到最好的结果。"效率限界"是一家帮助市场营销者在搜索引擎上设置

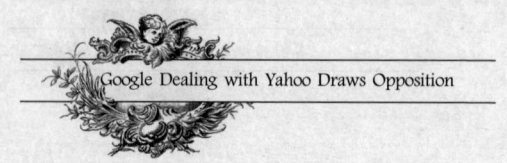
Google Dealing with Yahoo Draws Opposition

auction and the market dictates the price is not true," Mr. Norman said.

Even as major advertisers complain about Google's growing power, they are shifting more of their online spending to Google because its system delivers the best results for marketers. "Collectively, people would like Google to have less power," said Ellen Siminoff, the chairwoman of Efficient Frontier, a company that helps marketers place ads on search engines. "But individually, you will spend your money on Google, because you are responsible for your returns."

(1,119 words)

广告的公司,它的女主席埃伦·西米诺夫认为:"从个人角度来说,你还是愿意在谷歌消费,因为你必须对回报负责。"

知识链接

The Association of National Advertisers 美国广告主协会的主要职能是核查报刊发行量、核实、认证商业展览的观众人次、国际互联网站点的访问人次以及免费赠送的出版物和印刷品的净送量。

The WPP Group WPP集团是世界上最大的传播集团之一,仅次于Omnicom集团,总部位于英国伦敦。WPP集团拥有60多个子公司,包括:智威汤逊、奥美广告、精信集团、传立、扬罗毕凯广告、扬雅、United、伟达公关、朗涛形象策划、美旺宝、奥美公关、博雅公关和群邑媒介集团等。WPP集团主要服务于本地、跨国及环球客户,提供广告、媒体投资管理、信息顾问、公共事务及公共关系、建立品牌及企业形象、医疗及制药专业传播服务。

题　记

美联银行同意作价154亿美元将自身出售给富国银行，此项交易无需政府帮助。这一交易的达成使此前在联邦政府支持下的花旗集团收购案破裂，美联银行毫无悬念地另攀了高枝。原本稳操胜券却意外出局的花旗集团，考虑的不仅仅是关乎脸面的问题，而是自身在华尔街新的金融版图中的地位，即使撞得头破血流也要拿起法律诉讼的武器捍卫自身的利益。而富国银行以优渥的条件，将美联的银行业务收入囊中，其战略效益就是利用美联银行在东海岸拥有的强大分支机构，弥补富国银行的布局缺陷，并凭此交易跻身第一梯队的金融大佬之列。从长远来看，或许这块从花旗集团嘴里抢到的肥肉会为富国大厦的发展添砖加瓦，但富国银行在金融危机持续恶化的环境中显然也在艰难地消化并购的痛苦。而美联储和华尔街上的银行家们，希望关于美联银行的争夺战尽快平息，若一再纠缠不清，只会引发投资者和银行客户的恐慌心理，对市场产生负面影响，拉长盘活美联银行的时日。

Wells Bids for Wachovia

Wells Fargo & Co agreed to buy Wachovia Corp for about $ 15 billion, upstaging a government-backed Citigroup Inc bid for Wachovia's banking assets with a deal that would catapult it into the top ranks of national consumer banking. Citigroup demanded Wells Fargo drop its surprise bid, which comes four days after Wachovia preliminarily agreed to sell its banking assets to Citi for $ 2.2 billion with partial government guarantees on $ 312 billion of Wachovia's mortgages. Citi said Wachovia had signed an agreement to refrain from negotiating with other parties, even if the two parties had not signed a definitive merger agreement.

Wells Fargo Chairman Dick Kovacevich, in an interview with Reuters, said "We're confident that this deal goes through." "We get sued all the time, and many times the suits are meritless," Kovacevich said, adding that the company's lawyers are still reviewing the relevant documents. Wells Fargo said it has signed a definitive agreement to acquire Wachovia.

Regulators said they had not looked at the Wells Fargo bid, which would not require any government backing. The lack of government support may make the Wells Fargo bid more attractive for regulators, analysts speculated, and some even argued that Citi ought to walk away. "It's the right thing for the country for Citi to back off," Bill Hackney,

富国银行竞购美联银行

富国银行同意出价约150亿美元收购美联银行,抬高了政府支持花旗集团竞购美联银行资产的交易,花旗银行本想凭此交易跻身顶级国家消费者银行之列。花旗集团要求富国银行降低其出其不意的竞价,美联银行四天前曾初步同意作价22亿美元将银行资产出售给花旗集团,政府也承诺为美联银行3 120亿美元的抵押贷款做部分担保。花旗集团表示,美联银行已经与其签署了一项协定,即使双方尚未签署最终并购协议,也不可以和其他各方谈判。

富国银行主席迪克·科瓦舍维奇在接受路透社采访时说:"我们确信,这一并购能够顺利成交。"科瓦舍维奇表示,"我们一直面临起诉,而且多次的诉讼都毫无价值"。科瓦舍维奇补充说,公司的律师仍在审查相关文件。富国银行声称,它已经签署了收购美联银行的最终协议。

监管机构表示,他们还没有查看富国银行无需任何政府支持的报价。分析师们推测,没有政府的支持可能使富国的出价对管理者更有吸引力,有的甚至认为,花旗应该离场。大西洋资本管理公司的办事员比尔·哈克尼持有80亿美元富国银行的股票,他表示,

Wells Bids for Wachovia

managing partner at Atlantic Capital Management, which has $8 billion under management and owns Wells Fargo shares.

Citigroup's shares fell 18.44 percent, their biggest one-day drop since its history. The Wachovia acquisition would have helped it strategically, and the government-brokered deal also was seen as a vote of confidence from regulators. Lawyers said Citigroup has a real case, including an exclusivity agreement and the fact that it has been providing support to Wachovia. "Those are clearly strong facts on Citi's side," said Morton Pierce, chairman of the mergers and acquisition group at law firm Dewey & LeBoeuf. Dewey & LeBoeuf is not representing any of the parties in the transaction.

If Wells Fargo goes through with this deal, it will be taking a material risk. It will acquire $122 billion of "option pay" mortgages, where borrowers can choose every month whether to only pay interest on their mortgages, pay down some portion of their loan, and sometimes to pay less than the interest due. In a plummeting① housing market, such assets are seen as highly toxic, and Wells Fargo said it expects to write the assets down by $32 billion over time. These are big numbers for Wells Fargo, whose net worth as a company as measured by balance sheet shareholders' equity, was about $48 billion. Citigroup was just bidding for Wachovia's banking assets, but Wells Fargo is also buying brokerage Wachovia Securities and asset manager Evergreen as part of this deal. Those businesses could also be hit by economic slowdown.

But many investors downplayed the risk to Wells Fargo, whose

---

① plummet [ˈplʌmit] vt. 骤然跌落

富国银行竞购美联银行

"花旗银行的退出对国家来说是件有益的事"。

花旗集团的股价下跌了 18.44%,是有史以来的最大单日跌幅。从战略角度讲,收购美联银行对其有所帮助,政府促成的交易被视为来自监管者的信任投票。律师认为,花旗集团拥有足够的司法权利,包括排他性协议和对美联银行的一贯支持。杜威与勒伯夫律师事务所的合并与收购组主席莫顿·皮尔斯认为,"这些明显有力的事实有利于花旗一方"。杜威与勒伯夫在并购中并不代表任何一方。

如果富国银行完成这笔交易,将具有实质性的风险。它将收购 1 220 亿美元的"选择支付"抵押贷款,而借款人可以每个月选择是否只偿付抵押贷款利息,用现金支付部分贷款,有时还款比到期利息还要少。房地产市场暴跌时,这些资产被视为剧毒,富国银行声称,预计随着时间的推移,资产将减少 320 亿美元。对于富国银行来说这是个大数目,因为作为衡量公司股东权益的净资产,富国银行只有约 480 亿美元。花旗集团仅仅向美联银行的银行资产部分问价,但富国银行还要购买美联银行证券和资产管理,这是协议的一部分。这些业务也将受到经济增长放缓的影响。

但是,许多投资者淡化了富国银行的风险,其董事长对风险管理有良好的声誉,其最大的股东是沃伦·巴菲特的伯克希尔·哈撒韦公司。荷兰一家资产管理公司的主席迈克·霍兰德说:"我相信以科瓦舍维奇和巴菲特的经历,他们肯定严格评估过这项垃圾交易究竟有多危险。"霍兰德并不拥有花旗集团、富国银行或美联银行的股票。科瓦舍维奇对路透社表示,此次交易部分并未咨询巴菲特。

Wells Bids for Wachovia

chairman has a reputation for adeptly managing risk, and whose biggest shareholder is Warren Buffett's Berkshire Hathaway. " I believe Kovacevich's and Buffett's history indicates they've done their due diligence on just how toxic this junk is," said Mike Holland, chairman of asset management firm, Holland & Co. Holland does not own shares of Citigroup, Wells Fargo, or Wachovia. Kovacevich told Reuters that Buffett had not been consulted as part of this transaction.

Wells Fargo may be able to essentially get U.S. support for some assets through a $ 700 billion government program to buy bad assets that the House of Representatives approved. The strategic benefits to Wells Fargo are compelling to some analysts. Wachovia has a strong branch presence on the East Coast, patching① a major gap in Wells Fargo's network. U. S. banks have been scrambling to build or buy branches, which allow them to raise money from depositors. In a credit crunch, deposit funding can be cheap compared to borrowing in bond markets. Wells Fargo is one of the few major U.S. banks that has remained consistently profitable during the credit crisis, despite being headquartered in California, the state that has suffered most during the U.S. housing crisis.

Citigroup, meanwhile, has posted more than $ 17 billion of net losses in the last three quarters. Winning the Wachovia branches would have helped Citi bolster its relatively weak network of U. S. branches, which number about 1,000 compared with Wachovia's 3,300 and Wells Fargo's 3,400. "For Citigroup, this is a real loss. This was a deal that was going to save them as much as it was saving Wachovia," said Cassandra Toroian,

---

① patch [pætʃ] *vt.* 修补

富国银行竞购美联银行

富国银行本来可以得到美国政府的资产支持,众议院批准通过了7 000亿美元的政府收购不良资产议案。富国银行的战略效益激发了一些分析人士的兴趣。美联银行在东海岸拥有强大的分支机构,大大弥补了富国银行的布局缺陷。美国各家银行已纷纷建立或购买分支机构,这使他们有能力筹集储户的资金。信贷紧缩时,存款资金比债券市场要便宜。尽管总部设在住房危机中损失惨重的加利福尼亚州,富国银行是少数能在信用危机时保持盈利的几家主要美国银行之一。

同时,花旗集团在过去的三个季度中净亏损达到170亿美元。赢得美联银行的分行将有助于花旗集团加强其相对薄弱的美国分支机构布局,与美联银行的3 300个分支机构和富国银行的3 400个分支机构相比,花旗银行的分支机构只有1 000个左右。贝尔·洛克资本首席投资官卡桑德拉·塔罗伊安在宾夕法尼亚州的保利说:"对于花旗集团,这是一个真正的损失。因为这样的一笔交易在拯救美联银行的同时也帮他们实现了自救。"在一份联合声明中,美国联邦储备委员会和货币办公室的银行管理者表示,他们将协调各方,以取得最佳结果。美国联邦存款保险公司声称,支持先前花旗集团宣布的协议。

这是一笔大买卖。投资者拥有的美联银行的每股将获得0.1991股的富国银行股票,以富国银行上周五收盘价的34.56美元计算,相当于每股6.88美元。美联银行上周五收于6.21美元。合并后的公司将在夏洛特街主营东海岸的零售、商业和企业银行业务。路易

Wells Bids for Wachovia

chief investment officer at Bell Rock Capital in Paoli, Pennsylvania. In a joint statement, bank regulators at the U.S. Federal Reserve and the Office of the Comptroller of the Currency said they would work with all parties to achieve the best outcome. The Federal Deposit Insurance Corp said it stands behind its previously announced agreement with Citigroup.

This is a big premium. For each share of Wachovia, investors will receive 0.1991 Wells Fargo share, which is equal to $ 6.88 a share based on Wells Fargo's closing price on Friday of $ 34.56. Wachovia closed at $ 6.21 on Friday. The combined company will base its East Coast retail and commercial and corporate banking business in Charlotte. St. Louis will remain the headquarters of Wachovia Securities. Wells Fargo, which would retain its name once the banks combine, is based in San Francisco.

Wachovia shares closed up $ 2.30, Wells closed down 60 cents, and Citigroup closed down $ 4.15 to $ 18.35.

(901 words)

富国银行竞购美联银行

斯依然是美联银行证券公司的总部。一旦银行合并，富国银行仍旧保留其名称，总部设在旧金山。

美联银行的股票收盘时涨至 2.30 美元，富国银行收盘时下跌 60 美分，花旗集团收盘下跌 4.15 美元，收于 18.35 美元。

知识链接

Citigroup 花旗集团成立于 1988 年，是一家为消费者和企业客户提供一系列金融服务的综合性全球金融服务控股公司。该公司有四个主要部门：消费者银行、全球卡类、机构客户集团和全球财富管理，在 100 多个国家开展业务。

Wells Fargo 富国银行是加利福尼亚历史最悠久的银行，业务范围包括社区银行、投资和保险、抵押贷款、专门借款、公司贷款、个人贷款和房地产贷款等。富国银行是美国排名第一的抵押贷款发放者和小企业贷款发放者，是美国唯一一家被穆迪评级机构评为 AAA 级别的银行。

Wachovia 美联银行成立于 1967 年，是一家金融控股和银行控股公司，通过全套服务的银行业务办公室向客户提供商业和零售银行业务和信托服务，其他金融服务包括：按揭银行业务、投资银行业务、投资咨询、住房净值贷款、资产抵押贷款、租赁、保险和国际证券经纪业务服务。

题 记

在全球快递市场波谲云诡，跌宕起伏的时代，行业界内的竞争已成常态。德国邮政服务企业旗下的品牌敦豪快递携手美国联合包裹服务公司，为对手之间的合作赋予了新的竞争内涵。尽管敦豪快递建立了覆盖全美的空中和地面网络平台，但针对联合包裹服务公司和联邦快递无处不去、无所不包的业务模式所制定的"针锋相对"策略使敦豪快递付出了巨大的代价。由于单次航班的装载率过低，敦豪快递的人力和燃料开支一直呈亏损状态，最终选择将在美国的快递业务外包给联合包裹服务公司。对联合包裹服务公司来说，这无疑是一着妙棋，他们可以利用本次交易，更好地发挥在美国本土的精细运营布局和超强的优势。虽然敦豪快递和美国联合包裹服务公司的排兵布阵还需时日，在短期内并不会掀起正面冲突，但不能回避的是，新一轮的市场重组即将开始。

DHL Holds Hands with UPS

DHL Express entered the U.S. aiming to shake up the UPS-FedEx duopoly. After losing billions, it hatched a new plan: hold hands with UPS.

Shortly after DHL Express was purchased in 2002 by privatized German postal service Deutsche Post World Net, the yellow-clad global delivery service launched an ambitious assault on United Parcel Service (UPS) and Federal Express (FDX), the two mainstays of the U.S. express-delivery market. DHL acquired Seattle-based Airborne, the third-largest player, for a little more than $1 billion in 2003. And DHL made explicit appeals to customers of the more established competitors with marketing slogans such as "Yellow. It's the new Brown": a challenge to UPS' highly recognizable brown trucks.

DHL has made impressive strides in the past six years. It raised awareness of its brand. It built an impressive air and ground network covering the U.S. And it made a significant impact on the market's dynamics. "We've created a third choice which was not there before, a real threat to the competition," says John Mullen, chief executive of DHL's global business. Perhaps more important for DHL—a global giant with a presence in some 225 countries-the expansion represented a bigger footprint in the U.S.—the largest market in the industry by far.

敦豪快递携手联合包裹服务公司

敦豪快递公司进入美国市场,原本期望与联合包裹服务公司及联邦快递分庭抗礼。 在亏损数 10 亿美元之后,敦豪快递酝酿了一个新的计划——携手联合包裹服务公司。

敦豪快递 2002 年被私营的德国邮政服务企业——德国邮政世界网——收购之后,这家标志为黄色的全球快递服务公司就雄心勃勃地发起了与美国速递业务市场的两大巨头——联合包裹服务公司(UPS)和联邦快递公司(FDX)的竞争。 2003 年,敦豪快递以略微超过 10 亿美元的价格收购了当时的第三大快递公司,即西雅图空运公司。 与此同时,敦豪快递针对既有竞争对手的客户制定了更为直接的市场口号,如"黄色。 它是一个新的棕色"就是对联合包裹服务公司具有极大知名度的棕色运输卡车发起的挑战。

敦豪快递在过去的 6 年中取得了骄人的成绩。 它提升了品牌知名度,建立了覆盖全美的空中和地面网络平台,并且极大地活跃了市场。 敦豪快递全球业务总裁约翰·穆伦声称:"我们创造了以前不存在的第三种选择,这是对竞争的真正威胁。"对于这个已经在全球大约 225 个国家占有一席之地的巨头来说,也许更为重要的还是

DHL Holds Hands with UPS

But going head-to-head with the go-everywhere, do-everything models of UPS and FedEx proved costly. "They are so strong we have to maintain almost a similar scale of network to them, but with only 6% or 7% market share," admits Mullen. "Hence the reason for financial pain." DHL's U.S. business lost $ 3 billion over the past four years, according to a Dow Jones report, while market share never surpassed 10%.

Much of the losses stem from DHL's low load rate, or inability to fill planes to capacity. "The problem has been that DHL wasn't flying full. If the plane isn't full you can't just say 'I'm sorry those packages are going to be delayed for a day or two until we fill up the plane,' " says Doug Caldwell, executive vice-president of ParcelPool.com, an Orem (Utah) logistics provider. "I've heard some numbers that suggest that they were well under 70% of capacity." By contrast, UPS and FedEx will typically fill planes to around 80% to 85% of capacity. For every light load DHL flew, it lost money in labor and fuel costs.

Deutsche Post shareholders grew impatient. Personnel changes did little to appease①: Four different leaders have been hired for DHL's top U.S. post in the past four years. In recent years, the company began to mull a more drastic shift in strategy. The most obvious option was to sell the unit completely. "The easiest decision would have been just pack up and go home," says CEO Mullen. "The markets would have applauded us, because they would have seen the loss eradicated straight away."

But that move, management decided, would deliver a severe blow to the company's attempts to bill itself as a global player. Explains Mullen,

---

① appease [ə'piːz] vi. 缓和

敦豪快递携手联合包裹服务公司

如何能在美国这个目前最大的工业化国家中占据更多的市场份额。

但针对联合包裹服务公司和联邦快递无处不去、无所不包的业务模式所制定的"针锋相对"策略使敦豪快递付出了巨大的代价。约翰·穆伦承认:"他们太强大了,我们不得不维持与他们类似的网络规模,却只有6%到7%的市场份额。这就是财务问题的症结所在。"根据道·琼斯的报告称,在过去的4年中,敦豪快递在美国的业务共亏损了30亿美元,而其所占的市场份额从未超过10%。

敦豪快递的亏损绝大部分是由于载货率过低或者是飞机的装载量不足所致。犹他州奥勒姆市的后勤保障顾问、包裹运输联盟网站的执行副总裁道格·考德威尔指出:"问题在于敦豪快递的飞机一直不能满载飞行。如果飞机没有装满,你不可能说:'对不起,因为我们的飞机需要满载后才能飞,所以您的货物可能要延迟一两天才能送到。'我曾听说过一些数据,显示载货率一直在70%以下。"联合包裹服务公司和联邦快递与此形成鲜明对照,他们的绝大部分航班载货率达到80%至85%左右。由于单次航班的装载率过低,敦豪快递的人力和燃料开支呈亏损状态。

德国邮政的股东们逐渐失去耐心。频繁的人事更迭收效甚微:在过去的4年中,敦豪快递的美国业务总裁换了四任。近几年来,公司开始着手一系列重大的战略调整。最明显的抉择是整体出售美国业务。首席执行官约翰·穆伦说:"最容易的决定就是直接卷铺盖走人。市场会欢迎我们,因为他们曾经见证过扭亏为盈。"

但是,管理部门宣称,这样的决议与公司试图成为一家全球性企业的形象大相径庭。约翰·穆伦解释道:"我们是一个全球性的网络体系,这个体系中的每个国家每天都会与其他国家之间发生业

DHL Holds Hands with UPS

"We're a global network. Every country in the network trades with every other country every day. And the U.S. is the largest, most important market in the world. If we say to our U.S. customers that we want your volume in Asia, but we can't help you in your home country, are we going to get the volumes in Asia? We think probably not."

Deutsche Post announced a compromise solution, which would allow it to both retain its presence in the U.S. and slash costs. The company said it had begun talks to outsource all of DHL's airlift operations in the U.S. to a new partner. DHL plans to deliver, pick up, and track all cargoto and from the aircraft as usual. "The customer doesn't actually see a difference at all," says Mullen. That is, unless they pay attention to the color of the partner's planes: UPS brown.

DHL plans to pay UPS $1 billion annually to deliver its air freight, which DHL expects will help it to reduce annual losses from an expected $1.3 billion to $300 million—and put it back on the road to profitability in the U.S. As part of the restructuring, it will cut about 17% of its ground delivery routes and implement a new management structure that holds one person accountable for both sales and operations in each of four regions in the U.S.

For UPS, it's a huge win. "UPS had a very sophisticated network in the U.S. with excess capacity. And with this deal they better utilize that capacity," says Mullen.

But while clear winners and losers have emerged, other aspects of the deal are more opaque①. Will the substantial cost-cutting help DHL become

---

① opaque [əuˈpeik] *adj.* 难懂的；不透明

敦豪快递携手联合包裹服务公司

务往来。美国是世界上最大、最为重要的市场,如果我们对我们的美国客户说,我们可以帮你们投递亚洲的货物,却不能帮你们投递本国的货物,那我们还能得到客户在亚洲的业务吗?我想是不可能的。"

德国邮政宣布了一项折中方案,既可以保留其美国业务又可以大幅削减开支。公司宣称,正与一个新的合作者商谈敦豪快递在美国业务的外包问题。敦豪快递计划与以往一样,投递、收货、跟踪货物在飞机上的往返流程。穆伦认为,"事实上,客户完全看不出差异"。也就是说,除非客户留意合作伙伴载货飞机的颜色:联合包裹服务公司的棕色飞机。

敦豪快递打算每年支付联合包裹服务公司10亿美元左右的空投费用,敦豪快递据此预测,这会使公司的年度亏损从13亿美元降至3亿美元,使公司返回在美业务盈利的常轨。作为结构调整的一部分,公司将减少17%的地面投递路线,执行全新的管理架构,即在美国的四大区域中,每个区域派一个人负责销售和运营。

对联合包裹服务公司来说,这是一次重大的胜利。穆伦说:"联合包裹服务公司在美国具有非常精细的网络布局和超强的优势,他们利用这次交易更好地发挥了这种运营能力。"

然而,尽管胜者和败者已经明显浮出水面,这次交易的其他方面的影响却变得更加扑朔迷离。成本的大幅下降真能使敦豪快递在困难重重的美国市场上更具竞争力吗?敦豪快递和联合包裹服务公司的合作关系会给整个市场带来怎样的价格冲击?两家公司会在欧洲和亚洲等国际市场上再度联手吗?敦豪快递在竞争中在哪些方面更具优势呢?

DHL Holds Hands with UPS

a more competitive force in the tough U.S. market? What pressure will a DHL-UPS partnership put on prices across the market? And how will the alliance play out in international markets such as Europe and Asia, where DHL has more of the upper hand in the rivalry?

For the insight of experts and those close to the deal, read "The Analysis: DHL Saves Face."

(843 words)

敦豪快递携手联合包裹服务公司

专家和接近这次交易的人士对此做了深度解读:"分析结果:敦豪快递挽回了颜面。"

知识链接

DHL 敦豪快递公司于1969年成立,名称来自于三个公司创始人姓氏的首字母,他们是Adrian Dalsey, Larry Hillblom 和 Robert Lynn,主要业务为国际航空快递,通过飞机快速运送文件和货物。敦豪快递目前是德国邮政全球网络旗下的品牌。

UPS 联合包裹服务公司(United Parcel Service)起源于1907年在美国西雅图成立的一家信差公司,以传递信件以及为零售店运送包裹起家。通过明确地致力于支持全球商业的目标,联合包裹服务公司如今已发展成为全球最大的快递承运商与包裹递送公司,同时也是专业的运输、物流、资本与电子商务服务的领导性的提供者,拥有300亿美元的资产。

FedEx 联邦快递是一家国际性速递集团,提供隔夜快递、地面快递、重型货物运送、文件复印及物流运输,为全球超过235个国家及地区提供快捷、可靠的快递服务。总部设于美国田纳西州。

Deutsche Post World Net 德国邮政世界网是私营的德国邮政服务企业。欧洲地区领先的物流公司,共划分为四个自主运营的部门,即邮政、物流、速递和金融服务。

题 记

　　受次贷危机的影响,财政巨亏的美林证券摇摇欲坠,出售竟然成了摆在美林面前的出路之一。金融市场对美林的风险管理能力已失去信心,而美林为了避免不断深化的金融危机,同意作价500亿美元将自己出售给美国银行。这些令人羞辱的举动,重塑了美国金融界的版图,标志着动荡年代的最新篇章,曾经盛气凌人的金融机构,由于抵押贷款和房地产投资坏账造成的损失,已经一蹶不振。华尔街的银行家们挤在会议堆里昼夜谈判,美联邦储备大厦中召开的一系列紧急会议回天乏术。只是对收购混乱的抵押贷方全美金融公司的美国银行而言,收购美林使之登上美国金融的巅峰,成为最大的证券公司,并拥有最大的消费者银行业务专营权。

Merrill Is Sold

In one of the most dramatic days in Wall Street's history, Merrill Lynch agreed to sell itself to Bank of America for roughly $50 billion to avert a deepening financial crisis, while another prominent securities firm, Lehman Brothers, filed for bankruptcy protection and hurtled toward liquidation after it failed to find a buyer. But even as the fates of Lehman and Merrill hung in the balance, another crisis loomed as the insurance giant American International Group appeared to teeter①. Staggered by losses stemming from the credit crisis, A.I.G. sought a $40 billion lifeline from the Federal Reserve, without which the company may have only days to survive. The humbling moves, which reshapethe landscape of American finance, mark the latest chapter in a tumultuous year in which once-proud financial institutions have been brought to their knees as a result of hundreds of billions of dollars in losses because of bad mortgage finance and real estate investments.

The stunning series of events culminated② franticaround-the-clock

---

① teeter [ˈtiːtə] vi. 摇晃地站立
② culminate [ˈkʌlmineit] vt. 达到极点

出售美林

这是华尔街历史上最引人注目的日子之一,美林证券公司为避免不断深化的金融危机,同意作价 500 亿美元左右将自己出售给美国银行,而另一个著名的证券公司——雷曼兄弟,由于没有找到买主,申请了破产保护,并突然停业清算。就在雷曼兄弟和美林的命运安危未卜之时,另一场笼罩保险业巨头美国国际集团的危机似乎又岌岌可危。信用危机引起的损失给美国国际集团沉重的一击,只得向联邦储备寻求 400 亿美元的救命款,否则公司只能维持几天。这些令人羞辱的举动,重塑了美国金融界的版图,标志着动荡年代的最新篇章,曾经盛气凌人的金融机构,由于抵押贷款和房地产投资坏账造成了几十亿美元的损失,已经一蹶不振。

令人震惊的一系列事件在疯狂的昼夜谈判中达到顶点,华尔街的银行家们挤在会议堆里,应布什政府官员的要求,试图避免市场因信任危机引发的螺旋式下降。私人股权投资公司黑石集团的创办者、雷曼兄弟在 20 世纪 70 年代的负责人和尼克松政府的商务部长彼

Merrill Is Sold

negotiations, as Wall Street bankers huddled in meetings at the behest of Bush administration officials to try to avoid a downward spiral in the markets stemming from a crisis of confidence. "My goodness. I've been in the business 35 years, and these are the most extraordinary events I've ever seen," said Peter G. Peterson, co-founder of the private equity firm the Blackstone Group, who was head of Lehman in the 1970s and a secretary of commerce in the Nixon administration.

It remains to be seen whether the sale of Merrill, which was worth more than $100 billion, and the controlled demiseof Lehman will be enough to finally turn the tide in the yearlong financial crisis that has crippled Wall Street and threatened the broader economy. Lehman said it would file for Chapter 11 bankruptcy protection in New York for its holding company in what would be the largest failure of an investment bank since the collapse of Drexel Burnham Lambert 18 years ago. Questions remain about how the market will react, particularly to Lehman's plan to wind down its trading operations, and whether other companies, like A.I.G. and Washington Mutual, the nation's largest savings and loan, might falter①.

Indeed, in a move that echoed Wall Street's rescue of a big hedge fund a decade ago, 10 major banks agreed to create an emergency fund of $70 billion to $100 billion that financial institutions can use to protect themselves from the fallout of Lehman's failure. The Fed, meantime, broadened the terms of its emergency loan program for Wall Street banks, a move that could ultimately put taxpayers' money at risk. Though the

---

① falter [ˈfɔːltə] vi. 动摇

出售美林

得·彼得森说:"我的天啊。我在商界干了35年,这是我从未见过的最非同寻常的事件。"

是否出售总价值超过1 000亿美元的美林还有待观察,而控制雷曼兄弟的破产足以扭转持续一年的财政危机,这场危机已经使华尔街瘫痪,威胁到更广泛的经济领域。雷曼表示,将按照第11条例在纽约为其控股公司提交破产保护申请,这是继18年前德雷克塞尔·伯纳姆·兰伯特崩溃以来,投资银行的最大失败。问题是市场做何种反应,尤其是雷曼兄弟减缓交易业务的计划有何影响,美国国际集团和华盛顿互惠银行等其他全美最大的储蓄和贷款银行是否陷入摇摇欲坠的境地。

事实上,在重复华尔街10年前曾遭受过的一次巨大的对冲基金救市行动中,10家主要银行同意建立一个700亿美元至1 000亿美元的紧急基金,金融机构可以用此保护自己免受雷曼兄弟失败的影响。同时,美联储扩大了对华尔街银行的紧急贷款计划条款,此举可能最终使纳税人的钱处于风险之中。虽然政府已经控制了焦头烂额的抵押贷款公司房利美和房地美,投资者却已经越来越担心主要的金融机构是否可以收回损失。

最终的结局如何可能会对更广泛的经济领域产生影响,随着金融危机的恶化,经济已经在平稳地下滑,并随着国民经济增长速度的放慢而导致失业率增加。美林和雷曼兄弟的员工对即将发生的情

Merrill Is Sold

government took control of the troubled mortgage finance companies Fannie Mae and Freddie Mac, investors have become increasingly nervous about whether major financial institutions can recover from their losses.

How things play out could affect the broader economy, which has been weakening steadily as the financial crisis has deepened, with unemployment increasing as the nation's growth rate has slowed. What will happen to Merrill's employees or Lehman's employees remains unclear. Worried about the unfolding crisis and its potential impact on New York City's economy, Mayor Michael R. Bloomberg canceled a trip to California to meet with Gov. Arnold Schwarzenegger. Instead, aides said, Mr. Bloomberg spent much time working the phones, talking to federal officials and bank executives in an effort to gauge the severity of the crisis.

The humbled Lehman and Merrill Lynch and rewarded Bank of America, based in Charlotte, N. C., began in the first of a series of emergency meetings at the Federal Reserve building in Lower Manhattan. The meeting was called by Fed officials, with Treasury Secretary Henry M. Paulson Jr. in attendance, and it included top bankers. The Treasury and Federal Reserve had already stepped in on several occasions to rescue the financial system. The bankers were told that the government would not bail out Lehman and that it was up to Wall Street to solve its problems. Lehman's stock tumbled sharply as concerns about its financial condition grew and other firms started to pull back from doing business with it, threatening its viability. Without government backing, Lehman began trying to find a buyer, focusing on Barclays, the big British bank, and Bank of America. At the same time, other Wall Street executives grew more concerned about their own precarious situation.

出售美林

况仍然蒙在鼓里。由于担心出现危机及其潜在影响纽约市的经济，市长迈克尔·R.布隆伯格取消了前往美国加州与州长阿诺德·施瓦辛格的会面。其助手却称，布隆伯格先生花了大量时间打电话，与联邦官员和银行高官交谈，尽力判定危机的严重性。

卑谦的雷曼兄弟和美林证券与总部设在北卡罗来纳州夏洛特、盈利丰厚的美国银行，首次在曼哈顿下城的美联邦储备大厦召开了一系列紧急会议。美联储官员召集的会议由财政部长亨利·M.保尔森领衔，包括顶级的银行家。财政部和美联储已经插手了几次营救金融体系的行动。银行家们获知，政府不会帮助雷曼兄弟脱离困境，只能由华尔街自己解决问题。由于担心其财务状况恶化，一些公司取消了与雷曼兄弟的生意往来，雷曼的股票大幅下跌，并已威胁到其自身的生存。没有了政府的支持，雷曼兄弟开始寻找买主，主要是巴克莱银行、英国的大银行和美国银行。与此同时，华尔街的其他高管越来越担心他们自己岌岌可危的处境。

美林证券和雷曼兄弟的命运似乎不会有联系。美林拥有全美最大的经纪业务，名声威震美国城乡，而雷曼兄弟的主要客户是大机构。但是，在信贷繁荣时期，两家公司都挤进了存在风险的房地产市场，最后却落得实力严重削弱的下场——资金不足，资产中毒。美林的首席执行官、高盛集团和纽约证券交易所的前成员约翰·A.赛恩对投资者的焦虑心知肚明，开始与美国银行的首席执行官肯尼

Merrill Is Sold

The fates of Merrill Lynch and Lehman Brothers would not seem to be linked; Merrill has the nation's largest brokerage force and its name is known in towns across America, while Lehman's main customers are big institutions. But during the credit boom both firms piled into risky real estate and ended up severely weakened, with inadequate capital and toxic assets. Knowing that investors were worried about Merrill, John A. Thain, its chief executive and an alumnus of Goldman Sachs and the New York Stock Exchange, and Kenneth D. Lewis, Bank of America's chief executive, began negotiations. One person briefed on the negotiations said Bank of America had approached Merrill earlier in the summer but Mr. Thain had rebuffed the offer. Now, prompted by the reality that a Lehman bankruptcy would ripple through Wall Street and further cripple Merrill Lynch, the two parties proceeded with discussions. For Bank of America, which bought Countrywide Financial, the troubled mortgage lender, the purchase of Merrill puts it at the pinnacle of American finance, making it the biggest brokerage house and consumer banking franchise.

A leading proposalto rescue Lehman would have divided the bank into two entities, a "good bank" and a "bad bank." Under that scenario, Barclays would have bought the parts of Lehman that have been performing well, while a group of Wall Street companies would have agreed to absorb losses from the bank's troubled assets, to two people briefed on the proposal said. Taxpayer money would not have been included in such a deal, they said. Other Wall Street banks also balked at the deal, unhappy at facing potential losses while Bank of America or Barclays walked away with the potentially profitable part of Lehman at a cheap price. Lehman's filing is unlikely to resemble those of other

出售美林

斯·刘易斯举行谈判。 一名在谈判现场做笔录的人士透露，美国银行在夏季的早些时候曾接触过美林，但遭到塞恩先生的拒绝。 现在，面对雷曼破产波及整个华尔街、并进一步波及美林的现实，双方又开始继续谈判。 对收购混乱的抵押贷方全美金融公司的美国银行而言，收购美林使之登上美国金融的巅峰，成为最大的证券公司，并拥有最大的消费者银行业务专营权。

拯救雷曼兄弟的主要建议是将银行分为两个实体，即"优质银行"和"劣质银行"。 据两位在场记录的人士介绍，根据这种方案，巴克莱银行将收购雷曼表现突出的优质部分，而一批华尔街公司已同意吸收雷曼不良资产的损失。 他们说，纳税人的钱不会被列入这样的交易。 当美国银行或巴克莱银行以便宜的价格拿走雷曼兄弟潜在的利润部分之时，其他的华尔街银行也不愿意接受协议，不满面临的潜在损失。 雷曼兄弟的备案不太可能与那些寻求破产保护的其他公司类似。 由于联邦破产法对金融服务公司处罚更严厉，雷曼不可能指望改组和幸存。 政府是否任命一位受托人监督雷曼兄弟的清算或给予多大的财政支持还不清楚。 雷曼兄弟已聘请威嘉律师事务所为其破产辩护律师。

这些事件表明，美联储和财政部的高层官员正在采取更强硬的措施，给陷入困境的金融机构提供政府支持。 美联储主席本·S. 伯南克和鲍尔森先生两人都警告说，尽管政府对华尔街与雷曼兄弟的

Merrill Is Sold

companies that seek bankruptcy protection. Because of the harsher treatment that federal bankruptcy law applies to financial-services firms, Lehman cannot hope to reorganize and survive. It was not clear whether the government would appoint a trustee to supervise Lehman's liquidation or how big the financial backstop would be. Lehman has retained the law firm Weil, Gotshal & Manges as its bankruptcy counsel.

The events indicate that top officials at the Federal Reserve and the Treasury are taking a harder line on providing government support of troubled financial institutions. While offering to help Wall Street organize a shotgun marriage for Lehman, both the Fed chairman, Ben S. Bernanke, and Mr. Paulson had warned that they would not put taxpayer money at risk simply to prevent a Lehman collapse. The message marked a major change in strategy but it remained unclear what would happen. "They were faced after Bear Stearns with the problem of where to draw the line," said Laurence H. Meyer, a former Fed governor who is now vice chairman of Macroeconomic Advisors, a forecasting firm. "It became clear that this piecemeal, patchwork, case-by-case approach might not get the job done."

(1,209 words)

出售美林

被迫联姻提供帮助,他们不会仅为了防止雷曼崩溃而将纳税人的钱置于风险之下。这则信息标志着重大策略的转变,但仍不清楚到底会发生什么。前美联储理事、现任一个预测公司"宏观经济顾问"副会长的劳伦斯·H. 迈耶认为,"贝尔斯登事件之后,他们面临在哪儿划清界限的症结。很明显,零零碎碎、修修补补、逐案审查的方法可能于事无补"。

知识链接

Merrill Lynch 美林证券曾是世界最著名的证券零售商和投资银行之一,总部位于美国纽约。主要经营证券经纪、交易、承销;投资银行、策略咨询服务、合并与收购和其他企业金融咨询项目。2008年受次贷危机影响严重亏损,被美国银行收购。

题 记

尽管拥有近百年历史的美国国际集团的业务网络几乎覆盖了全球每个角落,但这位保险业的巨头面临金融风暴的来袭仍在奋力求生。它向美联储寻求政府的过渡性贷款,使公司能有喘息之机从而得以处置旗下的资产;它出席了纽约联邦储备银行主持的财政部代表、金融服务公司及州政府官员代表召开的会议,祈求找到"救命稻草",获得财务支援;股价暴跌促使评级机构下调其评级,迫使其为谋求生存提供更多的抵押品,并使保险合同失效;受信贷违约掉期等业务损失惨重拖累,全球各大央行纷纷向美国国际集团的银行系统注资。焦头烂额的美国国际集团不得不考虑出售或者拆分旗下的国际飞机租赁金融公司,同时可能出售其财产保险和灾难保险业务。重组美国国际集团远比人们想象的要难得多。

Fighting for Survival-Reorganizing AIG

With time running out on its finances, American International Group continues to plead for assistance in a meeting at the Federal Reserve Bank of New York. Scrambling① to raise as much as $75 billion in capital, the giant insurer needs either a bridge loan from the Fed itself or from a lending pool organized by a consortium② of banks. AIG, with 103,000 employees and more than $1 trillion of assets, is more than an insurance company. It is arguably the biggest player in the financial services industry; a collapse, many fear, could be catastrophic.

AIG's former chairman Maurice Greenberg said that without a loan or any other injection of capital from the outside, the giant insurance company would be bankrupt. "They need some confidence," he said during a television interview on CNBC. A Fed bridge loan would not be a gift or a bailout, he argued, because AIG would be able to sell valuable assets over time to pay it back. AIG is faltering on exposure to the

---

① scrambling [ˈskræmbliŋ] n.不规则性
② consortium [kənˈsɔːtiəm] n.(国际)财团;组合;共同体

奋力求生：重组美国国际集团

由于资金日益枯竭，美国国际集团在纽约联邦储蓄银行召开的会议上继续请求援助。这位保险业巨头的坏账多达 75 亿美元，不得不向美联储申请短期过渡贷款，或从各银行集资组成的资金池借款。美国国际集团拥有 10.3 万名雇员、超过 1 万亿美元的资产，远已不只是一家保险公司。它已无可非议地成为金融服务行业最大的参与者，许多人担心，它的倒闭将带来巨大的灾难。

美国国际集团的前任主席莫里斯·格林伯格声称，如果无法获得借款或者是外界的资金注入，保险业的巨人将面临破产的危险。他在接受美国全国广播公司财经频道电视采访时说："他们需要一些信心。"他指出，联邦短期过渡贷款不是礼物或救市行为，因为美国国际集团以后可以出售其有价资产来偿还贷款。由于持有的抵押资产和其他与市场紧紧相关的资产大幅贬值，美国国际集团面临破产的危险。它正试图稳定资本结构的调整和重新改组计划以出售部分

Fighting for Survival-Reorganizing AIG

plummeting value of mortgage holdings and other assets that get marked to market. It is trying to finalize a recapitalization and reorganization plan that would involve the sale of assets. Though with the pressure mounting, the company faces selling those assets at a steep discount.

Central banks around the globe pumped cash into the banking system, including a $50 billion injection from the Fed, to keep banks lending to each other in the wake of Lehman Brothers' bankruptcy filing. Rob Haines, an analyst at CreditSights, said that AIG needs to move quickly. A component of the Dow Jones industrial average, AIG's shares are off more than 40% in trading. "Without further management clarity, we fear that AIG's franchise could become impaired by the market sell-off as customers become increasingly concerned regarding the company's financial health," Haines wrote in a note.

AIG found a protector in the State of New York, which agreed to bend rules and allow AIG to borrow $20 billion from its operating subsidiaries. That could enable it to obtain some sort of credit facility or additional capital. It will be used to help maintain the company's credit rating. It may also be used as collateral①. New York's governor asked AIG as soon as possible to secure a injection of capital or a credit facility. If it fails to do that, the agreement to let it borrow from its operating subsidiaries is off the table. New York's insurance regulator, Eric Dinallo, is involved in discussions at the New York Fed about AIG, asking the central bank to provide the bridge loan.

---

① collateral [kɔˈlætərəl] *n.* 旁系亲属,担保品

资产。由于面临不断上升的压力，公司将只能以很低的折扣出售资产。

全球各大中央银行纷纷向美国国际集团的银行系统注入资金，其中包括美联储蓄银行注资的500亿美元，这是继雷曼兄弟破产后保持银行间相互借款的一种举措。信用展望公司的分析师罗布·海恩斯认为，美国国际集团需要采取迅速的行动。作为道琼工业平均指数期货的组成部分，美国国际集团的股票在交易中价格下降超过40%。海恩斯在备忘录中写道："如不尽快实行管理清晰化，我们担心，由于消费者变得更加关注该公司的财政健康状况，美国国际集团将会因为市场证券的跌价受到更大的伤害。"

美国国际集团在纽约州找到了保护者，该保护者同意改变规则，并承诺美国国际集团可以从其营运的附属企业获得200亿美元的贷款。这将帮助美国国际集团获得一些融通便利或者额外的资产。它将帮助公司维持信用度。它也可以用来做担保品。纽约州长要求美国国际集团尽快获得注入资金或融通便利。如果它无法做到，美国国际集团从其营运的附属公司获得贷款的协议也就失效。纽约保险规管当局的埃里克·迪纳罗在参与纽约联邦关于美国国际集团的讨论时，要求中央银行提供短期过渡贷款。

美联储和财政部似乎不愿意参与和拯救另一家公司。诚然，他们和雷曼兄弟划清了界限，拒绝按假定潜在损失条款提供实际的资

Fighting for Survival-Reorganizing AIG

The Fed, along with the Treasury Department, seems to loathe① to step in and rescue another company. Certainly, they drew a line with Lehman, declining to provide actual support in terms of assuming potential losses. Most of the problems with its balance sheet were caused by AIG Financial Products Corp., a division that, like many investment banks, participated in financial risk-taking, including investments in credit default swaps written on collateralized debt obligations. These investments are now considered to be toxic. AIG's total collateral related to this portfolio was $16.5 billion, and this figure is likely to climb. If AIG fails, it won't mean all of its underlying subsidiaries are unsound. The insurance divisions that make up its core would likely be salvaged, as they can be separated from the rest of the organization.

Fitch Ratings downgraded AIG's long-term and short-term issuer default rating, as well as its senior unsecured debt and commercial paper program ratings. Fitch said AIG's financial flexibility and ability to raise holding company cash are extremely limited due to recent declines in the company's stock price, widening credit spreads and difficult capital market conditions. Standard & Poor's lowered its counterparty credit ratings (including long-term) and financial strength ratings on most of AIG's insurance operating subsidiaries. Moody's Investors Service downgraded the senior unsecured debt rating of AIG as well as the ratings of several AIG subsidiaries.

It would be in the interest of public policy for the regulators to

---

① loathe [ləuð] *vt.*讨厌;厌恶

助。它的收支平衡表上的大部分问题来自于美国国际集团金融产品公司,这一分支机构与其他的投资银行一样,参与金融风险投资,包括建立债务抵押义务上的信用违约互换投资。而这些投资现在被认为具有高风险。美国国际集团拥有的与这种投资相关的担保品整体高达165亿美元,这一数据还有可能上升。即使美国国际集团破产,也并不意味着它旗下所有的附属企业都会不安全。构成其核心的保险部门可能获得救助,并从该组织的其他部门脱离出来。

惠誉国际评级下调了美国国际集团的长期和短期发行人违约评级,其优先支付的无担保债务和商业票据项目评级也分别下调。惠誉认为,由于近期该公司的股票价格下跌,信用危机扩散,以及恶劣的资本市场环境,美国国际集团的金融流动性和增加公司持现的能力受到了极大的限制。标准普尔下调了大部分美国国际集团保险附属企业的信用评级(包括长期信用评级)以及财政能力评级。穆迪投资服务公司下调了美国国际集团及其附属企业的优先支付无担保债务评级。

管理人员根据国家政策,将美国国际集团的不良资产和问题资产与应该、并可以继续运营的资产相脱离。这就意味着从金融产品部门将保险利润剥离出来。如果破产的话,保险实体继续运营是有利于维护公众利益的最佳方式,然而,这需要企业重组,甚至是清算在美国国际集团有价证券中的其他资产。美国国际集团是美国最

Fighting for Survival-Reorganizing AIG

separate the nonperforming assets and problematic parts of the company from those that should and can continue. This would mean separating the insurance interests from the financial product divisions. If there is an insolvency, it would be in the public's best interest to allow the insurance entities to continue, however it will require a restructuring and even liquidation of the other assets within AIG's portfolio. AIG is the largest commercial insurer in the U.S.

Should the company be split up, which is more than likely, it will probably hold onto its core property casualty business and spin off its auto insurance and life/annuities businesses while selling its aircraft leasing division. AIG was in discussions with Warren Buffett of Berkshire Hathaway. Speculation was that they were negotiating a sale of the aircraft-leasing division, and Buffett owns NetJets. But at the same time, Berkshire Hathaway owns several large insurance entities, including General Re and Geico, so it may be interested in buying some of AIG's insurance. It is doubtful, however, that Buffett would be interested in buying the whole enterprise.

(850 words)

奋力求生:重组美国国际集团

大的商业保险公司。

如果公司被迫分裂,这种情况更容易出现,它可能在出售飞机租赁公司的同时,维护其核心的财险业务,剥离汽车保险业务和人生养老金业务。 美国国际集团正在与伯克希尔·哈撒韦公司的沃顿·巴菲特举行会谈。 公众推测,他们在协商出售飞机租赁公司的交易,巴菲特拥有利捷飞机租赁公司。 但在同时,伯克希尔·哈撒韦公司拥有几家大型的保险公司,包括通用再保险公司和盖可汽车险公司,所以它可能有意购买美国国际集团的部分保险业务。 然而,也有人猜测,巴菲特可能有意于购买整个公司。

知识链接

Fitch Ratings, Standard & Poor's and Moody's Investors Service 惠誉国际评级、标准普尔和穆迪投资服务公司是国际三大齐名的评级机构。这三家评级机构各有侧重,惠誉国际评级侧重于金融机构评级,标准普尔侧重于企业评级,而穆迪投资服务公司侧重于机构投资评级。

题　记

　　丰田公司堪称世界上表现优异的成功汽车生产商的典范。无论经济处于繁荣期还是萧条期，丰田公司一直是全球汽车行业最盈利和最具创新力的企业。导致丰田持续增长的核心秘诀在于他们多年来形成的制造系统：它以低廉的生产成本制造出高质量的汽车，灵活地应对市场需求；它将生产手段变为"深度智慧"，发掘每位员工、经销商、业务合作伙伴头脑中的知识和经验；它开发出了一个适应知识经济时代工业生产的全新管理模式，把创新看做一个日积月累的过程。这就是为什么丰田推行稳妥渐进的市场方针，却培育出了快速而高效的运营体系。一般人看不透丰田公司的庐山真面目，就因为理解这个系统很容易，但要紧随其后却很艰难。

Toyota—The Open Secret of Success

In the current atmosphere of economic tumult①, the announcement that Toyota sold a hundred and sixty thousand more cars than General Motors in the first three months of this year might seem like a minor news item. But it may very well signal the end of one of the most remarkable runs in business history. For years, in good times and bad, G.M. has sold more cars annually than any other company in the world. But Toyota has long been the auto industry's most profitable and innovative firm. And this year it appears likely to become, finally, the industry's sales leader, too.

Calling Toyota an innovative company may, at first glance, seem a bit odd. Its vehicles are more liked than loved, and it is often attacked for being better at imitation than at invention. Fortune, which typically praises the company effusively②, has labeled it "stodgy③ and bureaucratic." But if Toyota doesn't look like an innovative company it's only because our definition of innovation—cool new products and technological

---

① tumult [ˈtjuːmʌlt] *n.* 混乱
② effusively [iˈfjuːsivli] *adv.* 热情洋溢地
③ stodgy [ˈstɔdʒi] *adj.* 平凡的;庸俗的

丰田公司成功的秘诀

在当前经济动荡的大环境下,丰田公司今年第一季度的汽车销量比通用公司多 16 万辆,这实在算不了什么大新闻。但是,这很可能表示商业史上最引人注目的运营之一的结束——多年来,无论经济处于繁荣期还是萧条期,通用汽车公司的年销量总是高于世界上的其他企业。而丰田公司则长期是汽车行业最盈利和最具创新力的企业。不过,丰田汽车今年的销量也很有可能最终跃居行业翘首。

乍看起来,说丰田公司很有创新力,似乎有点不可思议。人们对它的汽车还比较喜欢,但谈不上追捧,经常有人攻击它更擅长模仿而不是发明。财富杂志对丰田公司不乏热情洋溢的赞扬,给它贴上"庸俗而又官僚"的标签。然而,认为丰田公司不符合富有创新力公司的标准,仅仅只具有史蒂夫·乔布斯那样的空想主义者的创新定义,即酷炫的新产品和技术突破,这种观点未免太过狭隘。与其相反,丰田公司的创新集中在生产过程而不是针对产品,在工厂车间而不是在陈列室,所以这些创新很难被公众了解,但这并没有削弱他们的竞争力。

Toyota—The Open Secret of Success

breakthroughs, by Steve Jobs-like visionaries—is far too narrow. Toyota's innovations, by contrast, have focused on process rather than on product, on the factory floor rather than on the showroom. That has made those innovations hard to see. But it hasn't made them any less powerful.

At the core of the company's success is the Toyota Production System, which took shape in the years after the Second World War, when Japan was literally rebuilding itself, and capital and equipment were hard to come by. A Toyota engineer named Taiichi Ohno turned necessity into virtue, coming up with a system to get as much as possible out of every part, every machine, and every worker. The principles were simple, even obvious—do away with waste, have parts arrive precisely when workers need them, fix problems as soon as they arise. And they weren't even entirely new—Ohno himself cited Henry Ford and American supermarkets as inspirations. But what Toyota has done, better than any other manufacturing company, is turn principle into practice. In some cases, it has done so with inventions, like the andon cord, which any worker can pull to stop the assembly line if he notices a problem, or kanban, a card system that allows workers to signal when new parts are needed. In other cases, it has done so by reorganizing factory floors and workspaces in order to allow for a freer and easier flow of parts and products. Most innovation focusses on what gets made. Toyota reinventedhow things got made, which enabled it to build cars faster and with less labor than American companies.

But there's an enigma to the Toyota Production System: although the system has been widely copied,Toyota has kept its edge over its competitors. Toyota opens its facilities to tours, and even embarked ona joint venture

丰田公司成功的秘诀

丰田公司成功的核心在于他们多年来形成的生产体系,"二战"后,日本逐步重建家园,但很难得到资金和设备。丰田公司一位名叫大野耐一的工程师提出了一个系统,即尽可能使每个部件、每台机器、每位人工的效用最大化,将需要转化为功效。这些原理很简单,甚至显而易见——消除浪费,工人能及时拿到所需要的零件,问题一出现就能马上得到解决。这些理论并不全是新的,大野耐一的灵感受亨利·福特和美国超市的启发。不过丰田公司比其他制造公司高明的地方在于,他们所做的一切就是把理论运用于实践。公司在有些方面实施了这种创新模式,如安灯系统:任何一位工人发现问题时都能拉下吊绳,停止整条装配线;再如看板系统:工人需要新零件时能及时发出信息。公司在另一些方面又采取了别的方法,为了零件和产品的流通更自由和容易,公司改造了工厂的地板和空间布局。最大的创新之举集中在做什么。丰田公司重新确立了事情该怎么做,这使公司生产汽车的方式比美国公司更快,耗用劳力更少。

然而,丰田公司的生产系统存在着一种不可思议的现象:尽管这个系统被广泛模仿,丰田公司却一直保持优势,超越了其竞争对手。丰田公司开放工厂设施供参观学习,甚至准备和通用汽车公司合资,在一定程度上帮助通用公司改进生产系统。多年来,已有三千多本书和文章分析了丰田公司的运作模式,安灯系统之类的信息管理工具现在已是工厂车间常见的景象。丰田理念的传播已经产生了实际的效果。整个汽车行业的产能远远超过过去。那么丰田公

Toyota—The Open Secret of Success

with G.M. designed, in part, to help G.M. improve its own production system. Over the years, more than three thousand books and articles have analyzed how the company works, and things like andon systems are now common sights on factory floors. The diffusion of Toyota's concepts has had a real effect; the auto industry as a whole is far more productive than it used to be. So how has Toyota stayed ahead of the pack?

The answer has a lot to do with another distinctive element of Toyota's approach: defining innovation as an incremental process, in which the goal is not to make huge, sudden leaps but, rather, to make things better on a daily basis. The principle is often known by its Japanese name, kaizen—continuous improvement. Instead of trying to throw long touchdown passes, as it were, Toyota moves down the field by means of short and steady gains. And so it rejects the idea that innovation is the province of an elect few; instead, it's taken to be an everyday task for which everyone is responsible. According to Matthew E. May, the author of a book about the company called "The Elegant Solution," Toyota implements a million new ideas a year, and most of them come from ordinary workers. Japanese companies get a hundred times as many suggestions from their workers as U.S. companies do. Most of these ideas are small-making parts on a shelf easier to reach, say—and not all of them work. But cumulatively, every day, Toyota knows a little more, and does things a little better, than it did the day before.

The system doesn't necessarily preclude missteps-Toyota ran into a series of quality problems—and it's possible that the focus on incremental innovation would be less well suited to businesses driven by large technological leaps. But, on the whole, the results are hard to argue with.

丰田公司成功的秘诀

司是怎样保持领先地位的呢?

答案与丰田理念中的另一独特要素密切相关,即把创新看做一个日积月累的过程,它的目的不是制造巨大、突然的飞跃,而是在日常的工作中把事情做得更好。 人们熟知这种原则的日本名称——"经营方法改善",即持续不断的完善。 丰田公司似乎并不愿一蹴而就,而是依靠短期和稳定的盈利手段,步步为营。 因此,丰田公司拒绝将创新看成是少数几个人的事,而将其视作每个人都有责任承担的日常任务。 根据"最佳方案"一书的作者马修·E.梅关于公司的论述,可知丰田公司一年就有上百万的新创意,绝大多数来自普通工人。 日本公司与美国公司一样,从员工那里得到的建议多达百条。 这些想法的大多数似乎微不足道,如将零件放在一个更容易拿到的架子上,并非所有的创意都起作用。 但日积月累,丰田公司比原来知道得多一点,做得也更好一点。

这个系统不可避免地存在缺陷,丰田汽车曾经出现过一系列的质量问题。 集中于渐进性创新有可能不太适合突然转换大型技术的行业。 但整体上看,这些结果很难解释清楚。 创新模式也很难从表面上加以复制。 部分原因是大多数公司的组织管理仍然非常严密,很难将责任移交给一线的工人。 也可能因为"经营方法改善"的根本思想是缓慢而稳定地完善,与大部分公司求变的方式背道而驰。 很多公司希望,正确的理念能在一夜之间改变现状。 这就是人们称为的崩溃式节食法,即让自己饿上少许几天,就会一辈子瘦下来。 丰田公司的模式则更像一种有规律、一成不变的饮食方式,

Toyota—The Open Secret of Success

They're also phenomenally difficult to duplicate. In part, this is because most companies are still organized in a very top-down manner, and have a hard time handing responsibility to front-line workers. But it's also because the fundamental ethos of kaizen—slow and steady improvement-runs counter to the way that most companies think about change. Corporations hope that the right concept will turn things around overnight. This is what you might call the crash-diet approach: starve yourself for a few days and you'll be thin for life. The Toyota approach is more like a regular, sustained diet—less immediately dramatic but, as everyone knows, much harder to sustain. In the nineteen-nineties, a McKinsey study of companies that had put quality-improvement programs in place found that two-thirds abandoned them as failures. Toyota's innovative methods may seem mundane, but their sheer relentlessness defeats many companies. That's why Toyota can afford to hide in plain sight: it knows the system is easy to understand but hard to follow.

(958 words)

丰田公司成功的秘诀

缺少瞬间的戏剧性效果,但是,众所周知,坚持下去却很困难。麦肯锡在20世纪90年代的研究发现,把质量改革项目放在首位的公司有三分之二以失败告终。丰田公司的创新方式看上去很普通,但这种纯粹的义无反顾打败了很多公司。这就是为什么一般人看不透丰田公司的庐山真面目:它知道,理解这个系统很容易,但要紧随其后却很艰难。

知识链接

Andon systems　安灯系统是一种现代企业的信息管理工具。Andon也称暗灯或安灯,原为日语的音译,日语的意思为"灯"、"灯笼"。而现在的Andon系统不仅仅是灯光,而是一个声光多媒体的多重自动化控制系统,是一套专门为汽车生产、装配线设计的信息管理和控制系统。

Kaizen　"经营方法改善"。

Kanban　是个日语名词,表示一种挂在、或贴在盛装制品容器上或一批零件上的标签或卡片,或流水线上各种颜色的小球或信号灯、电视图像等,用于防止过量生产、并且保证关键部件在每一工艺步骤都有详细说明。

题 记

  亚马逊公司成立于1995年，一开始只是经营网络书籍销售业务，现在则将其多样化经营范围扩展到其他领域，特别是服装行业。网上购物时代为亚马逊的发展提供了机遇，服装行业的特性同样也对其提出了挑战。零售业成功的秘密是提供客户想要的东西，客户可能需要很多东西，对于保证每次愉快的购物体验，友好和快速的服务是最重要的。如何利用自身优势在激烈的竞争中脱颖而出是亚马逊公司亟待解决的问题。亚马逊可以在服装业的多样化经营中利用这些优势，因为亚马逊公司的品牌优势无疑将吸引消费者到新的服饰部门，但同时服装商店的长期成功将取决于亚马逊公司像一个聚合器一样，不断刷新自身的增值能力。

Amazon into Apparels

The move of Amazon into apparels came at a time of increasingly strong growth for online apparel, one of the biggest upcoming retail categories in e-commerce. With the apparel store in Amazon's fold, customers can shop the Amazon way, i.e., in one convenient place with easy-to-use shopping cart for well-known apparels, shoes and accessory's including kids and baby apparels. The Amazon's apparel store provides the customer with all the necessary tools and helpful information, such as customer review and rankings, similarities and lots more, giving them the benefit of the Amazon experience. The company is doing everything to make it click with the customers. It has also come out with some introductory offers and promotional certificates to attract customers.

Amazon has diversified into many businesses, since its inception. The question is why they chose apparel sector as their next diversification.There are quite a few important reasons for this seemingly inconsistent move of Amazon. The growing competition in the book sector seems to be one of the big reasons, because Amazon was incurring① huge losses and desperately wanted to substantiate their losses by diversifying themselves

---

① incur [inˈkə:] *vt*. 遭受；招致，引发

亚马逊进军服装业

亚马逊利用在线服装销售日益增长、即将成为电子商务最大的零售类商品之一的时机，强势推出进军服装业的举措。随着亚马逊服装商店的开业，客户可以在亚马逊网站购物，即在一个舒适的地方将知名服装、鞋和饰品，包括儿童和婴儿服装放入易于使用的购物车。亚马逊的服装商店为客户提供所有必要的工具和有用的信息，如客户的评论和排名，相似商品和更多的服务，使他们在亚马逊的购物体验中受益。该公司正在尽一切努力提高客户的点击率。为吸引顾客，它还发布了一些引导性报价和促销证书。

亚马逊自成立以来已经扩展到许多行业。问题是他们为什么选择服装行业作为下一个多样化经营的领域。亚马逊此次看似矛盾的行动有相当多的重要原因。图书销售日趋激烈的竞争似乎是主要原因之一，因为亚马逊损失惨重，迫切希望通过多样化经营进入盈利行业来弥补损失。来自其他出版商的竞争越来越激烈，约翰·威立、麦格罗·希尔、安德鲁·塔克、斯蒂夫·马提尼等多家出版商有自己的网站，客户可以上网购买他们想要的书，不用去亚马逊购

Amazon into Apparels

into a profitable business. The growing competition from other publishers is becoming more day-by-day, as many of the publishers like John Wiley, McGraw Hill, Andrew Tucker, Steve Martini etc., have their very own websites from where the customers can order the book they want, instead of going and buying it from Amazon. "When a company shows profit, investors start breathing faith on that organization again, and there is no better time than that to expand" according to Gaurav Chadha, a solution architect at NIIT and the co-author of the book eLearning. That's what exactly Amazon did.

The other reason according to Professor Rajeev K Tyagi, Graduate School of Management, University of California is that "the company has sunk its fixed cost of establishing an excellent ordering/delivering and tracking system. Expansion into any positive-margin product which can share the same ordering/distribution infrastructure, and which meets the above condition about consumer, purchases decision is a profitable strategy." And apparel is one of the biggest upcoming retail categories on the Internet with sales continuously going up years. In fact, it is the third most popular online sales category at present and is growing strong, according to Shop.org, the online arm of the national retail federation. The market segments in which Amazon is competing are rapidly evolving and intensely competitive, and they have many competitors in the online retail industry. The nature of the Internet as an electronic marketplace facilitates competitive entry and comparison-shopping and renders it inherently more competitive than conventional retailing formats. This increased competition may reduce their sales and operating profits. This fear would also have contributed to their idea of diversifying into apparel sector.

亚马逊进军服装业

书。印度国家信息技术学院的系统架构师和《学习》一书的共同作者格拉夫查·达哈指称："公司盈利时，投资者开始再次流露出对机构的忠诚，没有比这更好的扩张时间了。"这就是亚马逊这么做的原因。

根据加州大学管理学院拉杰夫·K.泰亚吉教授的观点，另外一个原因是"该公司已经投资固定成本，建立了优秀的订货/交付和跟踪系统。对可以分享相同订购/分销基础设施、符合上述条件的消费者的盈利产品，拓展是一个有利可图的策略"。服装业是互联网迎来的最大的零售领域之一，销售量逐年持续上升。事实上，根据购物在线旗下的全国零售联盟搜索引擎显示，它在当前最受欢迎的在线销售领域名列第三，并日渐强大。亚马逊参与竞争的市场份额变化迅速，竞争激烈，他们将面对很多网上零售行业的竞争对手。互联网作为电子交易市场，本质上具有竞争性和比较购物的特征，天生比传统的零售模式更具竞争力。日益激烈的竞争可能会减少他们的销售额和营业利润。这种担心也是他们多样化经营、进军服装业的原因。

与销售书籍和光盘相比，亚马逊打算如何从服装销售中获利？亚马逊有什么优势吸引客户造访他们的商店并购买服装？

高拉夫·查德哈认为，"第一个重要因素是亚马逊品牌，人们信任亚马逊公司的产品"。一般来说，人们趋向于从他们认识的人，

Amazon into Apparels

How is Amazon going to benefit from selling apparels when compared to selling books and CDs? What are the factors that are associated with Amazon, which will attract customers to visit and buy apparels from their store?

"The first major factor for Amazon will be its brand name and the peoples trust in Amazon's product," says Gaurav Chadha. Generally people tend to buy from someone they know, or from someone they had bought earlier, or from someone they had heard of before. When the word online buying comes, Amazon's name is right on top of the mind of the people. Amazon's customer satisfaction level is very high as it maintains a huge product inventory①, in order to ensure prompt delivery to its customers. It is regarded as the most customer-centric company that delivers the quality products at affordable price at the doorsteps of consumers. Amazon's brand recall will definitely help in its apparel sector. Another advantage of Amazon is its line up of branded items in its apparel store.

Amazon.com launched its apparel stores with lots of attractive schemes to lure customers. Amazon's move into the apparels already began to show results. The first few weeks' sale of Amazon's apparel store was very encouraging as in that short period only the customers ordered more than 9,000 trousers, about 1,500 shirts, 2,000 sweaters, 3,000 pairs of socks and many other items in bulk quantity.

Apparel and accessories store is the company's fastest growing store in terms of units sold in the first 60 days of operation. Since consumers are already comfortable with shopping on the site, Amazons involvement in

---

① inventory [ˈinvəntəri] n. 存货清单

亚马逊进军服装业

或早前做过交易的人,或以前听说过的人那儿买东西。在线购买的想法一出现,亚马逊的名字会最先在脑海中浮现。亚马逊客户的满意度非常高,因为它维持着巨大的产品库存,以确保向客户准时交货。它被视为顶级的、以消费者为中心的公司,以合适的价格将高质量的产品送到消费者的门口。亚马逊品牌效应肯定会助其服装部门。亚马逊的另一个优点是它的服装店拥有一批品牌商品。

亚马逊网站开办的服装商店推出了很多富有魅力的项目来招揽顾客。亚马逊进军服装业的举措开始初见成效。亚马逊服装店开业的头几周业绩令人振奋,因为就在这么短的时间里,客户订购超过9 000多条长裤,约1 500件衬衫,2 000件毛线衫,3 000双袜子和许多其他散装的商品。

服装和饰品店是公司在头60天营运销售单位中增长最快的商店。由于消费者感觉在网上购物很舒适,亚马逊参与服装销售将提高其整体销售额。这将极大地帮助那些经常浏览亚马逊网站的人购买服装,而不是到另外的网站购买相同的东西。亚马逊忠诚的客户们到这儿来非常方便。它有助于客户到亚马逊享受更好的购物体验,把所有的商品放进一个购物篮。亚马逊的主要优势在于它节约了客户的交易成本。如果客户清楚地知道他们想要什么,几分钟就可以买到。易于使用的网站、分类和跟踪系统进一步节省了客户的时间。

apparel sales will improve its overall sales. It will be of great help to those who regularly browse through the site of Amazon to shop for apparels, instead of going to another site to buy the same. The loyal customers of Amazon will come handy here. It makes for a better customer experience to go to Amazon and put everything in one shopping basket. Amazon's main advantage lies in the savings it provides to its customers in transaction costs. If the customer knows exactly what they want, they can order it in minutes. The ease of use of its websites and the ordering and tracking system further saves time for customers.

While all this is fine, there may be some hitches in the successful running of Amazon's apparel and accessory store.

Amazon's early success was built largely on selling items, such as books and CDs that a customer did not have to touch or feel or see in person before buying. Now, Amazon has diversified itself from books and CDs to apparels both having a vast difference between them. The key difference between books and apparels is in the urgency of need. Consumers across the world mostly buy books as collectables and apparels as consumables. The need for books is not usually immediate, i. e., consumers may not bother waiting for some extra days in case of a delay in delivery, but it's not the same in the case of apparels. A delay in delivering the apparels may lead to loss of customer in future.

Moreover, the two most important problems that prevent people shopping for clothing online are they are unable to try on clothes for fit and unable to feel clothes for the quality of clothes. Further, apparels reflect character of an individual and consumers select the basic fit only after a few trips to the trial room. It's not easy from a customer's point of view to

亚马逊进军服装业

尽管这一切无可挑剔,但在亚马逊服装和服饰商店成功运营的过程中,还会有一些障碍。

亚马逊早期的成功主要基于物品销售,例如书籍和光盘,客户在买前不需要亲自触摸或感觉或看到。现在,亚马逊的多样化经营从书籍和光盘转向服装业,两者之间差异巨大。书籍和服装的关键区别是需求的紧迫性。大部分世界各地的消费者买书作为收藏品,买服装作为消费品。书籍的需求通常不那么紧迫,也就是说,如果推迟交货,消费者并不在意多等几天,但服装的情况就不同了,延迟交付服装可能导致未来客户的流失。

此外,两个妨碍人们在线购买服装的最重要的问题是,他们无法试穿,不知道衣服是否合适,无法感觉衣服布料的质量。此外,服装反映个人的特点,消费者通常在逛过几次试衣间后才会初步做出选择。从顾客的角度讲,很难在网站看货就下订单。因此,卖服装不会像卖书籍和光盘那么容易。

亚马逊将面临大量的激烈竞争,因为沃尔玛和西尔斯等其他领先商家也在销售服装,在这场网购服装的战斗中,亚马逊可能错失实体商店。此外,总是有这样的可能性,即供应商有自己的网站,正如亚马逊也有自己的书籍网站一样。有些人可能会觉得浏览供应商的网站比浏览亚马逊的网页要容易得多。

Amazon into Apparels

just watch the item on the website and order it. So it will not be that easy to sell apparels as it was in the case of books and CDs.

Amazon will be facing a lot of stiff competition from various other leading players like Wal-Mart and Sears in selling apparels and it may miss the physical store in this battle of selling apparels online. Moreover there is always the possibility that the suppliers come up with their own websites, as they came up in the case of books. Some people may find it a lot easier to browse through these websites rather than browsing through Amazon.

(1,153 words)

亚马逊进军军服装业

知识链接

NIIT 印度国家信息技术学院（National Institute of Information Technology）成立于1981年,是总部设在印度的信息技术(IT)跨国公司。是专门提供教育、培训、软件解决方案和教育多媒体的上市公司。它是一家年收入超过3亿美元,每年按50%速度增长的IT公司。公司的国内收入和国外收入大约是各占一半,教育培训收入和软件解决方案收入大约是各占一半。

题 记

  在全球轮胎科技的领导者米其林的市场视野中,中国是将来世界上最主要和增长最迅速的市场之一。在与美国的固特异和日本的普利司通进行的激烈竞争中,米其林叱咤风云,纵横驰骋,以绝对的实力在中国轮胎领域独占鳌头,"滚动"出了一条经营奇迹。米其林对中国市场投资已经远远超出了公众的期望,是中国唯一为卡车和汽车提供绿色轮胎的制造商。米其林在上海成功举办了"必比登挑战赛",这项活动被认为是世界上促进清洁能源、道路安全和燃油节约发展的最重要的活动。米其林沈阳轮胎有限公司和上海米其林回力投资有限公司聚合起国际、国内的能量,组建了航行于中国轮胎市场的航空母舰。随着规模的不断扩大和业务的不断拓展,米其林绿色轮胎在中国不仅"滚动"出一条灿烂辉煌的金色坦途,也折射出一幅中国经济波澜壮阔、大步向前的发展宏图。

Michelin Green Wheels in China

It was far beyond the public's expectation that after only two years, his company Michelin delivered the 100,000th "green" truck and bus tire to Chinese consumers. Since it introduced its fuel saving tires to China's commercial vehicle market (the world's biggest), the French tire maker has made energy conservation and environmental protection a point of pride for its new products. China's 11th Five-Year Plan calls for cutting energy consumption per unit of gross domestic product up to 20 percent. Michelin is making its own efforts under the Chinese government's guidelines.

Michelin says that with more than 400 million sold since its European launch, the green tires represent three-fourths of Michelin sales in Europe. By replacing the carbon black in the tire treads with silica, the green tire guarantees a 3 percent saving on fuel consumption, thereby enabling the tire to maintain the same level of grip while reducing heat loss. Green tires take up two thirds of Michelin's replacement market in China. Most of the tires Michelin offers here are of lower rolling resistance.

Michelin is the only tire maker providing green wheels for trucks and buses in China. Industry forecasts say that the total tire demand in the Chinese market will be around 300 million units. The demand will

米其林绿色轮胎在中国

仅在两年之后，米其林公司就给中国消费者提供了第10万个"绿色"卡车和汽车轮胎，远远超出了公众的期望。自从它向世界上最大的中国商用车辆市场推出节省燃油的轮胎以来，法国轮胎制造商就为新产品的能源节约和环境保护引以为豪。中国的第11个五年计划要求，每单位国内生产总值削减能源消费量达到20%。米其林正在按照中国政府的指导方针做出自己的努力。

米其林承认，自公司投入欧洲市场以来，已卖出4亿多个轮胎，绿色轮胎占米其林在欧洲销售量的四分之三。通过用二氧化硅取代轮胎胎面的炭黑，绿色轮胎保证了3个百分点的燃料消耗节省，使轮胎在保持同等水平抓地力时减少热量损失。在中国，绿色轮胎占米其林替换品市场的三分之二。米其林在这里提供的大部分轮胎的滚动阻力较低。

米其林是中国唯一为卡车和汽车提供绿色轮胎的制造商。行业预测显示，中国市场的轮胎总需求大约为3亿个。这样的需求将不可避免地加快和加速环境友好型技术的应用。米其林认为，中国的道路流通正面临着巨大的挑战，这种挑战来自能源短缺和交通问

Michelin Green Wheels in China

inevitably speed up and also hasten the application of environmentally friendly technologies. Michelin thinks the road mobility in China is facing great challenges which result from a shortage of energy, as well as traffic problems. Michelin hopes the green tire will contribute to improving the road situation in China.

To publicize its efforts in China, Michelin chose Shanghai to host its Challenge Bibendum, considered one of the world's most important events promoting the development of clean energy, road safety and fuel economy. Michelin's late CEO Edouard Michelin founded the event in 1998 to celebrate the 100th birthday of the Michelin Man, the company's mascot and advertising logo, known to the French as "Bibendum". The event returned to China again later. The return to China was one way for Michelin and its partners to help the Chinese government chart the way forward for more fuel-efficient, cleaner, safer and less congested roads; an atmosphere that respects both people and the environment. In the future, Michelin will continue to contribute to local communities with very strict respect to the environment and concrete commitments① to local developments and specific needs. Michelin has sunk $ 440 million into the Chinese market, and the investment in China has proved to be the correct decision for Michelin.

Michelin was the first international tire maker to set up its office in China. After establishing its sales office in Hong Kong in 1988, Michelin set up its first mainland representative office in Beijing in 1989 to promote its products and prepare the distribution channels in major cities. It shows

---

① commitment [kəˈmitmənt] n. 义务

米其林绿色轮胎在中国

题。米其林希望,绿色轮胎将有助于改善中国的道路状况。

为了宣传其在中国的努力,米其林选择在上海举办"必比登挑战赛",这项活动被认为是世界上促进清洁能源、道路安全和燃油节约发展的最重要的活动。米其林公司已故的首席执行官爱德华·米其林于1998年创立该活动,庆祝"米其林轮胎先生"的百岁寿辰,公司的吉祥物和广告标识是法国人熟知的"必比登"。这项活动后来再次在中国举行。对米其林和其合作伙伴来说,重返中国是一种途径,可以帮助中国政府规划更节能、更清洁、更安全和减少道路拥挤的发展方向,形成尊重人类和环境的氛围。将来,米其林要继续为地方社区做贡献,非常严格地遵守环境和恪守承诺,满足地方发展和具体需求。米其林已经对中国市场投资4.4亿美元。对米其林来说,在中国投资已被证明是正确的决定。

米其林是第一个在中国建立办事处的国际轮胎制造商。米其林于1988年在香港建立销售办事处后,1989年在北京建立了第一个大陆代表处,以推广产品以及为其在主要城市的分销渠道做准备。这显示出米其林对中国和当地市场充满信心。改革开放的市场政策为米其林提供了良好的机遇,创造了有利的经营投资环境。

然而,米其林在早期面临如何平衡文化差异、将米其林的企业文化与中国的发展环境相结合的严峻挑战。米其林需要组建强大的本土管理团队。20世纪80年代末,大多数中国人还没有私人汽车,所以,中国轮胎行业处于起步阶段,专业人才匮乏。20世纪90年代初,大部分中国管理人员的管理知识相当有限,因此米其林集

Michelin Green Wheels in China

Michelin's confidence in China and the local market. The policy of market opening-up and reform offers a good opportunity to Michelin by providing a favorable business investment environment.

However, in the early times, how to leverage the cultural differences and combine Michelin's company culture with China's developing environment was the big challenge for Michelin. Michelin needed to build up a strong local management team. In late 1980s, a personal automobile was still out of reach for most Chinese people and as a result China's tire industry was in its infancy and professional talent was scarce. In the early 1990s, most of the Chinese managers' knowledge about management was quite limited, so Michelin Group sent over 10 managers from France. It leveraged the strengths and weaknesses between different cultures and the knowledge spread better and faster inside the company. The company later also sent Chinese employees to France for training. Michelin understood the challenge very well from the beginning. That's why most of the people that Michelin Group sent to China were not managers but technology experts. However, today, 15 Chinese are now working in high-level positions in France and other regional headquarters. In China, it has 5,500 employees and plans to hire more as its business expands.

In 1994, the Chinese government jump-started the country's auto industry development with a policy officially sanctioned[①] linking cars with the family, by first time putting forward that the private purchase of vehicles set to be encouraged to change the sedan consuming restructure. Before that, sedans in China are limited to be sold to public. They are

---

① sanction ['sæŋkʃən] vt. 批准

米其林绿色轮胎在中国

团从法国派来 10 位管理者。 这就平衡了不同文化之间的长处和短处，知识在公司内部传播得更好、更快。 公司后来也派中国员工到法国接受培训。 米其林从一开始就深刻地理解所面临的挑战，这就是为什么米其林集团向中国派送的大多数人员不是管理者而是技术专家的原因。 但时至今日，已有 15 个中国人在法国高级别的职位和其他地区的总部工作。 米其林在中国拥有 5 500 名员工，并计划雇用更多的人为其拓展业务。

1994 年，中国政府迅速启动国家的汽车产业发展，提出了官方认可的政策，将汽车与家庭联系起来，首次鼓励私人购买车辆，改变了轿车的消费结构。 在此之前，中国的轿车对公众限售。 轿车的生产使用权主要由官方掌控。 客车在 1995 年的产量比 1994 年增加 8.5 万辆，超过了 1991 年的总生产量。 1995 年年底，米其林公司在中国的第一家合资企业、米其林沈阳轮胎有限公司成立，并在 2003 年转成外商独资企业。 投资总额目前达到 1.5 亿美元。 1998 年，中国成为世界第十大汽车市场。 更多的汽车制造商来到中国，建立生产设施，以获得市场份额。 2001 年，米其林集团与上海轮胎橡胶有限公司组建了新的股份公司，即上海米其林回力投资有限公司，生产和销售子午线客运汽车轮胎，总投资 2 亿美元。 公司生产国内回力牌轮胎，并在 2002 年开始生产米其林品牌的轮胎。

米其林公司在中国的总部于 2001 年迁往上海。 同年，米其林（中国）投资有限公司在上海成立，这使公司有更多的机会发展和加强米其林在中国的长期承诺。 1990 年，中国的汽车库存为 550 万

265

Michelin Green Wheels in China

majorly produced for official usage. Passenger car production in 1995 increased 85,000 units over 1994, more than the total production volume of 1991. At the end of 1995, Michelin's first joint venture operation in China, Michelin Shenyang Tire Co Ltd was established and it was transformed into a wholly foreign-owned enterprise in 2003. The total investment currently reaches $ 150 million. In 1998, China became the tenth largest auto market in the world. More auto manufacturers came to China, establishing production facilities to grab market share. In 2001, Michelin Group and Shanghai Tire and Rubber Co Ltd formed a new joint stock company, Shanghai Michelin Warrior Tire Co Ltd, for the manufacture and sale of radial passenger car tires with a total investment of $ 200 million. The company produced domestic Warrior brand tires and started to produce Michelin brand tires in 2002.

Michelin's headquarters in China moved to Shanghai in 2001. In the same year, Michelin (China) Investment Co Ltd was set up in Shanghai, which gave the company more opportunities to develop and reinforce Michelin's long-term commitment in China. In 1990, the car inventory in China was 5.5 million. Now the number is up to 160 million. The fast developing Chinese market gave Michelin a big sales volume increase, though specific figures still remained unknown. But Michelin had to use different ways to solve problems. In Europe, it usually took Michelin half a year to make a decision since the market was quite stable and the strategies were often made for the long term. But in China, Michelin might make it in six weeks. The development and changes in China were very fast, so Michelin should make new decisions more actively and specifically.

Michelin's top rivals in China are US-based Goodyear and Japan's

米其林绿色轮胎在中国

辆。现在这个数字高达 1.6 亿辆。快速发展的中国市场使米其林的销售量大大增加，尽管具体数目并未对外透露，但是，米其林必须用不同的方式来解决问题。在欧洲，米其林通常需要半年时间做出决定，因为市场相当稳定，往往采用长期战略。但在中国，米其林可能只用 6 周就做出决定。中国的发展和变化非常迅猛，所以米其林应该更积极和具体地做出新的决定。

米其林公司在中国的主要竞争对手是总部设在美国的固特异和日本的普利司通。这三个品牌占据中国轮胎市场 60% 的份额。然而，米其林仍然具有极大的发展潜力。例如，中国拥有世界最大的卡车轮胎市场，而子午线轮胎仅占 25% 的份额。此外，国际品牌或地方品牌占有客运和轻型卡车市场，而卡车轮胎市场则由国产品牌主导，这就意味着此部分将是米其林的未来目标。米其林在客车和轻型卡车市场的目标是超过市场平均水平的增长速度，以保持其领先地位。

知识链接

Michelin Group 米其林集团是世界 500 强企业之一，全球轮胎业的领导者。在全球五大洲设有 74 间生产工厂，6 家橡胶种植园，所生产的轮胎行销全球 170 多个国家，全球雇员人数约 12.5 万人。1988 年进入中国以来，米其林在中国已成立了 4 家独资企业和 1 家合资企业。

Michelin Man "米其林轮胎先生"是法国米其林公司广告中的人物形象，它

Michelin Green Wheels in China

Bridgestone. The three brands occupy 60 percent of China's tire market. However, there is still huge potential for Michelin to develop. For example the truck tire market is the largest in the world, while the radial tire only takes 25 percent of the share. Moreover, the passenger and light truck market is held by international brands or local brands, while the truck tire market is dominated by domestic brands, implying the segment will be Michelin's target in the future. Michelin's goal in the passenger and light truck market is to grow faster than the market average to keep its leading position.

(1,126 words)

米其林绿色轮胎在中国

长得小小胖胖的,看起来就像是由轮胎做成的。

Goodyear 美国固特异轮胎橡胶公司始建于 1898 年,至今已有百余年的历史。固特异公司是世界上最大规模的轮胎生产公司,总部位于美国俄亥俄州阿克隆市。公司主要在 28 个国家 90 多个工厂中生产轮胎、工程橡胶产品和化学产品。如今固特异在全世界的员工达到 8 万多人。

Bridgestone 日本普利司通公司是世界最大的轮胎及橡胶产品生产商,也是世界轮胎业三巨头之一。目前,普利司通已经发展成为国际性的跨国公司,在 24 个国家和地区内设有 47 家轮胎工厂,65 家化工品及其他产品工厂,四家技术开发中心。公司 80% 的产品是轮胎,还生产工业橡胶及化学产品、体育产品,以及其他多样化的产品。集团从业人数超过 10 万。

题　记

　　具有233年历史、在全球范围内掌控270多亿英镑资产的巴林银行，一夜之间竟毁于一个年龄只有28岁的年轻人之手。事情表面看起来很简单，李森的判断失误是整个事件的导火线。李森当时看好经济呈现复苏势头的日本股市，在未经授权的情况下，他以银行的名义认购了价值70亿美元的日本股票指数期货，并以买空的做法在日本期货市场买进了价值200亿美元的短期利率债券，希望在日经指数上升时赚取大额利润。天有不测风云，突发的日本神户地震打击了日本股市的回升势头，股价持续下跌，导致巴林银行遭受巨额损失并最终倒闭。但这座在伦敦城乃至全球金融界消失的老牌商业银行，却使金融界开始关注如何约束机构内部成员的个人行为，从而避免由个人行为导致的无可挽回的巨大损失，并引发了业内关于完善监督机制、限制个人权限的大讨论……

The Lesson from Barings' Straits

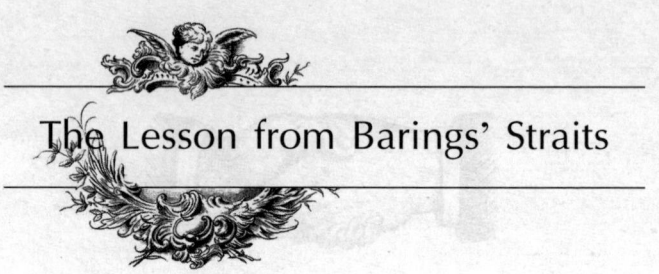

It's a long way from the dreary public-housing complex in the London suburb of Watford, where Nick Leeson grew up as a plasterer's son, to Singapore's exclusive Orchard Road section. The cocksure① head of futures trading in Barings PLC's Singapore office, Leeson earned a $1 million bonus, drove a Porsche, and sailed his yacht on weekends off Malaysia. But all that came crashing down with the revelation that Leeson, 28, had piled up $1.3 billion in losses on spoiled derivative deals in Singapore and Osaka.

In one humiliating blow, Leeson's huge trading loss wiped out the blue-blood investment bank's $900 million in capital and prompted the Bank of England to put Barings into bankruptcy. The collapse also sent shivers down the spines of bankers around the globe. "With so much money moving around so quickly, this is the kind of thing all of us worry about," says First Chicago Corp. CEO Richard L. Thomas. "It's stunning to think that a 233-year-old institution can be brought to its knees overnight."

Over the past year or so, one financial shock after another has hit the

---

① cocksure [kɔkˈʃuə] adj. 独断的;过分自信的

巴林银行陷入困境的教训

从泥瓦匠儿子的尼克·李森生长的伦敦瓦特福郊区沉闷的廉租房，到新加坡的高级果园路区，是一段很长的路程。作为巴林上市公司驻新加坡办事处分管期货交易的大权独揽的负责人，李森拿到了 100 万美元的红利，开着保时捷，周末驾驶着游艇前往马来群岛。但是，所有这些随着 28 岁的李森在新加坡和大阪衍生品交易中高达 13 亿美元损失的披露，彻底结束了。

在羞辱性的致命一击中，李森巨大的交易损失耗尽了这个贵族投资银行的 9 000 万英镑资产，并促使英格兰银行将巴林银行推向破产。巴林银行的崩溃也使全球范围内的银行家们感到脊柱发凉。芝加哥第一国民银行的首席执行官理查德·李·汤姆森声称："巨大的资金流动这么迅速，让我们所有人感到恐怖。一个拥有 233 年历史的机构竟然在一夜之间举步维艰，简直令人窒息。"

在过去一年左右的时间里，一场接一场的金融震动不断冲击着报纸的头版和美国有线新闻网络。一条共同的线索贯穿了全部：在 20 世纪 90 年代早期全球性流动资产繁荣期间，超过 1.5 万亿美元的

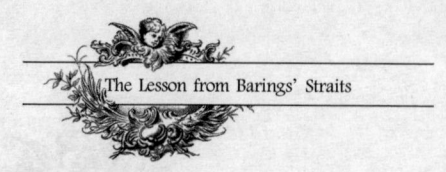

The Lesson from Barings' Straits

front pages and CNN. A common thread runs through them: In the global liquidity boom of the early 1990s, when more than $1.5 trillion in U.S. mutual-fund money flooded the globe, money was so available, markets so ebullient①, and profits so rich that simple safeguards and controls went by the board. Now, as interest rates rise and the margin for error narrows, many are paying a high price for inattention. Says New York economist Henry Kaufman: "Whether it's Mexico or Barings, these problems reflect inadequate monitoring and supervision."

By any standard, the list of financial accidents since 1994 is eye-popping. Hedge-fund manager George Soros, for example, dropped $600 million by misjudging the strength of the Japanese yen. Procter & Gamble Co. lost $102 million on leveraged derivatives purchased from Bankers Trust Co. The venerable investment house of Kidder, Peabody & Co. was sold off and dismembered after Joseph Jett allegedly ran up $350 million in paper profits on bogus bond deals. Wealthy Orange County, Calif., went bust when its treasurer made a spectacularly wrong bet on the direction of rates. And Mexico, the darling of emerging markets, had to seek a $53 billion international bailout after its debt-fueled economy ran out of hard cash.

Now, Barings joins the casualty list. Administrators from Ernst & Young are selling off pieces of the firm. The Dutch bank ABN Amro is buying Barings' corporate finance unit, and Merrill Lynch & Co. and Dresdner Bank may bid for other parts. But long after the disposal is over, regulators and financiers will still be asking whether Barings' situation was

---

① ebullient [iˈbʌliənt] adj. 沸腾的;热情洋益的

巴林银行陷入困境的教训

美国共同基金充斥全球,资金是如此容易获得,市场是如此沸腾,利润是如此的丰厚,以至于管理委员会对简单的防卫和控制不屑一顾。现在,随着利率升高和误差利润的缩小,很多人正在为疏忽付出高昂的代价。纽约的经济学家亨利·卡夫曼指出:"不管是墨西哥银行还是巴林银行,这些问题反映出管理和监督的缺失。"

不管用什么标准来衡量,1994年以来的金融事件名单都令人瞠目。例如,对冲基金经理乔治·索罗斯由于错误判断日元的坚挺趋势而损失6亿美元;宝洁公司在银行家信托投资股份有限公司购买的杠杆衍生品损失了1.02亿美元;在约瑟夫·杰特供认虚假债券交易的账面利润升至3.5亿美元后,德高望重的投资公司基德基金和皮博迪公司被廉价卖清和肢解;加州富有的奥兰治县在出纳员对利率走向做出彻彻底底的错误赌注后破产;墨西哥银行,这个新兴市场的宠物,被债务驱动的经济消耗完现金后,不得不寻求高达530亿美元的国际紧急援助。

现在,巴林银行加入了这个伤亡名单。安永会计师事务所的管理人员正在出售巴林公司的剩余资产。荷兰银行准备购买巴林的公司金融部门,美林公司和德累斯顿银行将竞标巴林公司的其他部分。但是,在这个处置结束很长一段时间后,监管者和金融家仍在询问,巴林的遭遇是否只是一个特例。很多人并不这么想。英格兰银行的督管艾迪·乔治警告说:"巴林银行发生的事件可能在世界上任何一家金融机构发生。"尤其是当个人被授予足够的权限、拿全

The Lesson from Barings' Straits

unique. Many think not. Warns Bank of England Governor Eddie George: "What happened to Barings could happen to any financial institution in the world." Especially if one individual is given enough leeway① to bet the entire store.

In the easy-money boom, too many securities executives lost the ability or will to scrutinize② high-energy traders or guard against unethical salespeople. Too many bankers and CFOs neglected to ask whether they understood the complexity—or the downside—of the highly leveraged derivatives they were using to hedge financial risks. And as an influx of some $300 billion in foreign portfolio money sent stock and bond markets soaring in developing countries, too many investors and fund managers stopped asking basic questions about disclosure, accounting, value, and risk.

Chastened③, the world's exchange officials, central bankers, and financiers also want to know how the Barings meltdown happened and how they might prevent another one. What they are learning is nothing short of remarkable. It shouldn't be possible, but a lone trader bought enough futures and options contracts in three weeks to amass a $27 billion bet. His local bosses, the exchange regulators in three Asian cities, and Barings' managers in London stayed in the dark.

Leeson's trading-floor peers knew something was up. But they didn't sound the alarm, because Barings had been taking huge positions for years

---

① leeway ['liːwei] *n.* 可允许的误差
② scrutinize ['skruːtinaiz] *vt.* 细察
③ chasten ['tʃeisn] *vt.* 磨炼；惩罚

巴林银行陷入困境的教训

部存储做赌注之时。

在银根松弛的繁荣时期,太多的债券经理丧失了审察高度活跃的交易人以及防备缺乏职业道德的销售员的能力和意愿。太多的银行家和首席财务官忽视了对他们的拷问:是否懂得他们用于防范金融风险的高杠杆衍生品的复杂性和下降趋势。对3 000亿美元左右、进入股票和债券市场、并在发展中国家猛增的外国组合资金的流入,太多的投资者和基金经理忘记了询问披露、清算、价值和风险等基本问题。

吃一堑长一智,世界范围内的证交所官员、中央银行家和金融家,都想知道巴林银行的彻底垮台是怎么发生的,以及他们如何去防范另一场灾难。他们接受的教训非常精彩。它本不应该具有可能性,但是,一个孤立的交易员在三周内购买了足够的期货和期权合同就集聚了一场270亿美元的赌局。他在当地的上司们——亚洲三座城市里的交易监督者和伦敦巴林银行的经理们,甚至都蒙在鼓里。

李森在交易所的同行知道出事了,但是他们却没有报警,因为巴林银行多年来在日经指数股票期货交易中占据巨大市场地位,并将其作为低风险套利操作的组成部分,以新加坡和大阪交易合同中的分秒价格差异获取利润。当时,李森神秘地从套利者转变为投机者。他将所有合同改为买进,很有可能认为,神户地震引起的破坏将会刺激经济并拉升日经指数。

The Lesson from Barings' Straits

in Nikkei stock-index futures as part of a low-risk arbitrage operation that tried to profit from minute price differences in contracts traded in Singapore and Osaka. Then, Leeson mysteriously switched from arbitrager to speculator. He converted all his contracts to buys—most likely in the belief that the destruction caused by the Kobe earthquake would stimulate the economy and push up the Nikkei.

When the stock market didn't cooperate, Leeson sold put and call options to raise cash for margin calls and bet that the market would settle into a narrow range. But as the Nikkei continued falling, Leeson is thought to have made one last roll of the dice. His losses had accumulated to about $700 million, and the exchanges wanted Barings to put up more cash to cover his deficit. The Bank of England says Leeson then fooled Barings officials in London into writing checks for margin calls, likely by saying the trades were on behalf of a corporate client whose funds would be deposited with Barings in a few days. When he couldn't produce the funds, Leeson fled, leaving behind a note saying: "I'm sorry."

What went wrong is simple: Barings allowed Leeson to wear too many hats. Preliminary investigations discovered that Leeson was both trader and manager, often settling his own trades. That was in violation of Osaka exchange rules and of industry practice, which keeps traders apart from back-office staffers who confirm transactions and write checks. " Leeson was the front office and the back office," says Graham Newall, head of futures trading at Barclays Bank PLC. "You can't stop someone from going berserk[①], but you can have a system to catch it in 24 hours."

---

① berserk [bə'sə:k] *adj.* 疯的；狂怒的

巴林银行陷入困境的教训

此时的股票市场并不配合,李森卖出看跌和看涨期权,筹措资金追加保证金通知,并打赌市场将会进入微量波动区间。但随着日经指数的持续下跌,李森最终只得孤注一掷。李森的损失累计约达7亿美元,交易所希望巴林银行筹措更多资金弥补亏损。英格兰银行认为,李森当时欺骗伦敦巴林银行的官员,为追加保证金通知填写支票,并可能声称这笔交易代表一位合作客户,其存款几天内入账巴林银行。李森拿不出这笔钱,他溜走了,留下了一张纸条:"抱歉。"

出差错的原因很简单:巴林银行纵容李森戴了太多的帽子。初步调查发现,李森既是交易员又是经理,经常清算他自己的交易。这种做法违背了大阪教育规则和行业惯例,即保持交易员与后台确认交易和签发支票职员之间的距离。巴克莱银行期货交易负责人格雷厄姆·尼瓦说:"李森既能操纵前台又能操纵后台,你无法阻止他人发狂,但是你可以有一个制度在24小时内抓住它。"

来自巴林的消息说,因为李森之前在摩根斯坦利做结算员的经历,他被获准清算交易。不管是什么原因,批评家们认为,巴林银行明显缺乏最基本的安全制度,跟踪交易员的活动范围。举例来说,伦敦国际金融期货交易所的首席执行官丹尼尔·霍森认为,巴林缺乏非正式的、与交易所沟通的后台渠道,也没有简单的随机抽查,了解其职员履行规则的情况。很多外部观察者认为,巴林银行的管理层过于疏忽,没有调查为什么公司的交易量激增。

The Lesson from Barings' Straits

A Barings source says Leeson was allowed to clear trades because of his previous experience as a settlement clerk at Morgan Stanley & Co. Whatever the reason, critics say Barings clearly lacked the most elemental of security systems to keep track of its traders' activities. For example, Daniel Hodson, CEO of the London International Financial Futures Exchange, believes that Barings lacked informal, back-channel communication links with exchanges, as well as simple random checks of how well its personnel followed rules. And many outside observers say Barings management neglected to investigate why the firm's trading volume was soaring.

Some of these will always slip through holes in the system. But as Barings executives found out too late, a far greater willingness—in good times and bad—might have kept the historic investment bank alive. When the market dishes out discipline, whether because of Mexico's economic misdeeds or Barings' trading scandal, punishment can be swift and severe. By refusing to bail out Barings, the Bank of England made that point crystal clear. Not every failure can be prevented. But a good deal more skepticism would go a long way toward limiting the losses.

(1,142 words)

巴林银行陷入困境的教训

有些差错总能逃脱制度的漏洞。但是,巴林银行的高管们发现得太晚了,无论顺境还是逆境,他们本来非常愿意维持这家具有历史意义的投资银行。当市场将纪律盛于盘中,无论墨西哥的经济犯罪还是巴林银行的投资丑闻,惩罚可能快速而严厉。英格兰银行拒绝拯救巴林银行,将这一点阐释得透彻明了。并不是每一次失败都能够避免,但是,对一桩好的交易持更多怀疑态度将会大大减少损失。

知识链接

Dresden Bank　德累斯顿银行是德国第三大银行,拥有德国第二大证券基金管理公司(德意志投资信托公司)和最大的地产基金管理公司。

ABN Amro　荷兰银行是一家享誉世界的国际性金融集团,有近两百年历史,其总资产约6 000多亿欧元。在全球60多个国家和地区拥有超过3 000家分行,全职员工约10万多名。

题　记

　　货币市场就像一条封闭的管道，一旦堵塞，后果不堪设想：受金融危机的冲击，全球银行同业拆借市场被有效关闭；银行的借贷成本高出美国官方利率3倍以上；由于银行缺少私营部门贷方的贷款，中央银行已经成为货币市场的重要供应商；贝尔斯登对冲基金对次级抵押贷款的投资组合造成的损害令市场猝不及防；利率幅度的猛涨或暴跌反映了投资者对银行的担心。如果货币市场的堵塞期超过一周，有些公司可能很难获得任何资助，这就意味着更多的破产和失业。市场昔日的美元资产宛若过眼云烟，投资者只能眼睁睁地坐在这堆日渐枯萎的资产里，凄凉如斯，梦想中的荣光急速瓦解。因此，可以毫不夸张地说，除非货币市场的表现更正常，否则金融危机不会结束。除非金融危机已经结束，否则全球经济可能无法恢复。

Money Markets—Blocked Pipes

Any good tradesman will tell you the importance of the bits of a house that you cannot see. Never mind the new kitchen: what about the rafters, the wiring and the pipes? So it is with financial markets. The stock markets are the most visible: as they soar or swoon①, the headline-writers get to work. The money markets, however, are the plumbing of the system. Normally, they function efficiently and unseen, allowing investment institutions, companies and banks to lend and borrow trillions of dollars for up to a year at a time. They are only noticed when they go wrong. And, like plumbing, when they do get blocked, they make an almighty stink.

At the moment, these markets are well and truly bunged② up. In the words of Michael Hartnett, a strategist at Merrill Lynch, "the global interbank market is effectively closed." The equivalent of a run on banks has been taking place, without the queues of depositors seen outside Northern Rock, a British mortgage bank. This stealthy run has been led by

---

① swoon [swuːn] vi. 下降
② bung [bʌŋ] vi. 塞住

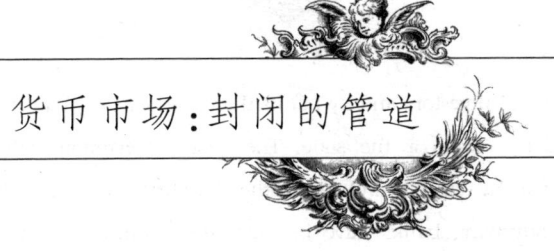

货币市场:封闭的管道

任何一位好心的商人都会告诉你,你不可能看到的房子中的细节非常重要,更别说是新厨房了,一定要了解橡子、线路和管道怎么样。金融市场也是如此。股票市场最为明显:随着它们的猛涨或暴跌,要闻撰稿人也马不停蹄。然而,货币市场却是这个系统的流通管道。通常情况下,它们有效且隐蔽地运作,一次性地给投资机构、公司和银行万亿美元,放贷和借款长达一年的时间。当他们出错时,才会受到关注。一旦他们真的像管道一样被堵塞,就会臭气熏天。

此刻,这些市场彻底被堵塞了。用美林银行战略家迈克尔·哈奈特的话说,即"全球银行同业拆借市场被有效关闭"。相应的银行挤兑从未停止,但英国抵押贷款银行诺森·罗克门外的排队储户却不见身影。这种暗箱操作一直由机构投资者和银行主导。许多银行不得不通过竞争对手或求助于国家来挽救自己。爱尔兰政府被迫出资保护国内 6 家最大银行的存款和其他负债。幸存的银行已变得极度谨慎,正如花旗集团的策略分析师马特·金所言:"一次只考

Money Markets—Blocked Pipes

institutional investors and by banks themselves. Many banks have had to be rescued by rivals or the state. The Irish government felt compelled to guarantee the deposits and some other liabilities of the country's six largest banks. Surviving banks have become ultra-cautious—"just taking things one day at a time," says Matt King, a strategist at Citigroup.

The effect has been most dramatic in the overnight rate for borrowing dollars. Bank borrowing costs reached 6.88%, more than three times the level of official American rates, while some were willing to pay a remarkable 11% to borrow dollars from the European Central Bank (ECB). Banks have become so risk-averse that they deposited a record 44 billion ($62 billion) with the ECB even though they could have earned more than two extra percentage points by lending to other banks. It was the last day of the quarter and, for balance-sheet reasons, banks were particularly keen to have cash on hand. Overnight rates fell back, but one-month rates rose further, indicating that the crisis had not eased.

In the absence of private-sector lenders to banks, central banks have become vital suppliers in the money markets. With the help of the ECB, the Bank of England and the Bank of Japan, the Federal Reserve agreed to lend a further $620 billion. That package, though of similar size to the administration's $700 billion bail-out plan, did not need congressional approval or attract public opposition. But central banks can only do so much. In particular, they tend to lend for short periods and then only against collateral with a high credit rating. That still leaves banks with the problem of financing their more troubled assets, an issue the administration's plan was designed to solve.

The money markets' difficulties began when two Bear Stearns hedge

货币市场:封闭的管道

虑一天的行情。"

效果最为显著的是借贷美元的隔夜利率。银行的借贷成本达到6.88%,高出美国官方利率3倍以上,而有些人愿意支付11%的高利率从欧洲中央银行(ECB)借入美元。银行已经变得如此规避风险,以至于他们在欧洲央行的存款已达到440亿欧元(620亿美元),尽管他们通过贷款给其他银行,已经赚取了超过2个百分点的收益。这是本季度的最后一天,由于资产负债表的缘故,银行特别渴望库存现金。虽然隔夜利率回落,但月利率进一步上升,这表明危机并未缓解。

由于银行缺少私营部门贷方的贷款,中央银行已经成为货币市场的重要供应商。在欧洲央行、英格兰银行和日本银行的帮助下,美联储同意进一步提供6 200亿美元的借款。尽管这个方案的规模与政府7 000亿美元的救市计划相似,却不需要国会的批准或引起公众的反对。但是,央行只能做这么多。他们特别倾向短期借贷,只反对抵押品高信用评级。这仍然给银行带来了更多不良资产的资金问题,政府的计划正是旨在解决这个问题。

货币市场的困境始于两个贝尔斯登对冲基金对次级抵押贷款的投资组合造成的损害。自那时以来,央行一直在进行干预,以维持他们的运转,并提出了"美国定期拍卖工具"等一系列计划。但是,雷曼兄弟的倒塌,以及随后欧洲和美国的一系列救援行动,似乎已经使货币市场陷入崩溃的边缘。即使立即通过美联储的计划,

Money Markets—Blocked Pipes

funds revealed the damage done to their portfolios by subprime mortgages. Sincethen, central banks have been intervening to keep them functioning, with a series of schemes like America's Term Auction Facility. But the collapse of Lehman Brothers, followed by the long series of rescues in Europe and America, seems to have brought the money markets close to breakdown. Even immediate passage of the Fed plan would not solve all their problems straight away, because it would take time to put the plan into place.

Why do these markets matter? First, the rates on loans paid by many consumers (adjustable-rate mortgages, for example) and companies are set with reference to the money markets. Higher rates for banks mean higher rates for everyone. Second, if the markets are blocked for more than a week, some companies may find it hard to get any finance at any price. That could mean more bankruptcies and job losses. Third, more banks could go bust if the blockage continues, making investors even more risk-averse. The downward spiral would take another turn.

It is widely assumed that central banks set the level of interest rates in their domestic markets. But the rate they announce is the one at which they will lend to the banking system. When banks borrow from anyone else (including other banks), they pay more. Every day, this rate is calculated through a poll of participating banks and published as Libor (London interbank offered rate) or Euribor (Euro interbank offered rate).

Normally, these are only a fraction of a percentage point above the official interest rates. But that has changed dramatically recently. Take the cost of borrowing dollars. Banks had to pay 4.15% for three-month money, more than two percentage points above the fed funds target rate. In theory,

货币市场:封闭的管道

也不可能马上解决所有的问题,因为需要时间将计划付诸实施。

为什么这些市场至关重要? 首先,许多消费者和公司支付的贷款利率,如浮动利率抵押贷款,都是参照货币市场而设置的。 银行的高利率意味着每一个人的高利率。 其次,如果货币市场的堵塞超过一周,有些公司可能很难获得任何资助,这可能意味着更多的破产和失业。 最后,如果堵塞持续延伸,更多的银行可能破产,投资者更加规避风险,减记恶性循环将再次发生。

人们普遍认为,央行在其国内市场设定了利率水平。 但是,他们宣布的利率是一个他们借给银行系统的利率。 当银行从其他渠道借款(包括其他银行),他们就会支付更多。 每天,这个利率按参与银行的人头计算,以伦敦同业拆借利率或欧元同业拆借利率对外公布。

通常情况下,这些利率只是比官方利率高不到 1 个百分点。 但是,形势在近期发生了翻天覆地的变化。 如美元借贷成本,银行为 3 个月的利率支付 4.15%,超过联邦基金目标利率 2 个百分点以上。 从理论上说,由于市场预期官方利率大幅上升,3 个月的利率有可能达到这种高度。 但是,如果危机的程度加深,这种情况不大可能发生。

相反,利率的幅度反映了投资者对银行的担心,尤其是这么多银行在翻云覆雨之间波动如此迅速。 要信任银行的经营健康状况,3 个月现在是一段很长的时间。 此外,银行正热切期望保存自己的现金,以防存款人大量提款,或他们的钱困在另一家破产的银行,

Money Markets—Blocked Pipes

three-month rates could be that high because markets are expecting a sharp rise in official rates. But that is hardly likely, given the depth of the crisis.

Instead, the width of the margin reflects investors' worries about the banks, not least because so many have faltered so quickly. Three months is now a long time to trust in the health of a bank. In addition, banks are anxious to conserve their own cash, in case depositors make large withdrawals or their money gets tied up in the collapse of another bank, as with Lehman. "We are at the juncture① where more widespread and permanent support is required to restore confidence in the banking sector," say analysts at the Royal Bank of Scotland (RBS). "Without it, the banks will be aggressively trying to contract their books and will be unable to provide credit to retail and corporate clients."

So it is safe to say that, until the money markets behave more normally, the financial crisis will not be over. And until the financial crisis is over, the global economy may not recover.

(948 words)

---

① juncture [ˈdʒʌŋktʃə] n. 接合点

货币市场:封闭的管道

如雷曼兄弟。苏格兰皇家银行（RBS）的分析师指出："我们正处于危殆关头，需要更广泛和长期的支持恢复银行部门的信心。没有信心，银行不会积极履行合同，不可能给零售和企业客户提供信贷。"

因此，可以毫不夸张地说，除非货币市场的表现更正常，否则金融危机不会结束。除非金融危机已经结束，否则全球经济可能无法恢复。

知识链接

Bear Stearns 贝尔斯登公司(Bear Stearns Cos.)曾是华尔街最赚钱的投行之一，成立于1923年，总部位于纽约，在2008年的美国次级按揭风暴中严重亏损，濒临破产而被收购。公司主要业务涵盖机构股票和债券、固定收益、投资银行业务、全球清算服务、资产管理以及个人银行服务。

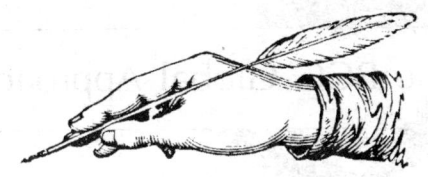

题　记

　　当人们将商业世界想象得充满血腥味道的时候，波士顿咨询公司的首席执行官汉斯·保罗·伯克却衣着朴实，以一个永不停歇的男人极端实用的态度和低调的行事风格，轻松优雅地领导公司追随自己的目标，认同自己的思想，创造一个又一个的商业奇迹。他采用了一套表面相似的方法经营与扩大波士顿咨询公司缓慢发展的全球业务；他要求员工做更多的旅行推销，从而赢得了比多数专业服务公司更多的声誉；他在保持美国本土业务持续增长的同时，相继在世界各地开设办事处，拓展公司的国际化业务；他正在准备前往亚洲，从一个不同于欧洲和北美的角度观察世界。波士顿咨询公司的全球业务在一批咨询界奇才雄心勃勃的管理下形成了一种独特的企业文化。

The BCG Global Approach

Hans-Paul Burkner has 10 blue suits. The chief executive of Boston Consulting Group also shies away from striped shirts and unusual ties. "Then I don't have to make choices," he says, over coffee in BCG's London office. "If you have certain rituals about what to wear and what to put in your bag, it makes life easier. My choice of ties is not necessarily the best, but most of the people I work with wouldn't notice." Mr. Burkner's unflashy clothing reflects not only the brutally practical attitude of a man who is constantly on the road, but also a deliberately low-key leadership style.

Unlike many of the chief executives who hire BCG to advise them on everything from restructuring to entering new markets, the 55-year-old does not try to light up the room or dominate every conversation. He personally serves his guests coffee and makes a point of calling every one of BCG's 550 partners on their birthdays. "He is really a totally unpretentious① leader, somebody who is leading from the middle," says Antonella Mei-Pochtler, a member of BCG's executive committee. Mr. Burkner has adopted a similarly outward-looking approach to running and

---

① unpretentious [ˌʌnpriˈtenʃəs] *adj.* 谦虚的

波士顿咨询公司全球业务巡礼

汉斯·保罗·伯克有 10 套蓝色的西装。这位波士顿咨询公司的首席执行官既不穿条纹衬衫,也不扎与众不同的领带。他端着咖啡,在伦敦的公司办公室说:"没有必要做选择。如果你有特定的习惯,即穿什么,包里放些什么,生活会变得更轻松。我挑选的领带并不一定是最好的,但和我一块工作的大多数人并没有注意到这一点。"伯克先生朴实的衣着服饰不仅表现了一个永不停歇的男人极端实用的态度,也反映了他低调的领导风格。

很多首席执行官雇请波士顿咨询公司,咨询从公司重组到进入新市场等各方面的建议,但 55 岁的伯克先生与他们不同,不会盛气凌人或主宰每次谈话。他亲自给客人冲咖啡,550 位公司合作伙伴中有人过生日时,他会特地打电话问候。波士顿咨询公司执委会成员安托内拉·梅·波彻特勒说:"他是一位完全没有架子的领导,与员工打成一片的领导。"伯克先生采用了一套表面相似的方法经营与扩大波士顿咨询公司缓慢发展的全球业务,公司共有 7 000 名员工,其中有 4 500 名咨询师,分布在全球 39 个子公司。

尽管他的工作地点主要在纽约和法兰克福,他却生活在公文圈

The BCG Global Approach

enlarging BCG's sprawling① global business, which encompasses 7,000 people, of whom 4,500 are consultants, in 39 companies worldwide.

Although officially based in New York and Frankfurt, he lives out of a briefcase. He takes four flights a week on average and tries to visit every office and meet every partner at least once a year. He has an assistant in Frankfurt and his 17-year-old son lives there, but he shares his workspace with another partner. In New York, the company recently cannibalized② his office to make room for more consultants. "I sit in a small conference room or the office of somebody else," he says.

In some ways, Mr. Burkner simply embodies the BCG approach to consulting. Founded by Bruce Henderson as the consulting arm of a Boston bank, it opened its first international office just three years later in Tokyo. With 77 offices, it has acquired a reputation for demanding more travel from its staff than most professional services firms. "We think of ourselves as an international company even though the origin is in the US," Mr. Burkner says. "In the past I would have described us as multi-local, but today we are increasingly global...eventually you don't know what kind of company it is and the headquarters becomes less and less relevant."

Born in Germany, he earned a masters at Yale University before winning a Rhodes scholarship to Oxford. He began his career in corporate finance at Commerzbank and joined BCG, then predominantly a US consulting firm. He opened BCG's Frankfurt office and led the company's financial institutions practice, specializing in bank turn rounds. After that,

---

① sprawl [sprɔːl] vt. 伸开
② cannibalize ['kænibəlaiz] vt. 拆用……的配件

波士顿咨询公司全球业务巡礼

之外。他平均每周要飞四趟,每年至少到每个办公室一次,至少和每个客户见一面。他在法兰克福有一个助手,他17岁的儿子也住在那儿,但他却与另一个合作伙伴共用一间办公室。在纽约,公司最近正在拆用他的办公室,以便为更多的咨询师提供空间。他说:"我在一间小会议室和他人的办公室里工作。"

在某些方面,伯克先生把波士顿咨询公司的业务仅定位于咨询。布鲁斯·韩德森成立波士顿咨询公司时,它还只是波士顿银行的一家咨询机构。3年后,波士顿咨询公司便在东京开办了首家国际事务所。如今,波士顿咨询公司拥有77间办公室,赢得了比多数专业服务公司更多的声誉,从而要求员工做更多的旅行推销。伯克先生说:"我们认为我们属于国际化的公司,尽管公司的起源地在美国。过去,我们认为自己属于多元本地化,但今天我们越来越国际化……最终,你不会知道它的公司,总部变得越来越不重要"。

伯克出生在德国,在耶鲁大学取得硕士学位,然后获得罗斯奖学金前往牛津。他从德国商业银行做公司理财起步,然后进入著名的美国波士顿咨询公司。他开办了波士顿咨询公司法兰克福办事处,主导公司的金融机构,专门运营银行周转业务。之后,他被推举为集团首位非美籍董事会主席和首席执行官。

在波士顿咨询公司的收入中,38%左右来自美国,44%来自欧洲和中东,15%来自亚洲和太平洋地区。尽管经济中涌现出许多新的机会,但波士顿咨询公司的美国本土业务仍持续增长。公司相继在阿布扎比、迪拜、基辅、明尼阿波利斯和费城开设了办事处。

虽然波士顿咨询公司与行业领导者麦肯锡相比要小很多,但10

The BCG Global Approach

he was elected as the group's first non-US president and chief executive.

Roughly 38 per cent of BCG's revenues come from the US, 44 per cent from Europe and the Middle East and 15 per cent from Asia and the Pacific. Many of the new opportunities are in emerging economies, but BCG continues to grow in its home base as well. It opened offices in Abu Dhabi, Dubai, Kiev, Minneapolis and Philadelphia.

While BCG remains much smaller than the industry leader McKinsey, its growth has outpaced the industry average for a decade and Mr. Burkner's ambitions remain large. "We want to change the world," he says simply. "It sounds a bit exaggerated but in a way we can really do this. We want to shape in some way the society we live in." For Mr. Burkner, one of the best ways of achieving this is by getting people in far-flung regions and countries to work together and build consensus. Under his leadership the firm has urged managers to look beyond the local office when putting together project teams. "By really working together, you are getting to know each other, by sharing values and sharing principles," he says.

Reserved by nature, Mr. Burkner can be hard to read. That often buys him the time to modify or change his position after hearing from others. "He is extremely careful to make sure everyone can voice his or her opinion, which is very important in a partnership," Ms. Mei-Pochtler says. At times that has meant abandoning dearly held proposals, including a recent attempt to establish a retirement age for BCG partners. Although Mr. Burkner believed the group needed a formal policy, he ran into strong opposition, particularly from some of the older partners, and ended up dropping the proposal. The same principles apply to the work BCG does for its clients, he says. "We really engage with their people and help mobilize

年来,它的增长率远高于行业平均水平。 伯克仍胸怀大志,他坦率地解释道:"我们应该改变世界。 这听起来有点夸张,但我们在某种程度上确实能有所作为。 我们应该在某种程度上改变我们生活的社会。"对伯克先生来说,达到此种目标的最佳方式之一就是使远在各地和各个国家的人们一起工作,凝聚共识。 在他的领导下,公司要求管理者组建项目团队时,要突破地域观念。 他说:"通过踏踏实实地一起工作,你们逐渐相互了解,分享价值观和分享原则。"

由于天性拘谨,伯克先生很难与人打交道。 这使他常常需要倾听别人的意见之后,再花时间修正或改变自己的观点。 梅·波彻特勒女士说:"他特别小心谨慎,确保每个人都能畅所欲言,这点对合作非常重要。"但这也意味着有时要放弃必须坚持的提案,包括近期尝试建立波士顿咨询公司合作伙伴的退休年龄的提案。 虽然伯克先生认为,集团需要一项正式政策,但他遇到强烈的反对,特别是来自年长的合作伙伴的反对,导致提案最终被弃。 他认为,同样的原则也适用于波士顿咨询公司对客户的工作。 他说:"我们真心与他们这些人打交道,动员他们去把事情做好,形成一个更强大的组织。 如果他们的头脑里和心中感受不到这一点,我们就是失败。"

由于很多大客户、特别是金融服务行业的客户,已经陷入金融困境,信用危机和金融衰退也打击了咨询公司。 公司收入去年增长了25%~30%,预计今年大约只有10%的增长。 但迄今为止,冲击远没有互联网泡沫破灭时可怕,那时许多公司大量缩减咨询工作。 波士顿咨询公司一直以能够通过帮助客户清理资产负债表上的不良资产和改善公司处理风险的能力而保持发展。

The BCG Global Approach

them to get things done, leaving behind a stronger organization," he says. "If they don't feel it in their minds and hearts, we have failed."

The credit crunch and financial slowdown have hit consulting as many of its big clients, particularly in financial services, have run into financial trouble. Revenues, which grew between 25 and 30 per cent last year are expected to rise only about 10 per cent this year. But so far the impact has not been as dire as after the dotcom crash, when many companies dramatically scaled back their use of consultants. BCG has been able to prosper by helping clients clean toxic assets off balance sheets and improve the way they manage risk.

A specialist in financial services, Mr. Burkner says he sees parallels between the credit crunch, the dotcom crisis and earlier emerging market debt troubles. Each time, he says, financial institutions violated their own risk management principles. "It's really about not only understanding your limits but adhering to them. How much did you pour into Russia or Latin America? How much did you bet on the dotcom bubble? How much did you put into real estate?" he asks. "If you see more opportunities in the market than your systems can take, you should say 'No'."

For future growth, Mr. Burkner is looking east. He studied Chinese at Ruhr University and did his doctoral work at Oxford on savings behavior in Thailand and the Philippines. If he were just starting out, he says, he would go to Asia: "See the world from a perspective you would not have from Europe and North America. It's good to have the perspective of a challenger."

(1,056 words)

波士顿咨询公司全球业务巡礼

作为金融服务行业的专家,伯克先生认为,他注意到信用恐慌、网络危机和早些时候出现的市场债务危机的相似性。他说,金融机构每次都背离了他们自己的风险处理原则。他质问道:"这不仅真正关系到你对自己的局限性了解多少,而且还要遵守这些局限性。你对俄罗斯或拉丁美洲的投资是多少?你在网络泡沫经济上的赌注是多少?你对房地产的投资是多少?如果你在市场上看到的机会比你的系统更多,你应该说'不'。"

为了未来的发展,伯克先生正在关注东方,他在鲁尔大学学习汉语,在牛津做博士工作,研究泰国和菲律宾民众的储蓄行为。他说,一旦起步,他就会前往亚洲:"从一个不同于欧洲和北美的角度观察世界。具备挑战者的观察能力是一种美妙的享受。"

知识链接

BCG 波士顿咨询公司(The Boston Consulting Group)创建于20世纪60年代,是一家全球性管理咨询公司,是世界领先的商业战略咨询机构,客户遍及所有行业和地区。波士顿咨询公司的四大业务职能是企业策略、信息技术、企业组织、营运效益。

McKinsey 麦肯锡公司(Mckinsey and Company)是世界级领先的全球管理咨询公司。自1926年成立以来,公司的使命就是帮助领先的企业机构实现显著、持久的经营业绩改善,打造能够吸引、培育和激励杰出人才的优秀组织机构。目前拥有分布于39个国家的79个分支机构及5 000余名训练有素的员工。

题　记

　　走在世界各大都市的街头，你会发现一个绿色的美人鱼标志；当你循着美人鱼的微笑进入店内，沁人心脾的咖啡香味和舒适优雅的环境会让你放松下来，轻松地享受一段美好的时光——这就是"星巴克"。星巴克的成功之旅是一段美妙而浪漫的文化传奇。星巴克的创始人是三位大学同学，他们创造了一个典型的、美国式企业成功的故事。而使星巴克脱胎换骨的人物则是霍华德·舒尔茨，他塑造出"星巴克"这个世界闻名的咖啡店品牌文化——极其重视消费者的"咖啡体验"，这使得它的品牌定位具备了独特的差异化竞争优势。舒尔茨让美国人体验到了欧洲咖啡馆温馨的氛围、高雅的环境以及放松的心境。如果说美国文化的典型特征是自由、舒适、随意，那么星巴克式的咖啡文化——"亲切、轻松和休闲"正是它的最好体现。

Starbucks Voyage of Success

It starts out like the classic American entrepreneurial success story. Three college friends get together from time to time and talk about what kind of business they could start. In this case, the three friends were Zev Siegl, Gordon Bowker, and Gerald Baldwin. The business they decided to start was gourmet coffee. It gets interesting. The company they started was Starbucks. And the story goes like this.

Way back in 1971, coffee didn't look like it was a great business. It didn't show signs of getting better, either. Coffee consumption in the United States had peaked in the 1960s, but it was on the decline since then. Part of the reason was that the coffee we had was awful. Most Americans drank something called "coffee" that came ground up very finely in vacuum-sealed tins. You scooped the stuff out of the can and put it in a percolator. Some coffee made this way was so weak you could read a newspaper through a carafe of the stuff. Sigel, Bowker, and Baldwin had traveled together to Europe where they discovered the rich dark coffee that was very different from the percolated① brown beverage that most Americans were drinking. But for a while they didn't connect that preference with any kind of business idea.

---

① percolate [ˈpəːkəleit] vt. (用渗滤壶)煮(咖啡)

星巴克成功之旅

故事的开头就像典型的、美国式企业成功的故事。三个大学朋友经常在一起聚会,探讨他们可以开创什么样的企业。这三个朋友就是瑟夫·思格、戈登·鲍克和杰拉德·鲍德温。他们决定从经营美食家咖啡起步。这真是非常有趣。他们创建的公司就是星巴克,故事就是这样开始的。

回到1971年,咖啡在当时并不像是赚钱的生意,也没有好转的迹象。咖啡消费在20世纪60年代的美国曾达到高峰,但之后却一直下降。部分原因是我们喝的咖啡味道很糟糕。大多数美国人饮用的所谓碾磨精细的"咖啡"装在真空密封罐里。人们要把咖啡从罐子里掏出来,然后放到过滤器上。这种方式调制的咖啡味道很淡,甚至透过装满咖啡的玻璃杯还可以读报。思格、鲍克和鲍德温曾一起游历欧洲,他们发现那里的深色咖啡与大多数美国人饮用的棕褐色咖啡大不相同。但是,他们当时并没有任何经营这种咖啡的想法。

故事转到加利福尼亚州的伯克利分校,那里一个名叫阿尔弗雷·皮特的人在步行店附近的葡萄藤和核桃街拐角处开了一间"皮

Starbucks Voyage of Success

The story shifts to Berkeley, California, where a fellow named Alfred Peet had started Peet's coffee at the corner of Vine and Walnut Streets, just around the corner from the Walk Shop. Peet had come to this country from Holland, where he was a coffee roaster, and he thought that most American coffee was pretty vile. Then he had started Peet's to offer something better.

Somehow a bag of Peet's dark blend found its way North, into the hands of Jerry Baldwin. It convinced Jerry and his friends that a gourmet coffee shop would be a good business for them to start. When they were pressed by their attorney for a name, their first idea was to call the place Starbo after an old mining camp. But after a bit of thought they settled on Starbucks to pay homage to Seattle's seafaring heritage.

They opened their first Starbucks in 1971. They weren't the only ones who thought a gourmet coffee business was a good idea, even in Seattle. Elsewhere in town Jim Stewart was starting The Wet Whisker, which later became Seattle's Best Coffee. Alfred Peet thought they were pretty good guys. He taught them about coffee roasting in his unbendable① European way. For the first year of their business he even roasted the beans for them. Starbucks started to grow.

In 1982 a young marketing manager for the Swedish kitchen equipment company, Perstorp, noticed that a small company in Seattle called Starbucks was buying a lot of special drip coffee makers. He stopped by to see what was going on. He stayed on to become a partner. The fellow's name was Howard Schultz. Shortly after joining Starbucks Schultz took a vacation in Europe. One day, sitting in a coffee shop in Milan, he

---

① unbendable [ʌnˈbendəbl] *adj.* 坚定不移的

星巴克成功之旅

特咖啡"。皮特从荷兰来到这个国家,曾是荷兰的一名咖啡烤制员,他认为大多数美国咖啡很差劲,于是,他开办了"皮特咖啡",以提供更好的品种。 一袋皮特深色咖啡莫名其妙地被运到北方,并落入杰里·鲍德温之手。 它使杰里和他的朋友确信,美味咖啡店对他们来说是经商的良好开端。 当律师要求他们给自己的咖啡店取名时,他们的第一个想法是采用老矿区营地"星博"这个地名。 略加思考之后,他们决定取名"星巴克",以表示对西雅图航海遗产的敬意。

第一家星巴克咖啡店于 1971 年开业。 即使在西雅图,他们也并不是唯一意识到经营美味咖啡是个好主意的商家。 吉姆·斯图尔特已在城里的其他地方开办了"湿晶须"咖啡店,后来成为西雅图最好的咖啡屋。 阿尔弗雷德·皮特以为,他们是非常好的伙伴,他教他们用独特的欧洲方式烤制咖啡。 在第一年的经营过程中,他甚至为他们烤制咖啡豆。 星巴克开始成长。

1982 年,一位年轻的瑞典厨房设备公司的市场营销经理柏仕德,注意到西雅图一家名为星巴克的小公司买了很多特殊的滴水咖啡壶。 他顺便造访了公司,查看发生了什么事。 然后,他留下来成为一名合作伙伴,这个人的名字就是霍华德·舒尔茨。 舒尔茨加入星巴克不久便前往欧洲度假。 有一天,他坐在米兰的一家咖啡馆,想象星巴克可能成为什么样子。 他设想星巴克应该是这样一个地方,服务员了解顾客,而精美的咖啡只是完美经历的一部分。 回到西雅图之后,他极力向鲍克和鲍德温兜售完整体验的理念。 然

Starbucks Voyage of Success

had a vision of what Starbucks could become. He imagined a place where the staff knew the customers and where the great coffee was only part of a totally wonderful experience. When he got back to Seattle he worked hard trying to sell Bowker and Baldwin on his idea of the complete experience. They remained unmoved so Schultz decided to do it on his own. He founded a company to create the experience that he'd seen in that Milan café. By 1987 he had three locations. Things might have gone on like that with him competing against Starbucks, but that was about the time that Gordon and Bowker decided it was time for them to sell out. Schultz arranged financing and became CEO of the company. Starbucks then had 17 locations in Seattle.

Schultz imagined that the customer's experience should be wonderful from the moment he or she walked in the door of a Starbucks. The Barista should recognize the customer and greet him or her by name. The Barista should also know the customer's regular order and start preparing it right away. To make that kind of experience happen, Starbucks has done a lot of training. Starbucks employees learn about making coffee, but they also learn how to remember customer names. Starbucks tries every way to have motivated employees, and gives even part-time employees full benefits and limited stock options. Starbucks controls what goes on in the stores, and holds that control by maintaining ownership of its stores. Starbucks stores are all non-smoking, even in places like Japan and Vienna.

That's what Starbucks wants to continue to do. So far the company has cruised through the business waters like a majestic sailing ship from Seattle's past. But they're coming close to the edge of the map and beyond that edge lies the legend, " Here be monsters." First, there's the generational monster. While lots of folks from Generations " X " and " Y "

而，他们仍然无动于衷，舒尔茨只好决定自己干。他成立了一家公司，创造出他在米兰咖啡馆曾见过的那种体验。1987年，他已有三家分店。事态继续如此发展就可能导致他与星巴克的竞争，但就在这时，鲍克和鲍德温认为，是时候卖掉他们的公司了。舒尔茨安排了融资，并成为公司的首席执行官。星巴克当时在西雅图有17家分店。

舒尔茨认为，顾客的美好经历应该从他或她进入星巴克的那一刻开始。咖啡生要熟悉客户，直呼其名来欢迎他或她。咖啡生也应该了解顾客的点单习惯，并马上开始做准备。为了让顾客享受这种体验，星巴克进行了大量的培训工作。星巴克的员工不仅要学会烤制咖啡，还要学会如何记住顾客的名字。星巴克想方设法激励员工，甚至给予兼职员工充分的福利和有限的优先认股权。星巴克控制了咖啡店里的一切，通过维持咖啡店的所有权达到掌控。星巴克所有的店内禁止抽烟，即使在日本和维也纳等地也是如此。

这就是星巴克希望持之以恒的经营策略。到目前为止，公司就像一艘宏伟的帆船，从西雅图的过去起航，成功穿越了商业水域。但他们正在接近地图的边缘，边缘之外就是"立地成魔"的传说。首先，这里有一代又一代的怪兽。虽然很多"X"代人和"Y"代人在星巴克工作，公司并没有真正受到这几代人的欢迎。他们可以在那里工作，但他们却没有家的感觉。X和Y代人中的核心群体已经告诉星巴克，他们在星巴克看到同类是柜台后的那些人。他们认为，星巴克属于自命不凡的雅皮士。正如一名X代人所称："我讨

Starbucks Voyage of Success

work at Starbucks, the company is not real popular with those generations. They may work there, but they don't feel at home there.

Focus groups of folks from Generation X and Y have told Starbucks that the only people they see at Starbucks like them are the ones behind the counter. They think Starbucks is for pretentious Yuppies. As one Gen-Xer put it, "I hate the Italian names for the coffee sizes, small, medium, and large are fine for me." If upcoming generations don't want to become customers, growth will stall.

Generations are just one monster. Another is growth itself. The bigger you are, the harder it is to generate high-percentage growth. That's not all. When a company grows fast it's usually hard to maintain good service. There's a real question about whether Starbucks can continue to find and train and supervise the people who deliver the Starbucks experience to customers.

The last monster that's out there is the Faustian bargain that public companies seem doomed to make with the stock market. The market loves Starbucks now, but what if growth starts to slow. Then there is bound to be pressure to cut corners, lower standards and change rules and practices.

Starbucks is not a perfect company. But it is a company who has managed to make the voyage to success without compromising key principles of the guiding vision. The voyage ahead is more treacherous. Will Starbucks be able to maintain the integrity of its vision.

(1,094 words)

星巴克成功之旅

厌用意大利名字标注咖啡的尺寸，小杯、中杯和大杯适合我。"如果成长中的几代人不愿成为顾客，增长就会停滞。

几代人只是一个怪兽，另一个怪兽是增长本身。公司越大就越难产生高比例的增长。这还不是全部，当一家公司快速增长之时，通常难以维持良好的服务。星巴克是否可以继续寻找、培训和监督将星巴克体验提供给顾客的人，这才是真正的问题。徘徊在那儿的最后一位妖魔是浮士德式交易，即公众公司似乎注定与股票市场相连。市场现在青睐星巴克，但如果增长开始放缓又会如何呢？其次是偷工减料、降低标准、改变规则和惯例带来的固有压力。

星巴克不是一家完美的公司，但这家公司已经设法踏上了成功的航程，对经营理念的关键原则毫不妥协。前面的航程更加变幻莫测，但愿星巴克能够保持完整的愿景。

知识链接

Generations "X" and "Y" 美国将1980年至1988年出生的人称为"Y代人"（80后），1965年至1979年出生的人称为"X代人"，1946年至1964年出生的人称为"婴儿潮代"，1945年以前出生的人则属于老一辈。

The Faustian bargain 浮士德式交易是一种心理障碍，指一个人对一种看似最有价值的物质盲目崇拜，从而使他失去了理解人生中其他有价值的东西或精神。这种症状使他永远沉浸在理念与结果的落差之中。